On the Mason-Dixon Line

On the Mason-Dixon Line

An Anthology
of Contemporary Delaware Writers

Edited by
Billie Travalini and Fleda Brown

DELAWARE

Newark: University of Delaware Press

Associated University Presses
2010 Eastpark Boulevard
Cranbury, NJ 08512

The paper used in this publication meets the requirements of the American National Standard for Permanence of Paper for Printed Library Materials Z39.48-1984.

Library of Congress Cataloging-in-Publication Data

On the Mason-Dixon line : an anthology of contemporary Delaware writers / edited by Billie Travalini and Fleda Brown.
    p. cm.
  ISBN 978-0-87413-030-0 (alk. paper)
  1. American literature—Delaware.   2. Delaware—Literary collections.
I. Travalini, Billie.   II. Jackson, Fleda Brown, 1944–
PS548.D305   2008
810.8′09751-dc22   2007052996

PRINTED IN THE UNITED STATES OF AMERICA

Contents

Acknowledgments

T HE EDITORS OWE A HUGE DEBT OF GRATITUDE TO DELAWARE'S emerging and professional writers, and to writing groups around the state, from whose ranks come much of the good work in this collection. We are especially grateful to the Delaware Literary Connection, particularly to Merle Shao, Helen Ohlson, and Sally Rinard, for encouraging the project and believing in its value as a cultural record of a diverse group of people. Thanks also to John Traino and Gina Travalini for hours of typing and proofreading.

We are equally grateful to the Delaware Division of the Arts for its tradition of promoting Delaware writers. And to Cruce Stark and Bernie Kaplan for their constant support and their willingness to listen to questions and offer good advice; and to Julianna Baggott for her enthusiasm, and for digging up for us the names and addresses of many of Delaware's best writers. And finally, Jerry Beasley has exercised a generous and unerring editorial eye, for which we are profoundly grateful.

This book is dedicated to the writers of Delaware.

Some of the novel excerpts, short stories, and poems in this anthology have appeared in other publications, and are reprinted here with the permission of the author or of the publisher.

Baggott, Julianna. The excerpt from *The Miss America Family* (New York: Simon and Schuster, 2002) is reprinted here by permission of the publisher. "Living Where They Raised Me" is from *This Country of Mothers* (Carbondale: Southern Illinois University Press, 2001), and is reprinted here by permission of the author.

Balingit, JoAnn. "Comfort, Cape Henlopen" was first published in *Smartish Pace*, Issue 13 (April 2006), 124–25, and won Second Prize in the 2006 Beulah Rose Poetry Contest; it is reprinted here by permission of the author.

Blaskey, Linda. "Loading Hogs for Market" is published here for the first time, by permission of the author.

Brown, Fleda. "Anatomy of a Seizure" is reprinted from *The Journal*, 28 (Spring/ Summer 2004), 7–19; the essay won the William Allen Prize in Creative Nonfiction. "Delaware" appears in *Reunion* (Madison: University of Wisconsin Press, 2007), and is reprinted here by the permission of the publisher.

Claire, William. "An Archaeological Dig: My Unwanted Third Century Monk" was first published under the title "In the South of France," in *Chelsea*, No. 38 (November 1979), 131, and is reprinted here by permission of the author.

Colwell, Anne Agnes. "Playing Chicken on the Tracks" is published here for the first time, by permission of the author.

Coyne, Tom. The excerpt from *A Gentleman's Game* (New York: Grove/Atlantic, Inc., 2002) is reprinted here by permission of the publisher.

Creasy, Deborah. "Pelican Sky" is published here for the first time, by permission of the author.

Davis, Robert Hambling. "Death of a Deer" was first published in *American Writing*, 16 (Summer 1998), 65–69, and was reprinted in *Delmarva Quarterly* (Winter 2004), 53–54; it is reprinted here by permission of the author.

Dee, Ed. "The Tailman" was first published in *Mississippi Review*, 19: 1 & 2 (1990), 70-76, and is reprinted here by permission of the author.

de los Santos, Marisa. "Poem for a Birthday" appears in *From the Bones Out* (Columbia: University of South Carolina Press, 2000), and is reprinted here by permission of the author. The excerpt from *Love Walked In* (New York: Dutton, 2006) is reprinted here by permission of the publisher.

Dolan, Liz. "The Lady of Annie B Street is Gone" is published here for the first time, by permission of the author.

Fischer, Maribeth. "Stillborn" was first published in *The Iowa Review*, 24 (Winter 1994), 161–75, and was reprinted in *The Pushcart Prize Anthology XXV* (Wainscott, NY: Pushcart Press, 1995), 241–55; it is reprinted here by permission of the author.

Funk, Allison. "Downstate" is published here for the first time. "Afterimages" was first published in *The Knot Garden* (Riverdale-on-Hudson: Sheep Meadow Press, 2002), 14–15. Both poems are reprinted here by permission of the author.

Garrett, Dana. "From the Seventh Floor of the Carvel State Office Building" is published here for the first time, by permission of the author.

Haley, Vanessa. "For a Former Student Found at Fleming's Landing After Two Years at the Bottom of the Smyrna River" was first published in *Southern Poetry Review*, 27:2, Fall 1987. "George Stubbs's 'Plate for the Sixth Anatomical Table of the Muscles, Fascias, Ligaments, Nerves, Arteries, Veins, Glands and Cartilages of a Horse, Viewed in Front, Explained'" appeared in *Dogwood: a Journal of Poetry & Prose*, 6 (Spring 2006), 2–3, and won the Dogwood Poetry Prize for that year. Both poems are reprinted here by permission of the author.

Hanna, Gary. "The Visit" was first published, in a slightly different version, in *Heart*, No. 1 (Spring 2007), 15, and is reprinted here by permission of the author.

Ingersoll, Wendy. "The Practice of Scales" was first published in *Passager*, online at http://raven.ubalt.edu/features/passager/issue40.htm as one of the "2005 Winners on the Web," and is reprinted here by permission of the author.

Jenkins, McKay. "And None Came Back" was first published in *The Outside Magazine*, 25:2 (February 2000), 40–47, 97, and is reprinted here by permission of the author.

Keegan, James. "Mule" was first published in *Southern Poetry Review*, 34:1 (Fall 1994), 31–32, and is reprinted here by permission of the author.

Kimball, Amanda. "Levittown, 1951" is published here for the first time, by permission of the author.

lanyon, e. jean. "some metals tarnish" is published here for the first time, by permission of the author.

Lloyd, Emily. "*Jane Eyre*, Unbanned" was first published in *Bloom*, 2:2 (Fall 2005), 50, and is reprinted here by permission of the author.

Long, Alexander. "Unfinished Love Poem" appears in *Vigil* (Kalamazoo, MI: New Issues Press, 2006), and is reprinted here by permission of New Issues Poetry & Prose.

MacDougal, Bonnie. "Out of Order" appears in *Out of Order* (New York: The Ballantine Publishing Group, 1999), and is reprinted here by permission of the publisher.

Maxson, H. A. "Slug" is published here for the first time, by permission of the author.

McCafferty, Jane. "Delivered" is published here for the first time, by permission of the author.

McMillian, Franetta. "Martin Luther King at 75" appeared in *Prints* (Wilmington, DE: 2nd Saturday Poets, 2004), and is reprinted here by permission of the author.

Miller-Duggan, Devon. "Elvis Is an Angel Now" is published here for the first time, by permission of the author.

Morea, Douglas. "Winkle" was first published in *Prints* (Wilmington, DE: 2nd Saturday Poets, 2004), and is reprinted here by permission of the author.

Peale, Tracy Steven, Sr. "Route 82, Above the Brandywine" is published here for the first time, by permission of the author.

Pifer, Drury. A different version of "Fruitcakes and Fiction" was commissioned by and first published in *The News Journal*, Wilmington, Delaware. This version appears here by permission of the author.

Poole, Francis. "Lost Springs" was first published in *Southern Poetry Review*, 44:1 (2006), 16, and is reprinted here by permission of the author.

Pruett, Lynn. "Shouting Nazarene" is published here for the first time, by permission of the author.

Rowe, Maggie. "Wexford Boy" is published here for the first time, by permission of the author.

Ruark, Gibbons. "A Vacant Lot" and "Waiting for You with the Swallows" appear in *Passing Through Customs: New and Selected Poems* (Baton Rouge: Louisiana State University Press, 1999), and are reprinted here by permission of the publisher.

Schappell, Elissa. "The Green Fairy" appears in *Food & Booze* (Portland, OR: Tin House Books, 2006). "That Sort of Woman" appears in *The Mrs. Dalloway Reader* (New York: Harcourt-Brace, 2003). Both are reprinted here by permission of the publishers.

Schumacher, Julie, "Resurrection Hockey" was first published in *Ms. Magazine*, 10:4 (June/July 2000), 84–91, and is reprinted here by permission of the author.

Scott, David. "Delaware" was first published in *Red, White and Blues* (Iowa City: University of Iowa Press, 2004), 166, and is reprinted here by permission of the publisher.

Snodgrass, W. D. "Cherry Saplings" and "The Marsh" appear in *Selected Poems 1957–1987* (New York: Soho Press, 1987). Both poems are reprinted here by permission of the author.

Stark, Cruce. "Getting Out More" is published here for the first time, by permission of the author.

Travalini, Billie. The excerpt from *Bloodsisters* (Lewiston, ID: LC Press/Lewis-Clark Press, 2005), was the winner of the 2005 Discovery Prize. It is reprinted here, revised, by permission of the author. "To My Quaker Grandmother" is published here for the first time, by permission of the author.

Varallo, Anthony. "In the Age of Automobiles" was first published in *Epoch*, 54:2 (2005) 218–28, and is reprinted here by permission of the publisher.

Walker, Jeanne Murray. "Driving North to the Headwater" appears in *Nailing Up The Home Sweet Home* (Cleveland: Cleveland State University Press, 1980). "Betting in Bright Sunlight at Delaware Park" appears in *Fugitive Angels* (Port Townsend, WA: Dragon Gate Press, 1985). Both poems are reprinted here by permission of the author.

Zeises, Lara. "Me and the Bean" was first published in *Rush Hour: Face*, Vol. 3 (New York, NY: Delacorte Press, 2005), 21–33, and is reprinted here by permission of the author.

Introduction

Billie Travalini and Fleda Brown

"ALL GOOD WRITING SHOULD CUT TO THE BONE," JAMES BALDWIN said. Such writing requires intensity and focus, to allow us to see ourselves, our community, and our world with unexpected clarity. We trust that the fifty-two poems, stories, and essays in this anthology offer a new clarity of vision about this small but extraordinarily diverse state their authors have called home. For Delawareans, different worlds have always come together like turbulent winds, competing, then augmenting, blowing first one way, then the other. This is not a criticism, but an explanation. The Mason-Dixon Line marks the western border of the state—we're Yankee, but barely. We're a state that hardly knows whether it's Northern or Southern. Stretching ninety-six miles along the eastern coast of the United States, Delaware, the first state to ratify the Constitution, and one of four border states during the American Civil War, is as diverse and interesting as any state in the nation.

Delaware was nicknamed the "Diamond State" by Thomas Jefferson because he said Delaware was a jewel among states. Talk to any native Delawarean, and you'll hear about Caesar Rodney riding horseback eighty miles in driving rain to reach Philadelphia in time to cast the deciding vote for the Declaration of Independence. You'll also hear about Eleuthère Irénée Du Pont coming all the way from France to live along the Brandywine River, produce gunpowder, and get rich. A century later Al Smith had his presidential campaign headquarters up the road in Claymont at the Raskob estate, but not many people know about that one. But they do know about the Perdues and their chickens. Sussex County is full of chickens—chickens, and carloads of vacationers driving to Rehoboth and Bethany and Fenwick to swim in the Atlantic Ocean, lie on miles of white sand, and eat Dolle's saltwater taffy and Grotto's pizza.

Editing this anthology was an exercise in coming to terms with the question of what it means to be a Delaware writer. When we started this project we had to decide whether living in Delaware now was a requirement for inclusion, or whether having once lived in the state was enough—and for how long. Was it enough that a writer had just dropped by, the way Edgar Allan Poe is rumored to have stopped overnight at the Deer Park Tavern in Newark? As we looked at poems, stories, and essays, the question began to take care of itself. We selected writers who live in Delaware presently or who had lived or worked here long enough to allow Delaware to touch them in some important way. Sometimes their Delaware-ness is reflected in the setting or language of the poetry or prose, sometimes not.

And, oh yes, this anthology is edited by a Northerner and a Southerner, sort of. Fleda Brown grew up in Arkansas and Billie Travalini grew up in Delaware. Neither state is definitively North or South—both Delaware and Arkansas seem very Southern in their southern region, very Northern in their northern region.

Besides a Delaware connection, our only criterion was good writing. We sent e-mails and made calls to solicit manuscripts from every state writer we had contact information for. We sought out writers whom we knew had left Delaware. From what came to us, we chose the most lively, original, and skillfully written work. We're sure we've missed people whose work could have been included, but at some point, anthology-collecting must end.

The writers here range from internationally known storytellers and poets to emerging professionals such as former Bronx school teacher Liz Dolan and Newark's curmudgeon at-large, Douglas Morea. Many of the contributors are faculty members at major universities. Others are associated with writing groups throughout Delaware. Together they are a diverse group, but cohesive in an unusual way. Delaware is a small state. Everybody knows everybody, and tries to be helpful. When Pulitzer Prize-winning poet W. D. Snodgrass was asked to contribute to the anthology he immediately suggested his poems "Cherry Saplings" and "The Marsh." Gibbons Ruark, Jeanne Murray Walker, and Allison Funk, nationally known poets with many books to their credit, enthusiastically offered their work. Popular novelist and poet Julianna Baggott provided a novel excerpt and poems and helped locate several of the writers represented in this collection.

A few words about the prose pieces a reader will find here—and those mentioned represent only a random sampling: In Julie Schumacher's poignant story, "Resurrection Hockey," a high school women's hockey team gets back together to play again after twenty-four years. Elissa Schappell's essay, "The Green Fairy," describes her and her husband's decision to drop out of their lives in New York and the publishing world to live in Portugal, where they fall under the dangerous spell of absinthe. In her companion piece, "That Sort of Woman," Schappell is reading *Mrs. Dalloway* and finds herself connecting to the story in unexpected and powerful ways. The first chapter of Bonnie MacDougal's novel, *Out of Order*, shows us an ominous beginning to a Greenville marriage and the kidnapping of the thirteen-year-old son of an influential senator. Lynn Pruett's "Shouting Nazarene" takes us along on a date between a lonely old black professor of religion and a young white woman who answers his online ad. "Stillborn," Maribeth Fischer's Pushcart Prize-winning essay, delves into the profound pain a young woman feels when her mother suddenly leaves home to be with an old high school sweetheart. Drury Pifer's "Fruitcakes and Fiction" pits a marvelously sadistic lie against plain facts—and the lie wins. McKay Jenkins gives us a condensed, magazine-version of his bestseller, *And None Came Back*, about the ill-fated climb of five boys up a mountain in Glacier National Park.

With both the prose and the poetry, we were happy when a writer mentioned Delaware, but didn't insist on it. As is true of the prose, many of the poems reflect Delaware's mix of past and present, agricultural and urban. For example: the "old ways" are viewed from different angles in Julianna Baggott's "Living Where They Raised Me," David Scott's "Delaware," and Vanessa Haley's "For a Former Student Found at Fleming's Landing After Two Years at the Bottom of the Smyrna River." In "Poem For a Birthday," Marisa de los Santos has readers visit the Brandywine River in summer through the eyes of a young woman confronting both love and loss. The images in Gibbons Ruark's "A Vacant Lot" and Allison Funk's "Downstate" bridge the past and present, giving new meaning to both. And there's Dana Garrett's meditation on law and lawlessness, "From the Seventh Floor of the Carvel State Office Building." Other poems don't focus on Delaware. Maggie Rowe goes back to her roots in Ireland to write "Wexford Boy," a poem about a young boy and his grandfather trying to understand each other and the world around them. Devon Miller-Duggan imagines that "Elvis is an Angel." Linda Blaskey connects the act of "Loading Hogs for Market" and the act of war. Deborah Creasy's "Pelican Sky" gathers a father, a speaker, and grief into one bundle of words that can hold them all. Each poem we chose "cuts to the bone." Each offers a truth from some new or interesting angle.

Of course no collection of writing can define a people or place. But a person's imaginative landscape is always formed, and informed, by real landscape. It has its roots there, no matter where it branches. The richness, diversity, and complexity of the essays, stories, novel excerpts, and poems included here add up, in some strange yet real way, to Delaware.

On the Mason-Dixon Line

JULIANNA BAGGOTT

This excerpt is taken from the very beginning of *The Miss America Family*. The novel is co-chronicled by Pixie, former Miss New Jersey, and, as you see in this section, her sixteen-year-old son, Ezra, who's just home for the summer from St. Andrew's, the boarding school in Middletown, Delaware. The novel, which takes place primarily in Greenville, spans the summer when Pixie becomes dangerous and the family loses its bearings completely. In this section, Ezra is just beginning to feel that things are a bit off.

The Miss America Family

Ezra, 1987
Greenville, Delaware

Rule #1: Have a set of rules to live by like a monk or an Army general or a debutante so that you always know just what to do and say.

I'll start just before the beginning, just before the incident with Janie Pinkering and her father's French tickler. I believe you should lead up to sex. And I'll get to death, too—an almost-death, at least, how someone changes when they're about to die. Their mouth and eyes can be wide open like a child's again as if singing the "oh" of one of their favorite songs. That's how Mitzie put it, my little half sister, who's probably a better person than everybody I know put together.

This was just this past summer, six months ago now. Everything started to happen all at once, as if all my life I was waiting for the beginning and finally there it was, like I was leaning against what I thought all along was a wall, and then it gave in, and I realized it was a door, swung wide open to bright dazzling sun. This was when my mom, for all intents and purposes, left my stepdad, Dilworth Stocker, and Mitzie decided to live with our neighbors, the Worthingtons, a nice, squat but well-postured couple who eat things that Mrs. Worthington has made from scratch, who, you can tell just by looking at

19

them, think all children are precious gifts from God, even though God didn't bless them with any of their own. (The household's fertility seeming to be wasted on the cats, hundreds of them wandering in and out of a kitty door on the side of their house.) All at once, it seemed like people had decided to tell their lousy secrets. My grandmother told hers, things that I've never really understood except that they were dark, too dark to pass on any further than they needed to be, and I guess she decided, in a weakened post-stroke condition, that they needed to be passed on, at least to my mother, who reacted with calm irrationality. And my real dad, too, unburdened himself to me in a convertible a few blocks from a stranger's house, telling me that he's a faggot, after all, not even bisexual, but purely gay, despite the fact that he married my mother and, evidently, had sex with her at some point. Although he pretended that he didn't know I'd been kept in the dark, it was, in fact, a secret and came as a complete shock. Even Mr. Pichard, an old man I met who could sing opera, spilled his guts. And I had to start sorting all this shit out. But I've got to start before everything happened, because you have to know how much bullshit I was dealing with in this intensely dull way. I have to explain what the wall was like before it swung open as a door.

My stepdad was the one who made my short-lived affair with Janie Pinkering possible and that's really when the wall gave a little under the weight of my shoulder. It wasn't his intention to get me laid—although I think he was kind of proud of me in that tough, boys-will-be-boys way when all of the facts came to light—but I'll give him credit, since there isn't much else that's redeeming about him. Dilworth Stocker turned out to be a sad specimen, after all. I remember him that summer rumpling my hair like he was Santa and I was a five-year-old on his lap, rapping his glass of scotch to get our attention throughout dinner, like a little gavel in between his president jokes, his priests and rabbis, his talking cows, the little gavel always passing judgment. When he introduced me to his friends, he always pulled them slightly aside and whispered hoarsely, "Well, they don't make boys like they used to." Sometimes he'd get on this kick where he'd call me a puny runt, usually when he and my mother had had a fight, when he'd said enough mean things to drive her from a room, with him laughing in that full-bellied way so she couldn't really get upset, or he'd start in on her delicate psyche, and I was the only one left standing there. He's a tan, bullish man with thick forearms and a tight, toothy smile, a jackass.

In any case, he charged into the kitchen one day to inform me and my mom that I was going to stop being sickly and pale like some British kid. He hates the British, mainly, I think, because in his mind they've confused the term *football* for *soccer*, American football being holy, and because they always think they're right. He told me that I was going to work for a living that summer as Bob Pinkering's gardener. Bob Pinkering was my mother's podiatrist, my stepdad's golf buddy, and still is Janie Pinkering's father.

The day my stepdad showed up at the back door of the kitchen to announce my new-found employment, I was eating French toast that my mom had made for me, and she was flipping through one of her fashion magazines but keeping an eye on me at the same time, filling my juice when it got low, and sometimes reaching over the table to press down a wayward curl in my hair. Mitzie was up in her bedroom, practicing her tap dance routine. Above the clatter of her tap shoes on the hardwood floors, we could still hear her tinny, sharp voice, narrating the steps, "Shuffle, ball-chain. Shuffle, ball-chain."

This happened after I'd loafed half the summer away. I was home from St. Andrew's, a boarding school smack in the middle of Delaware cornfields and strip malls. The school is only a little less than an hour from our house in Greenville, a couple towns north. Dilworth insisted I go away to school somewhere. He'd voted for a good, far-off military academy, but my mother would have none of that. So I ended up at St. Andrew's, and my mother consented because it's the best school around, hands down, and I do exceptionally well on standardized tests. Just give me a sharp number two pencil and a piece of paper covered with little bubbles and I can solve just about anything. Unfortunately, Dilworth likes to remind me, life isn't set up that way. I didn't know it at the time, but things would go off-course and I wouldn't be going back to St. Andrew's in the fall.

Of course, I'd set out with good summer goals. I was going to make a list of Rules to Live By, my own set of guidelines that would take me through life. I had a blue spiral pocket-size flip pad to write them down in. But the only rule I'd come up with so far was to have my own set of rules and to stick by them without question, like the only member of my own military or priesthood or something. Instead of coming up with more rules, I'd eaten a lot of fruity cereal and watched reruns of "Gilligan's Island" and stupid stuff like that, and felt all the while really bad about not being a better person with rules. I was down on myself. The morning Dilworth gave us the news about my job, I'd looked in the mirror after splashing my face with cool water. I'd stared at myself, my too-big eyes, and narrow head, my skinny neck, puffy lips, and oversized teeth, my ears sticking out just enough to get sun-burned if I don't coat them in lotion. And I was wondering where it all came from and what I could possibly look like to people who met me for the first time.

You see, I come from good-looking genes. My mother was once Pixie Kitchy, Miss New Jersey. But it never did her any good. The pageant stuff happened before she eloped with my father, Russell, a long-haired, door-to-door household cleaner salesman from Wiscon-sin, and had a sickly four-pound son, me, Ezra, with weak, fluid-filled lungs, and webbed toes. They thought that they were naming me after a great literary figure, Ezra Pound. Of course, I'd since figured out at St. Andrew's, where they had a Pound scholar, that the original Ezra was a huge Fascist with a thing for Mussolini. It's something that probably neither of my parents has ever figured out. I've heard my mother say, "And this is Ezra, named after Pound, the great literary figure." She's never read any of his books, I bet. My mother subse-quently left the long-haired, door-to-door household cleaner sales-man and gave up on the string of so-called boyfriends who followed the divorce—men she'd bring home where she'd serve them drinks at the green kitchen table and then disappear with them behind her locked bedroom door—before she married a Catholic dentist, Dilw-orth Stocker, when I was seven, and had a daughter, Mitzie. My moth-er's talent for the beauty pageants was the accordion. She could play only one song, "Moonlight Serenade," practiced to perfection. She didn't make it all the way to Miss America, not even to the final ten. Some bimbo from Michigan won that year, probably because she let it slip during the interview with Bert Parks that her sister was brain-damaged. Up to that point, Susan Anton, the blond California giant, was the obvious favorite. But my mom was a knock-out. And I'd like to say, right here, that it's not easy when your mom's a knock-out. I'm not bragging. In fact, if I could unmake my mother Miss New Jersey, I think our lives would be a lot easier. But there are other things that I know about now, or at least have pieced together about my mother's life, darker, meaner things I'd unmake for her first, if I could. It's just that my mother's being Miss New Jersey is an important fact. It's key to understanding my mother and, if you don't understand her, you'll misunderstand all of this altogether.

I've got to be up-front, though, and admit that I don't really under-stand my mother. People don't *like* her really, but she doesn't seem to want friends. They respect her. She's very frank, and this makes her scary. I've heard her advise Mitzie, who's only nine and has got this high-pitched, screechy voice, "You must *sound* pleasing to be pleasing." But I don't think she believes it. I get the feeling she's handing down a known evil, because, well, at least it's known.

When I think of my mother the first half of that summer, before all of the craziness with Janie Pinkering and my grandmother and then the gun, I think of her as being held together simply out of habit. She was on the verge of something, like at the edge of a cliff, but having a picnic perched right there, a chic little picnic from a Longaberger basket bought at one of those stupid at-home Tupperware-type parties. She knew the edge was there, maybe, but ignored it all the same. I knew that my mother was dangerous despite the fact that she seemed like a normal person, not especially happy but resigned to her life, kind of like a commie who's bought into the whole idea of things being for the common good. But I knew that she had a gun in her bedside table. She got the gun when she left my real dad and decided to use her body to make a political statement, a statement that was never clear to me, but obviously hinged on the practice of having sex with a lot of men. She was armed before she gave up this so-called political life to marry Dilworth Stocker who charged in to sweep us off our dirty bare feet into the land of upper-middle-class suburbia. I was with her when she bought the gun in a pawn shop in Bayonne. And I always kind of knew that she could pull it out.

That summer it had begun to dawn on me how strange she really was. First of all, she seemed to be two very different people. In the daytime, she was amply gracious, refined, generally connected and straightforward. But she rarely slept—as far back as I remember—because she suffered from terrible nightmares that made her wake up screaming. And so she usually prowled at night. I remember her that summer in beautiful sheer nightgowns with delicate sheer drawstring robes, her long legs swiftly shifting underneath. I was up, too, sometimes, wandering into the kitchen for a late-night snack and when I'd find her, she was strange, confused sometimes, distant.

Secondly, I'd just started to notice how bizarre our relationship was, the way she'd never allowed anything to be too itchy or tight on me, and still snipped the elastic around the waistband of my underwear and the thick edge around the leg holes. "It might diminish your circulation," she claimed. I assumed she meant the circulation to my balls but was never clear on that. I was once called to the principal's office in seventh grade because she couldn't remember if she'd peeled the waxy edge off of my bologna sandwich or not, and, afraid that it might be toxic, she wanted me to check first. The secretary told this to me, trying desperately to keep a straight face. My mother had, in fact, peeled off the waxy edge. And she was still at it, cutting my fruit for me in small pieces to minimize the risk of choking. I was born sickly and she never got over it, but it's more than that, too. I mean, when I was Mitzie's age, for example, I wanted a cat and she wouldn't let me have one, but she offered to let me pet her slippered feet while she purred. What was stranger was that I liked petting her fuzzy slippers, liked listening to her purr. And I still felt this way, drawn to her, and I hated the feeling. I wouldn't even mention this embarrassing stuff if I didn't think it was important, somehow, to show how things would eventually play out.

JULIANNA BAGGOTT

Living Where They Raised Me

Delaware is ripe with cancer—
its shallow fields and factories without run-off,
but we don't speak of it, the home-towners,
because we aren't going anywhere.
From here, Ohio sounds exotic.
But we wonder how it will settle in,
where the curdled cells will take root.
In school, I was impressed
by the filmstrip of the woman born armless,
who could do everything with her feet—
trim her son's bangs, swat flies,
stir cake batter with her rump on the counter,
one leg around the bowl,
a wooden spoon hooked in her toes.
A nervous child, I prepared,
practiced the barefoot art
of turning pages, scrawling my name.
But my arms never fell off.
In fact, they are still here,
my feet still holding ground,
my pink organs turning this into that,
and Delaware, surrounded by the rumor
of mountains, is still flat,
its back unbroken, refusing to attempt
that sort of useless resurrection.
It's easy to blame the land,
to think if we lived somewhere else—
Hackensack or Damascus—
believing would be so easy.

JOANN BALINGIT

Comfort, Cape Henlopen

As the moon set, I saw a big toad smashed in the road, entrails popped
from its side.
Then a smaller toad, then an even smaller toad, all flat in a line, on a
road-longitude

which made me fear that someone I knew—or a stranger I'd said Hello
to, who'd said back warmly Hello—had meant to kill them. That is,
let a little evil scoot out. I came on two men

in silhouette at sunrise standing on top of a picnic table in morning
conversation, gesturing
with coffee cups, one flicking a fly from his trunks, the other passing
binoculars, both

gazing in their pauses out to sea. Friendly—they said Good
morning—and I understood
they were studying the waves, as they understood I was studying the
waves from the top

of my picnic table, for when to get our boards. They asked me if I
knew what time's low tide.
Then I saw a horsefly fat as a toad, wings like guitar picks, the
Horsefly-Huge-as-Knowledge

dead in the road, and I said to me, I am glad about that. Like last night
I clapped for my
Buddhist friend when she smashed a nasty, pesky fly. With her fine,
fast hand. Her deft

heavy hand. Like those fishermen down there casting flies that tap the
sun-glassed water.

Their lines float out flimsy as spider silk, they sail, what a wayward
    way back. I'm told it's

the heaviness of those lines—the dumb weight forges flight. And the
    men's hard wrists
are supple, their delicate movements precise. They sweet-wrangle
    ropes into whispers.

Same way a stranger's smile, conjured up or cast off, buoys me toward
    comfort. Goodness
or illusion of goodness? It's not for study. I say Hello. Because I
    cannot know, if I want

to know. And I am moving toward glad about that. Last time a spider
    got in my car, I chose quick-with-a-shoe. There are reasons one
    man brings his rockfish in, the other man lets his go.

LINDA BLASKEY

Loading Hogs for Market

The young man runs them
through the chute   up the
ramp of the truck Those
that escape have to be tackled
wrestled to the ground   He has
to be quick   face pressed
to bristled back   Chest   belly
legs ride the bristles   He eats
their dirt

Good practice for the war in his
future   for the steam and the mud
he will fall down in   to avoid being
caught   to camouflage himself
Good practice for the stiff reeds he will
walk through   for the jungle that
will attack his skin   rot his feet
liquefy his bowels   parasite his mind

Good practice   many years
later   for the war he will reflect on
while he sits on the sprung couch
in the shaded house   in the dark
little valley   listening to the grunts
and snorts of the hogs in their pen
the metal door of their automatic
feeder banging shut   banging shut
banging shut   like a rifle report

FLEDA BROWN

Anatomy of a Seizure

Ontogeny

Probably when my mother carried the blue-knitted bundle of my brother through our door for the first time, he was already brain-damaged. I don't know. It was like my parents not to have bothered to help my sister and me understand what little they did know. My father says now that he worried from the beginning. Even in the womb, he says, Mark seemed to hold very still, then jerk unnaturally, as if he were having seizures. But then, my father has always lived within his own inexplicable womb of worry. It is possible my mother's bad case of German measles when she was three months pregnant caused Mark to be born retarded—no one knew back then what damage German measles could wreak. It's remotely possible, however, that he was bitten by a mosquito when he was about three months old and caught encephalitis, with its high fever, which damaged his brain. "Your mother naturally prefers to believe this," my father would say, with his frightening way of objectifying feelings. No matter. They did what had to be done, changed diapers, cleaned up spills.

Anxiety I

What I remember is as vague and fuzzed with anxiety as the rest of my childhood. I was nine when Mark was born; my sister Melinda was six. Already we had moved from Columbia, Missouri, to Middlebury, Vermont, where my grandfather had pulled strings to get his eldest son his first academic job, then when it appeared the college didn't want to keep him, to Akron, Ohio, for the same purpose, and when that failed, back to Columbia, where my father reluctantly finished up course work toward a Ph.D. in economics. We lived in his parents' house while his economist father was off lecturing around the country.

My mother's parents lived next door: a study in contrarieties, the academic and the businessman. When my father proved to be difficult, childlike, and socially impossible, my mother's parents stiffened against him, but with as much Christian grace as they could muster. All of this seeped under my skin, started a lifelong war inside me. Nana would invite my sister and me over in the afternoons and use something called "Baby Touch" on our legs, to get the first signs of dark hair off. "Sandpapering your legs," my father would say, furious. She wanted us to be ladies; my father wanted. . . . well, I don't know that he wanted anything but to go hiking, sailing, and flying kites. And sex with my mother. My mother wanted. . . . well, her wants were pretty simple, a hot fudge sundae, a new vacuum cleaner, a little approval. All she got was a mother who frowned at the life her daughter had let herself in for and pursed her lips at her daughter's awkwardness, her inability to sew or cook creatively. And she got a husband who mostly reacted, who made as few decisions as possible. Let her ask him to change his shirt, and he flew into a childish rage. Rage was his middle name. But when he wanted sex, he was all over her, purring. She naturally pushed away. More fights.

Description

Into this edginess, Mark was born, the third child, the only boy. I only remember the questions, the budding of a new kind of tension, his diarrhea, the dirty diapers over and over, the beginning of a life of diapers. Mark started out a handsome child, blonde and blue-eyed, fine bone structure. His thin body seemed intended to be strong. Until he was two or three, it wasn't immediately obvious to look at him that he was retarded. At least not much. I can't remember. Until the last years, except when he was having seizures, his blue eyes sparked with what seemed like the possibility of intelligence. I think he would have been very smart. As he grew, the anti-seizure drugs made his gums swollen and red. His lips got fat from the pummeling they took when he had seizures. His chin and forehead became as scarred as a prize-fighter's, his teeth chipped. His head seemed gradually to grow too large, the way it leaned to one side, bobbling on his weakening, thin neck.

He scooted around in a walker until he was maybe three, then he walked like a toddler, on his toes, his feet unable to lie flat. Gradually, his wrists also drew up, his fingers didn't want to uncurl. He was able to walk until he was fourteen. He got a bad case of the flu, I think it was, and when he recovered, he'd lost so much strength in his legs that he couldn't walk any more. He spent the rest of his life propped up on the couch, or flat in bed.

Anxiety II

Mark was going to have a spell. No one knew when, but they were likely to come on two or three times a week. It could happen at break-fast when he was sitting at his high chair, his long legs dangling below the leg-rest. It could happen on a long, hot car-trip to Michigan. For the few years he was potty-trained, it could happen when he was sit-ting on the toilet, so he had to be held, in case he slammed suddenly forward. His seizures stand for my own private anxieties, my family's anxieties. Something was always about to happen, and it wasn't good. Something was going to break down, money would be gone, someone was going to get strep throat, my parents were going to fight, my mother was going to lie on the bed and cry, my father was going to rant.

To Seize

To take possession of, to arrest, to confiscate, to grasp. Beginning with blankness in the eye, a stillness, a kind of aura you could sense, a slight whitening of the skin. This was all so quick, but still, my parents would say "Markie's having a spell," before it happened. Actually, it was al-ready in process, inevitable, the electrical storm begun. All his muscles would suddenly be strung tight, he would lurch forward from the waist, throw his head down and arms out in front of him. He would be rigid enough to break. He would barely seem to breathe, his eyes rolled up in his head, his mouth open and drooling. If there happened to be anything in front of him, he would slam down on it as hard as possible. He would bleed. We would hold his head, we would put a cold towel on his forehead. We would wipe the saliva from his mouth and chin. He would hold his position, quivering with rigidity for min-ute after minute. "My god, I don't see how he can keep that up," my father would say, chewing on his tongue. There would be a hopeless desperation, and a kind of ironic distance, a survival distance. My mother would sometimes be the one to stroke with the towel, speaking softly to him over and over. She would almost be crying, but not—the terrible not, the not that wanders in pain's wilderness and has no one

to tell. Mark appeared to hear nothing. Where was I? Anywhere, nowhere, wetting the towel, holding his head, or in my room trying to
get through my Algebra with the left-over parts of my brain. Did the
seizures hurt? Possibly. Sometimes he moaned as if in pain. Sometimes he whimpered. Gradually, he would begin to soften, gradually
to collapse. Color would return to his lips. He would be exhausted,
but calm, his circuits blown, like a person after electroshock, I imagine. He would sit quietly for a while, and it would be an hour or so
before he was himself again.

Voice

There's a quality of voice that carries the weight of awareness within
it. It's rich, steady, resonant. Actors can mimic it, but it takes a full and
conscious life to have it. There's the thin head-voice of the afraid-and-
afraid-to-reveal-it; there's the breathiness of the utterly held back;
there's the loud frontal voice, skilled at argument, that uses the body
like a weapon at the service of the mind. The most unnerving voice,
though, shoots upward from the animal center, the body crying out in
its own language while the mind remains asleep. Mark would cry out
now and then, a sudden bleat—the tone of which was pain, delight,
frustration, or simply assertion of being—but unalloyed, bypassing the
cerebral cortex, as if it emanated from the ragged ingredients of the
soul before they figured out how to merge. The precious few times we
ate in restaurants, my father would carry him in, a gangly, half-grown
boy. He would be fastened into a booster seat, his bib tied. Suddenly
he would call out to the universe as if he and it alone understood each
other, a raven's cry, a beacon. How easily I disappeared, then, moving
through the vacuum that would have been shame, had I not sucked all
the life out of it. At night, too: a wail, a screech, a reminder of how
dearly silence is bought, how quickly it can be taken away. As his voice
deepened, it came up from a cave I imagined as dark, dank, full of all
his slow, sodden years.

Treatment

First there was only phenobarbital, before it began to lose its effec-
tiveness. Then dialantin, which never worked as well for him. And cel-
ontin, which made him seriously depressed, crying, tense, so that was
stopped quickly. Others I can't remember, all ground up with mortar
and pestle and mixed in his oatmeal, or mashed vegetables. Some-

times, when a medicine was working less well, or when doctors were experimenting with a new one, he would have *grand mal* seizure after seizure. He would fling himself over and over into his own abyss, gasping for breath. Now there's surgery, a bisection of the brain that disconnects the cerebral hemispheres, which can be performed on people whose seizures can't be controlled by drugs. Exactly the right metaphor, it seems to me: sever connections; compartmentalize the suffering, break it down into its component parts; don't let the excitatory neurotransmitters broadcast all over the place and overpower the inhibitory ones; don't let the dendrites react to what the axons are shouting. This, then that—each aspect completed and coming to rest within itself, not whipping on the others to a frenzy. It's a kind of enlightenment.

Iron Curtain

The seizure trembled at the center of our existence. It was the meaning of family: our concerted alertness to the helplessless in our midst, the vulnerable core of each of us, exposed—the bedraggled unloveliness we suspected lay at the heart of each of us—our anger, our selfish desire for this all to go away. We lurched from day to day inside the borders of necessity. My parents never looked up long enough to see what help there might have been for his care, for his expenses, until several years after I left home. Probably it was when he turned twenty-one that a social worker came to the house and explained to them the possibilities. As a child, I hardly knew there was a world out there. When my brother Mark was born, it was 1953. Ike was President, the Beats were beginning their underground surge against the man in the gray flannel suit. Nuclear bombs were being tested. Guatemala was invaded, to "liberate" the people and to fend off communism. Communism loomed as the great world seizure, ready to make its move at any moment. America's tension may have infiltrated our own, but how could I know?

Priests

If the seizure was the center of our existence, doctors were its priests, Dr. Patrick in particular—young, handsome, and sympathetic. My mother needed someone to notice her, a surrogate parent, ten or fifteen minutes of undivided attention in a small room. My father needed science, a cool eye, a dispassionate physician's assessment, to distance himself. Dr. Patrick was not inclined, however, to offer his prediction of the worst, and perhaps we were all grateful. We needed and needed, but what we needed wasn't exactly clear. We needed—if I can see from this distance what it was—a few medical words embedded in ongoing Godlike concern. We didn't want him to forget about us, to let us slip from his everlasting presence. We were taken to see Dr. Patrick at the slightest provocation, and we were sick a lot: earaches, colds, flu, sinus infections. The delivery car from Collier's Drug Store pulled up in front of our house several times a week. When I wasn't sick, I invented an ailment, or exaggerated its severity. Oddly, perhaps, I wanted to stay home from school: the tightly self-absorbed system of our household was more familiar, more comfortable than the outside world. Dr. Patrick represented the blessing of that outside world on our complexities, an omniscient understanding.

Potty Training

For the infant-fold diaper, one doubles the entire length of cloth, ending up with a tight little triangle. Then, as the child grows, one begins the initial fold not at the half-way mark, but only one-third down the rectangle, and the corners are not brought so closely together, leaving more room for the legs. Soiled diapers are rinsed in the toilet, flushing and swishing. They're wrung out and stored in a plastic bucket. Each time the lid is opened, the ammonia smell jolts into the room, stronger as the child grows older. Just when the whole process begins to seem tedious and awful, there's potty training. Even for Mark, after a long while. For several years, before he became weaker and couldn't get out of bed, he wore training pants. But when he couldn't get up any longer, he wore several diapers at once, not folded at all, but flattened out and tucked down in the front. Safety pins would get rusty and dull from urine and would have to be stroked across a bar of soap to get them through the layers of diaper. He would need glycerine suppositories every day to have a bowel movement: the house would fill with the odor. By this time, he was fully developed and had to be washed carefully each time, his pubic hair kept clean and powdered.

Normal

I was beginning to understand something about normality. Normality wasn't normal. It couldn't be. If normality were normal, everybody would leave it alone. They could sit back and let normality manifest itself.

So says the main character, a hermaphrodite, in Jeffrey Eugenides' novel that won the Pulitzer Prize this year. Ah, those of us who grow up in "abnormal" homes are the ones to consult when it comes to worrying normality to death! We know exactly what it is, where it is to be found—at Little League games, Dad grilling on the patio, Mom headed off to bridge club—images always receding on our horizon. We believe with our whole hearts in *Saturday Evening Post* covers, in Ozzie and Harriet, in the rest of the world—the not-us—living their lives within a halo of society's approval.

Missy was born in 1958. I was fourteen, Melinda eleven, Mark five. Missy never knew Mark as a smiling little blonde boy, babbling his words. She doesn't remember him walking. To her, he was a large, thin, almost-man lying in a hospital bed in her parents' room, emitting random eerie cries, terrible smells. Our parents—isolated people, afraid of the outside world themselves—couldn't help her find ways to explain to her friends. Her isolation fed the dream of normality, as it did for all of us, and the horror of being stranded outside that dream. She told no one about her brother. She avoided bringing friends home. On the rare occasion when she did, Mark would suddenly cry out from the bedroom, and all would be lost. Once, on a camping trip to Kentucky Lake long after Melinda and I had left home, Missy was put in charge of watching Mark, who lay helplessly in the tent, while our parents went for a sail. Some of her new campground friends came by and asked her out on their boat. She went. She was only twelve— having to admit to the existence of her monstrous brother in the tent was more awful than the consequences of leaving him alone.

Baby-talk

While we were living in Arkansas and Mark was seven or eight, his teacher Mrs. Laverty reported that she'd cataloged three hundred words he could say. A vast number. He was potty-trained and could say that many words. He could run with the neighborhood children, his own head bobbling far above them, lurching and laughing. "Tee-dah," he called me. There was a kind of hope, a belief in progress in the face of certain collapse. The doctors knew what they knew—for the duration of each seizure, oxygen to the brain is cut off, gradually destroying more brain cells. What was our hope made of? Of one good day, of word after word, for the record. I am coming home from school. Mark is on the couch. He has had a seizure but is now calm and beginning to perk up. His face brightens when I walk in. "Tee-dah," he calls out, and lurches toward me. I love him with the same old miserable love that's followed me since. Things can't be fixed. Nothing can be nice, or clean. I don't know exactly who I am, yet I am asked to be this person, this "Tee-dah," and so I am, the roiling of my mind quieted for a moment as I hold him and kiss the top of his head.

I can see my mother in his latter years, before he went to the nursing home, sitting beside his hospital bed in their bedroom. She keeps a tall stool with a back on it next to the bed, to save her own back. She's talking baby-talk to him. She's worn out with trying to shift his weight enough to change his diaper, to clean him up. She's using the voice, the baby-talk he knows. She's stuck there; he's stuck there; we're all stuck, seized, gripped. Those of us who can, pull loose and get out. Those who can't, stay with the sweet language of the past, that once had meant beginnings.

Nourishment

It doesn't matter how old he is, here. He's fastened in his scratched, wooden highchair, tied with a rag to hold him more securely. He is being watched carefully for signs of seizure. The highchair, actually, is a good place for it, if there's enough advance warning to get a pad on the tray, because he's protected against falling. My mother's on one side of him, my father's on the other, to quickly grab his head if he jerks forward. On his highchair tray are bits of pork chop and green beans, cut small as beads to prevent choking. He picks up a handful and shoves them in. Some miss. He throws some of them. He's fed some of them. He likes it when we're all at the table. He babbles. We are not unhappy. Even my father, who has ducked his head and re-peated the prayer my mother begs him to say before meals, even though he believes in science instead. "Bless this food to our use and us to thy love and service amen," he's intoned for her, with his flat, ironic edge. My mother asks for the applesauce, content enough. What is happiness but the nest we make for ourselves out of the tangle of troubles?

Thelma

Thelma Smith is hired to help my mother when Mark gets too heavy to handle. Thelma, barely literate, lives in a miserable hovel on

Olive Street, with her drunken, abusive husband and her children, including one retarded son who roams the streets, dirty, whooping and mumbling. Sometimes, she reports, one of her children is bitten by a rat while sleeping. Thelma's husband won't let her take birth control pills, so she hides them at my parents' house and takes one there each day. She and my mother drink Pepsi and watch soap operas in the afternoons when Thelma is supposed to be folding diapers or washing clothes. "Why don't you make her do what you pay her for?" we ask over and over, but they just keep sitting, two women in silent rebellion.

Rescue

(1) Mark is on the sailboat, happily dangling his hand in the water. He falls overboard. My father dives in after him, grabs his leg. My father's leg catches on a rope. They dangle there for a moment, both of them underwater. The rest of us are watching from the dock. My father makes a superhuman lunge upward. They're both saved. (2) Mark is lying in a tent at Kentucky Lake. He is overheated, burning up with fever. My father carries him to the water and swabs him over and over with a wet diaper. He is okay. (3) He is in the nursing home. They call to say he's very ill, that he may not live. My father suggests that they give him intravenous fluids, which revive him so that he lives a while longer. My father writes me, "It is unfortunate that we prolonged his misery as long as we did." He says, "I recall at the nursing home, there was one young boy who was almost totally a vegetable, and could do nothing but lie on the floor and salivate. Why we insist on keeping such people alive is more than I am able to understand. If 'God' intends them to die, how can we interfere with his divine plan? But if 'God' intends someone to live, and we help him to die, then we are guilty of the gravest sin and probably will have to spend an eternity in a lake of fire (according to some idiots like Saint John, the author of 'Revelation')."

Consolations

We're coming for Christmas. We've driven eight hours. We turn onto South Garth, three houses from Nana's, but Mark's about to have a seizure. My mother says we should drive around for a while so as not to upset her parents. And so we do, and finally he has the seizure, and my mother pats his face with a wet cloth until he eases. We drive up the driveway. My mother makes my father honk, as if we had just arrived, as if we're all excited.

"They have a poor afflicted boy," Granddaddy often says to their friends, borrowing that evangelist word, taking our lives out of our own hands, as if Mark is a visitation upon us.

Nana sits in her chair, watching the Lennon sisters on the Lawrence Welk Show. She says she would like my sister and me to be like them. They're singing about love, but their harmonies sound to me like humming about nothing, the kind you do when your mind's on something else, or if you were being forced to hum at gunpoint. My Uncle Bob's perfect family is here for Christmas, too, with their perfect, fiercely Christian children. They tell us secretly that our father is going to hell because he's not a Christian. Mark is sitting on the ottoman in front of Nana. She takes his head between her hands. She concentrates hard, closing her eyes. She squeezes and says "Be Healed," twice. We hear her say it. I want to kill the Lennon sisters, smash their TV faces with my foot. I want to raise the ugly, bitter, and dark world in front of her and make her eat it, bite by bite. I want her to get diarrhea smeared on her hands, to wipe up blood, to open her eyes, to know who we are, who I am, with my hard knot of love and rage. Anger forms a glorious sea-wall against my misery.

Indications

Mark is lying in his casket, in his pajamas, a full-grown man, still soft-skinned and no whiter now in death than in the last years of his life. He's more carefully shaved than usual. There are only a few dozen people here, a former teacher, a nursing home staff person, a few friends of my parents, and my sisters and me. Mark's been completely lost so many years that the minister can muster no anecdotes for his sermon, no personal comments, only clichés. So I am left with my own feelings, whatever it is I feel, mine alone, and with Mark alone, inscrutable for all his twenty-four years, mirror of my best feelings and my worst, dear child I have held and comforted, needing comfort myself, dear child I have hated, hating myself, dear child I have cheered on with every new word, pushing myself to achieve, achieve, not to waste a minute of my life.

Now almost thirty years later, my sorrow still feels private, my personal relationship with it as silent and respectful as that moment in which I sat in front of the plain coffin, closed at last. Sorrow remains within me like a closed box, the contents I know so well there's no need to keep checking. Still, sometimes one wants—one deliberately opens the past and lifts out, one by one, its small radiant objects. One suddenly thinks of sorrow with fondness, the way it keeps on being itself, no matter how it's been anatomized, analyzed. Sorrow is easy to love, actually, the way it asserts its own clear presence that one can't dispute, can't wish away, for the way it insists on being included, along with everything else.

FLEDA BROWN

Delaware

An old Candid Camera skit: two men
stop cars at the border. "Delaware's closed
today," they say, and the drivers docilely turn away.

That's me, I'd be still driving around looking.
The way you ought to find a state is, things
change. Fields, then you get to a difference

that stays different, not this compass arc carved
out of Pennsylvania, this right angle drawn away
from Maryland. On a map, its name drifts

in the Atlantic, neither here nor there. It lies
inward like a cove on a creek, twigs and leaves
swirled in, and sludge, and a faint orange ring

you know is pollution, and then in a hard rain
it all moves on and starts again: cancer
slipping boundaries—highest breast cancer rate

in the country, no one takes the blame, everyone's
from somewhere else, like New Jersey, the other side
of the hypotenuse across the bay. In the middle,

Salem Power Plant steams upward, refuses
to take sides. In the south, the long slow marshes,
cypresses, snow geese, herons. Good and evil

cancel each other out—Dela*where?*—
the way the ocean tries to cancel out the shore,
and the shore walks inland and forgets itself in relation

to anything else. I don't know where I live.
You need a breath between states, to be sure
the next one's coming. "Welcome to Oklahoma,

to Missouri," for instance. I remember Arkansas that way,
as being *not those other states.* There has
to be limits, skin and bones. The poetic version

of home can open the mind like a trick-
or-treat bag and endlessly drop things in: Wilmington,
Newark, Middletown, Smyrna, Lewes, Rehoboth,

names our children learn, meaning their own
caches of grief and joy, the resonances
their ears have collected by now. But me, did I

mention my hearing's getting worse? Words
grow softer, doing tricks and transformations.
I could be in a hotel room, soft clicks

in the hallway, a rumble. I can't remember the number
on the door, the sheets are empty pages. I try
to identify the boundaries, as the Buddha says, separate

the strands of experience until there is no self, while
the self is full with the moment, riding the waves
of its own impermanence. I've said farewell, God knows,

many times. The day we left Fayetteville, the three
neighbor children lined up on the sad little mound
of grass to wave goodbye to our son. It was summer,

and the sun took everything out of my eyes
and kept moving. Like a fool, I've believed, though,
in each place. The little creek behind our house

runs clear, now rusty, now clear. Who or what
causes this I do not know. Runoff from lawns,
I'd guess, growing feathery weeds underwater, here,

then gone. Still, there are minnows. And oh yes,
you, my utterly specific love, and our children,
and our children's children, ringing and crashing like deer

to our salt lick, appearing in the morning mist as if
through holes in the universe—their innocence
and light—leaving small berries of scat, and tracks.

WILLIAM CLAIRE

An Archaeological Dig: My Unwanted Third Century Monk (Nice, France)

I chip around the avocado-shaped skull
of a third century monk after being told
earlier by museum heads from Grasse
they do not collect remnants this recent:
the entire monastery remains common
as sunlight on the Riviera where motorists
will find still another road after it's paved;
bulldozers will come tomorrow.
With noble aspirations we came
to uncover what was going under for good . . .

Our leader announced, midway the dig,
nothing here save for amateurs . . .
Years later I still play in my mind
songs my monk sang and sacrifices
he offered, and pray as I scraped
I added another rung up a desert ladder
which one day will lift me from the dust
face to face with an unwanted man I touched.

ANNE AGNES COLWELL

Playing Chicken on the Tracks

Three boys leap against the shivering chainlink,
kick themselves over the wire.
Stepping sideways, sneakers skittering gravel,
they slip down the steep embankment
to the tracks. December cold, brown
weeds, strewn trash, a plastic grocery bag
caught on a sapling, like a white lung,
fills and deflates with sharp air.

Three boys, fourteen maybe or fifteen,
curse, dare, kick at angry cans, smoke,
talk, call each other pussy until they're
all playing chicken with the next one
that comes, no matter what. Waiting
for it, squinting down the double line,
the youngest shoves red hands
in the flannel pockets of his jacket.
There's a piece of jasper in the left
he picked up for its color.

Three standing together, touching, they
feel what is coming for them shiver
through the weeds and trash, through
the rails, through their bones.

All three, in the selfsame instant,
leap against the force that holds them in,
the vacuum in front of a speeding train,
the keening of the brakes, this fence of skin.

TOM COYNE

A Gentleman's Game is the story of young Timmy Price, whose mastery of the game of golf inspires awe among the adult membership and envy among his peers on the shaded fairways and immaculate greens of exclusive Fox Chase Country Club. But when his self-made father forces Timmy to become a caddy at the club to teach him a lesson in humility, he is thrown into the hardscrabble world of the behind-the-scenes workers who make the game possible. And when his best friend and fellow looper, Jamie Byrne, abruptly stops showing up at the caddy hole, it begins a series of events that will force Timmy to confront the dark secret that hides behind the community of Fox Chase. This is an excerpt from that novel.

A Gentleman's Game

The air was April, cool and bright and everything smelling like a fresh towel in your face when you step from the shower. The days began to stretch themselves, and the return of those late afternoons was everything to a golfer. A few more hours, a few more holes. There would be enough light, my father told me, for a quick round after school if we hurried along. Meet at the tee at three o'clock, get out and back in three hours because my mother was making her pot roast. This time she asked us not to come home with excuses.

It was the kind of spring day when things move on a little quicker without trying, the April afternoon when I was eleven years old and I first beat my father.

Three o'clock sharp. We stretched on the tee box, our quiet twosome, and he smiled at the way I was stretching the first hole, looking to see where my drive was going to land. Charlie Logan once explained to me that it was the thing separating those who played golf from those who were golf. It distinguished weekend golfers from those who played the game like it was all buttons and switches, those who made the questions fit inside their answers.

"It's the difference between the likes of you, and the likes of this old bag talking to you," Charlie Logan said, swallowing a mouthful from his Styrofoam cup. "When I move on the ball, Christ, I'm just hoping for contact. You," he said, pushing his cup toward me, "you smooth-as-silk sons a bitches, you fellas aren't thinking about where it's going to end up. You're *seeing* it. There's not one damn smidge of fear in your swing," he said, his eyes staring out at nothing. "Give anything to know what that feels like. Give my left nut. And that's the bigger one." He laughed, the folds of his face lifting into a smile.

On the first tee that afternoon, my father slid the headcover off his wooden driver, its lacquer worn yellow, the face chipped and softened around the edges. "That's not where you're supposed to hit it," he would say when I pointed out the wear and tear around the sweet spot, "and they don't make them like this anymore, Timmy. This is what Ben Hogan used to swing, an old spoon just like this."

In our garage, hanging above my father's neglected tool bench, there was a black-and-white framed photograph of Ben Hogan's one-iron shot at Marion. The picture was cracked and bowed from the yard sale where he'd picked it up. My mother wouldn't let it in the house. It was a view of Ben Hogan's backswing from behind, his stature perfect in a way that cannot be held longer than an instant, that cannot be posed or drawn or sculpted. I agreed with my father when he talked about golf being the one game that allowed for those singular moments, those small visions of pure success, pure purpose, pure unity of effort. Other games blur past, run, score, win, lose. But golf is a flow of pauses, a pace of moment after moment, and sometimes, at some point in that progression from tee to green and green to tee, there is a Ben Hogan at Marion, a club set straight across his shoulders like a carpenter's balance, his cap tipped humbly on his head, a white ball rising toward a gray green deep in the distance.

My father teed up his ball and asked me if I wanted any strokes. I told him I didn't.

"And what are you playing for?" he said.

"I don't know. What do you usually play for?"

"The fellas usually play for drinks. Or money. Or real estate. Do you have any of those?" He smiled.

"I've got some money."

"Not that I don't give you, you don't. What fun would that be for me, taking my own money?"

"We can play for drinks," I said.

"Right. We'll stop for a round on the way home. And your mother would cook me instead of the pot roast. I'll tell you what, we'll have ourselves a gentleman's bet."

I slipped my hand into a crusty leather glove, the fingers shriveled from rain and sweat. "What's a gentleman's bet?"

He took a slow practice swing and watched an imaginary ball move out into the afternoon light. "It's a friendly bet. A bet for honor."

My father's swing wasn't like the one hanging in the garage. It was chopped in half, his arms and legs disagreeing on what they were trying to do. His driver struck the ball with a heel thud. It knuckled over and dove down into the rough.

"Jesus Mary and Joseph," he muttered through clenched teeth.

I bruised a drive that rolled to the stop the hole suggested, right center of the fairway to get back to a pin tucked left. When I used a pitching wedge to drop my second shot six feet below the hole, my father looked at me like I had changed colors.

"Who showed you how to do *that?*" He pointed to my ball as we marched up to the green.

I shrugged my shoulders and didn't look at him and tried not to cough on the pride swelling in my throat. I rolled the ball into the bottom of the cup, and it went down with the sweet rattle *gulp* that only birdie putts have.

The fifth hole was a tight snaking par five, a tunnel of trees bending right then left. A dry creek bed ran down the left side of the fairway, and the other side of the ditch was marked out of bounds. White stakes were placed back in the woods there, in the shadows and the leaves where no one went to look for lost balls. It was too deep and it was dark in the daytime. It was where Fox Chase ended and somewhere else began.

A soggy black carpet of autumns past, a million leaves, and my father's ball was beneath one of them.

"You should probably just drop one," I told him.

"I'll find it. Golf balls don't grow on trees. That was a brand new ball."

He inched down into the ditch, stepping onto a loose stone and almost breaking his ankle. He kicked over rocks and I walked ahead to my ball. I dropped my bag in the fairway, and to my right I spotted someone standing on another fairway. Through a crowd of blue pines, I saw a boy in jeans and sneakers standing a few paces beyond the tree line. I knew that at dusk, fence-members would hop their way onto the course and play a few holes at Fox Chase in the last bits of daylight.

They were usually guys from the public courses, older men with soft-ball cleats instead of golf shoes, carrying sticky old golf bags from the trade-in sports shop. If a member spotted a fence jumper, he would usually look the other way, happy to allow a Joe Sixpack a couple of holes, ten minutes of night golf for the workingman. But I didn't look the other way, and I stared at the figure until I recognized the boy and remembered his name, Jamie Byrne, the kid with straw-blond hair poking out from under his caddy cap. He was trying to hit a golf ball, and as I watched him I understood how that kid carried bags twice his size, sweating that ring of salt into his cap. He was all try. He didn't stop once, not once to think or reconsider as he whiffed shot after shot. Jamie Byrne just whipped the club around his body like he was throwing back a sledgehammer, the club falling down to the ball and missing again.

He grabbed another club off the ground, swinging and holding on with eight fingers and finally knocking a dribbler along the grass that ran ten yards and sat down in the rough. Another ball came out of his pocket, and Jamie set it up on a tee. He waited over the ball, turning his chin, teeth clamping the tip of his tongue, perhaps thinking of the next shot and trusting it to be perfect.

That pause before the swing begins is a small moment of simple faith. It's one of the reasons we play, for that quiet before contact when it might all go right, when we might believe we were better than ourselves. And as Jamie lifted his club back, then threw his body forward to pull it on through, I watched that moment slip through his fingers, the club getting loose from his hands, banging and twisting across the fairway.

"Jesus Christ! Get the hell out of here!"

I turned to see my father waving his five-iron like a sword. He stomped his foot at the ground and spat as he yelled. "Go, get out of here!" A dozen yards in front of him, a fox stood frozen at the edge of the fairway, a gray squirrel hanging limp in its teeth. The fox was small with sharp ears and dark eyes, burnt-orange fur the color of my brother's hair. It shot its eyes from my father to the woods beyond the creek bed, then to me across the fairway. Two hundred acres of open grass and this animal found itself in a corner.

When I turned to look for Jamie, I saw him running hard for the shade of the tree line where the link fence was lowest. He left his golf balls behind, no bag, running with golf clubs cradled in his arms like a bundle of twigs.

"Go on, get out of here!"

The fox dropped the squirrel from its mouth and sprang across the creek bed. It scratched its way up the bank and disappeared into the woods, twisting through the tree trunks until it was just a sound of fast-beating paws on leaves that were still wet from winter.

"That thing could have had rabies," my father said. "Somebody's going to have to do something about that." His hands were shaking when he reached into his bag, taking out a new ball and dropping it in the fairway.

You would hear the talk about there still being foxes at Fox Chase, but it seemed like such an obvious myth that I had not believed it. I had seen the paintings in the clubhouse, men in red coats leaping fences on white horses, a little red blur trying to escape the corner of the frame. And now I had seen a fox, and I thought that there must have been something better to chase, something bigger to hunt that they could kill and stand over. It seemed as pointless as chasing a dog around the backyard or a cat around the kitchen. I wondered why they needed all those people in a mob, why they needed all those horses.

On my sixteenth hole, my father stood over a perfect lie in the heart of the fairway with a three-wood in his hands. He made two poetic practice swings, then took one sideways rip at the ball, sending it worm-burning along the turf and into a muddy creek that crossed the fairway. I had never heard the work *fuck* come from my father's mouth before. It sounded accidental, two syllables like he wanted to stop halfway, fu-*uck*. He wrapped his three-wood around his knee, bending the shaft into a boomerang. It didn't bend back. I looked away as he snapped it in two and dumped the pieces into his bag. I slowed and let him walk out ahead of me, watching him kick and curse and crawl his way in. He looked old, which he did sometimes, but with all that ungraceful anger I thought for the first time that my father looked like a fool.

I only let myself think it for a moment.

By the time we finished, the light was just a cold blue shadow between the trees and the night above us. After eighteen holes, there were two scores. Mine was lower by five.

My father looked over the scorecard, adding up the numbers. "Eighty," he said.

"I think it was seventy-nine."

He looked at the scorecard again, his brow tight over a short list of simple numbers that were somehow tough to put together. He ran his fingers over and down his chin and said, "Right, seventy-nine. Well done."

He tucked the card into his back pocket and said, "You are eleven years old, Timmy. *Eleven.*" It sounded like an accusation. "I have never broken eighty in my entire life."

Eyes lowered against the breeze, my father turned and headed back up to the clubhouse. I watched him pull the scorecard out of his pocket and turn it over in his hands, looking to see if the numbers had changed.

We drove home in a silence that said we had both had enough for one afternoon. My father walked into the kitchen and set the scorecard up on its side on the breakfast table. It took us a minute to notice the smell of electric heat and to see the slippery pink loaf of beef waiting in a black pan on the counter. The kitchen was warm like the oven had been broiling for hours.

My father didn't panic when he saw her in the family room, sleeping sideways in her chair, grape juice dripped down the front of her blouse. Her hair fell over the armrest, and her shoulders, small and crooked, stretched at the corners of her shirt. One knee faced in, one faced out. Her face lay on the edge of the chair, her lips open and pushed against the upholstery. The sound upstairs of my brother's stereo. She slept, drums throbbing against the ceiling.

My father helped her off the chair and up the stairs, holding her by her waist, and she apologized until she cried while he told her not to worry. We had eaten already, he said, a quick bite on the way home.

She stopped crying, and she lifted her head and said, "You promised you wouldn't." He said it didn't matter, we could save her roast for tomorrow.

My father came downstairs and made a pile of peanut butter and jelly sandwiches. We ate dinner across from each other in silence, a scorecard for a centerpiece. My father mashed up the bread in his mouth, eyes studying his sandwich like it was covered in fine print. I tried not to think about the boy on the course and his hands and they told us grip's the thing. I didn't stare at the roast on the counter, thinking about why we were eating sandwiches again. I didn't wonder if the man across from me wished he had beaten his eleven-year-old son.

My father and I sat there eating our dinner, both of us not thinking the exact same things.

DEBORAH CREASY

Pelican Sky

Where does music come from and where does it go when it's over—the child's unanswered question about more than music.
Lisel Mueller, "Place and Time"

This poem is my father.
This poem is the chair
he was sitting in when he died.
It is his favorite chair.
This poem is me,
stranded in a flood,
slogging through high water,
trying to reach higher ground
before dark.
This poem is a day in February,
its grey sky cracking open,
a red brick church, the white rose
I plucked from the sidewalk,
the poem that fell
from the coffin spray
as the pallbearers struggled
down uneven steps.
This is the poem that won't go away,
that grows like tickweed
along the railroad tracks.
This poem is a vine with tendrils
that tangle in my hair.
It is a striped sparrow
fluttering inside my ribcage.
When I take a walk,
this poem hides behind a tree,

it dances above my left shoulder,
just out of view.
I can see its shadow
when the sun shines.
When I lie down at night,
it is there, under my bed.
I hear its small
animal breathing.
It will stay there
until I am asleep,
then crawl into bed with me,
and burrow into my dream—
Sometimes, this poem
will take me by the hand
and reveal itself to me,
though it is clear
as a raindrop.
Today, it leads me
to a sandy bluff
above the sea
and we watch
five pelicans
skim the waves
in single file,
only a whisper
between their wings
and the water. Then,
in an almost imperceptible
shift of flight,
the second two in line
fly side by side,
and we see
for a moment,
a cross,
a cruciform
of five pelicans
before they disappear
into the mist.
This poem knows
where those birds are going,
though I don't,

and when I beg this poem
to tell me, it refuses,
and instead leads me
to my own hard chair
and makes me sit,
until I learn
the sparrow's music.

ROBERT HAMBLING DAVIS

Death of a Deer

Late afternoon, Thanksgiving Day, and from the hill I could see Middle Run Creek through its canopy of sassafras, poplar, maple, and oak. The gray birch was the only tree with leaves. Furled like tiny parchment scrolls, they would rattle on their winter branches and not fall off till spring. The barely clouded sky was loud with geese and starlings flocking in the cold wind.

Three gunshots rang over the valley. The starlings hushed and veered as if caught in a gale, and the geese drove higher in flight. Hunters in the cornfield on the far side of the woods? It was goose season, and someone had stripped the no hunting signs from the trees along the bridle path. Hunting was illegal, but in the ten years since the Greenways Project had saved this land from New Castle County's housing boom, I'd seen and heard many poachers who shot at whatever they thought they could kill without getting caught.

I was a hunter of a different breed. I scoped deer and geese with my naked eye, and tracked the bloodless trails of coons and rabbits. I flushed quail and stood in the wake of their beating wings long after they'd gone. And I stalked red foxes to watch them run through tall grass like the wind.

I'd seen geese shot out of the sky. A badly wounded goose comes down hard and flails about till a hunter breaks its neck. But one that's been winged will stop trying to fly after a few painful attempts. If the grounded bird can walk, hunters surround it with decoys till it has served their purpose. The last time I saw this was in the cornfield of the Brown's Farm, two years before Tri-State Bird Refuge acquired the land.

An Indian summer day, and I'd been walking over an hour and hadn't heard any shooting, when I noticed a tentative flock of geese circling the cornfield bordered on one side by a hedge. Downslope, I couldn't see but suspected why the birds were reluctant to land. I walked up to one end of the shoulder-high hedge and peered over it. Sure enough, parked on the other side was a Ford pickup with a gunrack and tailgate of beer.

There were four of them. They had their shotguns raised at the hungry flock and a lame goose trapped among the decoys in the corn stubble. Whenever the goose tried to stray, the poachers shifted their positions and blocked its escape. At the far corner of the field, fat guy blew on a goose call. About sixty yards from where I was, blackbeard slugged from a bottle without lowering his gun. I figured they'd shot the goose from behind the hedge, and now their best decoy was so convincing they didn't need a blind.

I was a mile from my house and phone. I took out my notebook and wrote down their license plate. Then, as the flock neared gun range, I leaped from behind the hedge, flapping my arms and screaming, "Yaahhh! Yaahhh! Yaahhh!" Fat guy opened fire on the spooked geese and the two nearest him followed suit. Blackbeard came at me with his gun.

I lowered my head and ran along the outside of the hedge. The range of a shotgun is forty-five yards: I had plenty of lead time but cringed with each shot. When I got to the middle of the hedgerow I stopped for another look. Fat guy stumbled in a circle, still blasting at the sky. The other two ran upfield as blackbeard turned the corner behind me.

I ran to the end of the hedgerow, crouched down and looked back. Fat guy staggered toward the pickup. With his gun and head hanging, he looked too depressed to chase the bastard who'd stopped him from bagging an all-time high. On the other side of the hedge his buddies had caught up to blackbeard who had the speed and grace of a beerbellied ex-marine. All three ran toward me with their weapons at present arms.

Over the woods the geese yodeled in a ragged line. The centers jockeyed for point—one, then another, edging by a necklength. At last one pulled ahead and the flankers trailed across the harvest sun.

I waited till my game neared the middle of the hedgerow, then I raced through the cornfield. Fat guy, slouched over a can of beer on the tailgate, barely looked up as his buddies howled at me from behind the hedge. When I reached the creek they sounded like sports fans in a distant arena.

-<+-

I watched on the hill for the hunted geese to come over the woods. But none came, and the starlings were gone, and except for the wind and few cirrus clouds, the Thanksgiving sky was clear and silent.

I went down to the creek and splashed my face with water. Was it still safe to drink? The springhead was a mile upstream in what used to be Nelson's cowpasture. I dipped and raised my cupped hands and felt the cold stream all the way down my throat and into my stomach. Then I crossed over and climbed the hill through the woods, letting the wind dry my face.

When I reached the bridle path I stopped. Had a triggerhappy goosehunter strayed from the field and flushed an eight-point buck? Or blown off the rump of a fawn? A silver maple was spattered with blood and more lay on the fallen leaves. I followed its trail back down to the creek.

On the muddy bank were bootprints, size eleven or twelve, and deer tracks pooled with blood. I checked my watch: a half-hour since the gunshots. I figured the poacher was gutting the deer by now.

I heard voices and looked up through the trees. In the field on the other side of the creek, volunteers for the park's reforestation were putting wire-mesh guards round the saplings planted that spring.

I went down to a shallow rocky place, crossed over and backtracked along the far bank, but couldn't find the trail. When the deer saw the people, had it run a ways through the creek before coming back out? If so, which way? The same sized bootprints led along the bank upstream. Hoping the poacher had taken a wrong turn, I went downstream.

When I came to the spot where I'd crossed, I flashed on the deer stumbling through the blood-red creek. What was I doing? If I found it alive, what then?

The previous summer I saw the bald eagle that made the news. He was found in a muskrat trap by a creek near Millsboro. Predators had stripped the flesh from part of his head, and one eye was gone. He arrived at the bird refuge, dehydrated and in a coma. Vets did surgery and monitored his condition round the clock. Some people griped about the small fortune in taxes it cost to keep him alive. Others said the treatment was inhumane, especially if he lived. A half-blind eagle was better off dead.

I was painting the frames of the outside cages when I saw him a month after his rescue. With his talons in the dirt and wings by his sides this fierce, scar-faced creature stood over a lunch of dead rats.

Did it matter that he lived? He'd lose his fierceness in the cage and become a still-life of himself.

I was wrong. A month later the Tri-State staff released him, and I was there when he spread his wings and went soaring over the woods.

Where was the nearest deer refuge?

I'd gone at least a quarter mile along the creek, searching the brush for blood and tracks. My legs were cut, I had a thorn in my thumb, and now the bank was dark with moss and evening shadows.

The deer wants to die alone, I told myself. It doesn't want you. It wants to die alone, in the silence of these woods. This is the only death it knows. It doesn't want to be put out of its misery. It knows nothing of that. Go home and let it die.

I looked back. Through the rustling trees came the cry of a hawk. I turned and pushed on along the bank. Crouching every few feet, I rubbed the moss with my hands and looked at them.

I stood cold and dizzy. My breath flew in the wind over the creek. Something was there. I waded out to the rock and looked at the stains.

It was hard to believe the deer had run this far in the creek.

On the bank I crawled around, scouring the moss with my hands, and soon found blood. I could barely see it on the spongy moss, but the moss was torn and along the fringe where it gave way to the pines I found the trail and followed it uphill.

An owl cried in the distance. I stopped again and looked back, shivering in the twilight. I scattered the bloody pine needles with my boot and walked on, and had nearly reached the top of the hill when I found the deer.

A doe with a sleek wet coat and youngish face, she lay in a grove of cedar, her bent legs jerking. She raised her head and made a low sound as I drew near. Her muzzle was frothy. Her body shuddered and twitched. Did she know why her legs no longer worked? I wanted a big rock to put her out of her misery.

I took off my hat so I wouldn't look like her killer, and stared at her wounded flank. Higher up, her rump was a torn mass of muscle and cartilage.

I was shaking. I wanted to kill her killer and go home and forget about this. I held back a scream and felt unworthy of my outrage as she trembled at my feet. What funeral rite could I perform that would not make me feel like an accomplice to this crime?

I knelt and touched her. I stroked her neck and heaving ribs and imagined rubbing a cool salve into her body. "It's okay," I said as she shook beneath my hand.

It wasn't okay. All my old cats had gone off to die alone. I was denying this deer's right to die in peace. I was another two-legged beast spooking her. A sadist pawing over her pain. My feet were wet, my teeth chattering. Get away! Get lost! Go home!

I settled myself on the ground and kept stroking her. Her life was ending at nightfall on a soft bed in the pines in late autumn, before her grazing lands froze and were covered with snow. This was the only good thing about her death. Maybe, somewhere inside her, she knew this. Maybe it relieved some of her pain.

She stopped shaking and her coat felt soft and cool. I rested my hand on her head and watched her die.

ED DEE

The Tailman

Guys like me need to get shot at once in awhile. Just a sudden blast, but close enough to see the muzzle flash and inhale the burnt metallic smell. It's a wake-up call. Slow down, it says. Act more like the next guy, the cautious soul who white-knuckles the steering wheel as he creeps past a grisly highway scene of twisted metal and crushed bodies. But guys like me are different; we fly past those scenes because grisly is second nature. Guys like me talk about lunch or women at a time like that, because we've been there, seen it all . . . lived our lives in the worst ten minutes of that other guy's life. Also, the next guy's life. And the guy after him.

I spent thirty-two years in the NYPD and I was thinking about all this while sitting on the front bumper of my '73 VW in section B104 of this mall-in-the-desert parking lot at four o'clock in the afternoon, the heat around one hundred and fifteen degrees. I was also thinking: Why the hell am I living in Arizona? My wife was in the goddamn mall and no way was I going to join her and wind up sitting on a bench with a bunch of old men, chewing on toothpicks, staring into space. She told me, "So stay out here and roast." Off she went; a regular comedian, that lady. Left me there, another retired cop, pissed-off in the hot sun.

It wouldn't kill them to plant a few trees out here, I was thinking; then I saw the little girl. She was about eight or nine years old, but don't quote me, I can't tell kids' ages anymore. A man was pulling her by the arm across the desert parking lot. Her face was slack, mouth open, numb with fear. Not the Daddy's-going-to-spank-me fear, but that pale, sweaty look you see in hospital corridors and the morgue waiting room. I got behind the wheel of my VW.

The girl wore tan shorts and a white Minnie Mouse T-shirt. Her pink flip-flops slapped against the steaming blacktop. The guy was big, six-three, a fleshy two-twenty, dark brown hair moussed back. Well dressed. He was yanking her by the arm, hustling down the line of cars. Moving fast, but I knew he wanted to go faster.

It was the look on her face that struck me. Not that she was crying, some kids never cry. And maybe I'm not college educated, or even as sharp as I used to be . . . but I know fear. I fished through a box of pens near the gearshift, trying to find one that hadn't dried out in the goddamn heat.

The man put her into a brand new white T-Bird, Hertz rental sticker in the window. He took time strapping her in. I found a space on my sun visor and wrote down his plate number. The sun visors on every car I ever owned were covered with license plate numbers— that's how the argument started. That's how I came to be sitting and sweating in this bake-oven of a parking lot in the first place.

About an hour earlier the wife and I had stopped at a Seven-Eleven where I bought a can of Bud and walked outside. She stayed in the store, leaning on a stack of Coke twelve packs going through her weekly lottery ritual: a formula of our grandchildren's birthdays that never came out the same way twice. I was enjoying my brew, watching her through the window, when three scuzz balls pulled up in an old black Camaro. Instantly, I knew they were trouble. Instantly, I knew these guys were only currently unincarcerated. The situation reeked of a stick-up.

You think I overreact or I'm prejudiced, right? Listen to this: all three were sporting Hell's Angels wardrobes; they parked the Camaro sideways blocking all the other cars. *Motor running.* One stayed behind the wheel, two got out. They slithered into the store. And you *know* how these sleaze balls slither. Scuffing along in slippers or sandals, doing the institution shuffle, clearly escapees from *something.* Stick-up was the only conclusion. Who could think otherwise?

So I strolled back to the Camaro, scoped out the back seat for shot-guns, maybe a shooter prone across the backseat. I saw nothing but the mook behind the wheel. By the time my wife came out of the store I was back in the car writing the Camaro's license plate on my car's sun visor. She said, "Aren't you ever going to stop being a cop?" I was about to explain the situation when the two geeks slithered out with nothing but forty-four ounce Big Gulps. So okay, I said to myself. No harm, no foul.

I didn't say anything more to the wife. I backed the VW out and headed for our next exciting destination. On the way there, God only knows why, I decided . . . okay, I'll explain it.

"Are you crazy," she yelled. "You have no gun, no authority, nothing." I said, "You're missing the point." Although I knew she wasn't missing anything.

I drove to the mall while she stared into space. She was thinking hard, probably for another reason why I should like retirement in the goddamn hot sun. She waited maybe ten full minutes, then said, "Let's eat Mexican tonight." That was it. Case closed.

I admit I haven't adjusted well to retirement. But some things you can't get out of your blood that easily. Like getting back to the kid. I kept thinking that the guy never looked back over his shoulder. A kidnapper would check over his shoulder. This guy didn't. All he took was one glance at me, an overweight, white haired guy sitting on the bumper of a rusted VW . . . with PBA stickers on the windshield. The stickers are the point here; plus, I still looked like a cop. A pro would-d've picked that up. But, this guy looked through me, like I wasn't even there. It's these little details that mean everything.

For that reason, and for the sake of family tranquility, I told myself it was nothing. My wife was right: I still had cop paranoia. After all, my alleged kidnapper was out of a Dean Witter commercial: grey slacks creased stiletto sharp, a blue button-down oxford shirt wrinkled in the lower back like he'd been sitting. His tie was a rep, green and blue stripes. Shoes were those ridiculous brown tassel loafers. But then a surprise: an earring, a small diamond stud? What did that say about Mr. Young Republican? And don't forget the look on the little girl's face. I don't know about you, but it was enough for me. I started the car.

I didn't say this before but I was one of the best tail men in the history of the NYPD. I'd crawl over broken glass to keep from losing my man. I made a tire-screeching, horn-blaring, wild left out of the mall against the light. A big-haired blonde in a Beemer convertible held her middle finger high, like a rude golfer checking the wind. I threw her a kiss-my-ass smile.

As soon as I cleared the intersection I took a hard left, then slammed on the brakes. Blinking orange construction signs funneled us into one lane. Dean Witter was already beyond the construction, six cars in front. I saw the T-Bird dip right onto the freeway ramp, so I swung around the blinking barriers, spraying pebbles like buck shot. At times like this you can't sit with your balls taped to your leg. I gunned the VW onto the freeway begging for all the guts it had.

It took me three miles to catch the T-Bird. I moved into safe tail position, same lane, four cars between us. I put my Arizona State hat on to change his rearview silhouette. Perfect. My heart beat steady and powerful, like a Rolls Royce engine.

My wife said that what I missed most was drinking and carousing with my friends. True, I missed that, but it was the action I longed for. The romance of the chase.

The black rainy nights, three a.m., parked on the edge of a garbage-filled alley, radio crackling, waiting for a move, a pass of drugs or more—then the adrenaline-pumping, all-out chaotic strike. Or laying on my stomach on a Harlem rooftop, sipping coffee from a paper cup, and staring through binoculars at the lips of an olive-skinned man in a black cashmere overcoat as he whispers the right words into a puff of steam in the air.

I won't bore you with the details of this tail. Tailing on a freeway is so easy it's an insult. All you need is a car with some punch and no pink pig on the roof. No experience necessary. All this sunlight takes the cloak out of crime, new technology steals the dagger. I know how the Swiss watchmakers felt when someone invented digital. In fact everything is easy now, computerized and cloned, craftsmanship means nothing.

My wife says I'm always looking for something to bitch about these days. My wife is stranded at the mall.

The T-Bird swung onto I-10. We cruised a couple of miles when he made a move to the right. Airport exit. I knew it wasn't a kidnapping, but it was close. It was a custody snatch.

I hung back a little, not wanting to go directly on his bumper. But Dean Witter goosed the T-Bird and left me trapped behind a dripping cement truck. He was flying now, jumping from lane to lane, missing bumpers by the skin of his ass. The guy wasn't a half-bad wheelman, but I caught him at the airport entrance—he was a dozen cars in front.

The arrow went green for him, then red for me. Crunch time. I jumped into the oncoming lane, the VW screaming in second gear as I pulled abreast of a shocked white-haired lady in a four-cylinder Caddy. I should've been only six cars behind Dean Witter but he'd floored it on the straightaway. He was gone.

Ten minutes later I spotted the T-Bird abandoned at the America West arrivals gate. I double-parked the VW, blocking in the T-Bird. I ran into the terminal. It took only thirty seconds of my dead-leg trot for the crowd to open a wide path. Maybe the Mets T-shirt helped, with the enchilada sauce spills that appeared to be bloodstains. I headed for the All-Gates sign telling myself I was in good shape for my age. I tried to spot a cop as I ran up the escalator stairs squeezing past nice people in shorts and loud shirts. I wedged between two smiling stewardesses, all hair and bone. But I wasn't smiling or nice. I was homesick for sincere, overweight obnoxiousness when I attempted a long stride up and over a Nogales shopping bag. Its owner jammed her experienced elbow into my ribs in the true spirit of mass transit.

Then I saw Dean Witter. He was riding the down escalator, coming toward me, carrying a small piece of luggage. The little girl was with him. Her face was buried in the skirt of a pretty dark-haired woman. At the top of the stairs I swung over to the down side and grinned at the faces of those I'd just bulldozed. Fraternity stunt, I said. I followed the trio out to the street.

Outside, a female cop was putting a ticket on my windshield. I looked at my watch, slapped my forehead in apology, and graciously accepted the ticket. Dean Witter glanced over at me as he tossed the luggage into the T-Bird's trunk. The little girl was calling the dark-haired woman "Mommy." Good result, I thought. I was a guy who loved a happy ending.

The sun began to set as I headed home. I snapped in a Sinatra tape. He was midway through "Here's That Rainy Day." I listened to his voice, the voice of a man who understood pain and loss. I thought about the look on that little girl's face. That face was going to nag me. Something was still wrong there.

I stopped at the first Seven-Eleven and called the house. I knew my wife would get home just fine. This wasn't the first time we'd gone through this. "What's your story this time?" she said. I told her I met a guy I knew, retired cop from Bronx Homicide. We went for a couple of beers, and time flew by. She knew it was bullshit. "Are you okay?" she said.

Our entire thirty-year married life I'd put her through different versions of this same scenario. I leaned back and listened while she told me that the cab home cost nineteen bucks and if I wasn't home immediately, forget about it. I was half listening; I already knew she was right. But I was also watching a guy with greasy long hair and a tattoo on his bicep. The tattoo had a spear going through an angel. He was parked near the street, but staring at the front door of the Seven-Eleven. My wife said, "With or without you I'm going out for Mexican food."

"Where?" I said.

"Find me," she said.

A girl who looked too young to drive came out of the Seven-Eleven and got into an Audi. Tattoo started his Grenada and fell in behind her. I was on the case. I pulled down the visor as I wrote down the license plates. I was laughing out loud, shifting, talking to myself. "Find me," she'd said. What a piece of work my wife is.

The Grenada and Audi were going in my direction, so I followed. Palm trees were moving in a soft evening breeze. The sun slid past white puffy clouds and down behind the mountain. The sky had that pink glow you only see in the west. I was in place behind my tattooed quarry, as he was in place behind his.

She led both of us through a left on the arrow, her head bopping to a tune I'd never know. She had a young face, but it had that soft, sweet beauty of someone I loved. I grabbed my Yankee hat from the clothes stashed on the back seat. I pulled a Hawaiian shirt with it; you can't change silhouette too often. I snapped Sinatra back on. The light ahead turned green and we floated through. The breeze was lovely; we all had our left arms out the window. Tires hummed under our little convoy.

My life was different now, and I was a guy who didn't like change. But things change, ready or not. Life doesn't let anyone off the hook. Some of my old cop friends in New York . . . lost souls . . . their lives are horror stories. I was lucky, really. I still had the most important thing. Whenever things got bad, all I had to do was find her. That says it all. I looked at my watch, it was enchilada time.

MARISA DE LOS SANTOS

Poem for a Birthday

What my mind pushes back toward is irresponsible
summer, nightfall, bright, singing syllables

of insects, all the folded birds, invisible sleepers
in dense trees, and what's at the center, what keeps

insisting itself is one long brown arm, mine, dangling
out the car window as I drive the narrow, angling

road because it was just that careless, all of it, the whole
thing, driving with the windows open, twenty years old,

how something as easy as honeysuckle, the knots
and small stars, the unasked for sweetness in a hot

month made *I love you* the only right words to say,
not so much to the man beside me, as to the red, clay-

banked road itself, its onwardness, and to hidden vines
radiating scent into the dark.

                                        Now, what's most mine is
familiar dazzle: cerulean-washed sky, sun stitching
sequins on the Brandywine's tawny satin, beating

a tiny, pointed water tower to sterling. On my balcony,
I grow eggplants in orange pots, fingering suedy

leaves, awaiting the swell, the black-purple, vegetable
weight. Today, I hold, like handfuls of silt, palpable

absence: once five ducklings, uneven, breaking line
of fidgety paddlers, followed their mother across the shine.

There are four now. My husband and I have watched
them for weeks, full of wanting to scoop up one splotched

bundle. He leans out over the railing and tosses down
a whole loaf's-worth of crumbs, too much for a family now

reduced, too much for ten ducks. I'm quiet, looking
at his lifted hands, the falling bread. O duckling,

eggplant, husband, careless girl. At thirty, love is focused,
grown distilled, feeding both the living and the lost.

MARISA DE LOS SANTOS

When *Love Walked In* opens, thirty-one-year-old Cornelia Brown is treading water. The manager of a Philadelphia coffee bar, she exchanges witty banter with her customers by day, watches classic films by night, and waits for her real life to walk through the door. When Martin Grace, charming, funny, and a dead ringer for Cary Grant, enters her café one morning, Cornelia believes it's the start of something big. The two begin a relationship that unfolds like an old-fashioned silver screen romance, so old-fashioned that at one point, Cornelia's best friend Linny asks, "Did someone pass a law against sex?" and Cornelia has to admit that she has a point. Then, Martin and Cornelia's seventh date rolls around, a little date that Cornelia likes to call *Date Seven* or *It Happened One Night*. Like most things in their relationship, it doesn't go quite the way Cornelia expects.

Cornelia

If you've ever considered having a conversation about your sex life in a South Philadelphia cheese shop, stop that thought in its tracks right now and wring its scrawny, little neck. Why?

I'll tell you why, you know I will. But first I should say that I have nothing against such cheese shops, in general. In fact, I love one particular South Philadelphia cheese shop—the very one that figures into this story—with a love so exalted and sweet that the place has shown up more than once in my dreams. A couple of years ago, when I succumbed to overwhelming peer and societal pressure and took a yoga class, the instructor asked us to begin by imagining ourselves in a beloved, familiar place. While others were probably mentally transported to the seashore or their grandparents' farm or their childhood tree house, I settled in among the wheels of Parmigiano Reggiano, the semisoft wedges of Bel Paese, the gorgeous white fists of Mozzarella di Bufala, and the giant provolones dangling from the ceiling like punching bags.

It's not that I am on familial terms with the people who work there.

I can't keep them all straight, to tell you the truth, as there seem to be a great many of them in rotation, all loosely or closely related to each other, all equally nice. They talk about cheese, and not just cheese, but olives, charcuterie, pâté, and so forth, with that combination of offhandedness and passion more commonly associated with reference librarians. ("We all know *The American Heritage Dictionary of Idioms*, but have you tried *Brewer's Phrase and Fable, Millenium Edition?* Well, hold onto your hat; you're in for the ride of your life!") It's the plenty of the place that speaks to me, and the language—"artisan," "ash-coated," "washed rind,"—and the unlikeliness of it all. From some-one's hands in France, Wisconsin, Italy, Argentina, Ireland, Greece to this single, singular, well-lit store on South 9th, to me, if I can afford it. My head knows this to be true of many stores, that it's the result of making phone calls, placing orders, but in this particular store, my heart sees only serendipity. In this store, I believe in luck.

Except, this time, the day after *Date Seven*, I'm unlucky enough to enter the store with Linny, who decides in her maddening Linny way to pick up the thread of a conversation we'd started two streets back, the thread she'd dropped in order to rush into a shop and buy a neon green watch cap right off a window mannequin's head. The manne-quin looked glad to be rid of it.

Anyway. For reasons that will soon become clear to you, I prefer to tell this story in the third person, thus keeping as much distance as possible between it and me. Here we go. The cheese store on a quiet afternoon. Two middle-aged men behind the counter. Linny and Cor-nelia enter. And boom:

"So, I'm sorry sex with Martin was no good," chirrups Linny.

The middle-aged men smile sympathetically at Cornelia.

Cornelia hisses, "The sex wasn't no good."

Middle-aged Man Number One says, "Any good. The sex wasn't *any* good."

Cornelia protests, not shrilly, not yet, "The sex was fine!"

An ample, elderly woman, possibly the mother of the aforemen-tioned men, drifts in from the back of the store to smile sympatheti-cally at Cornelia.

"Fine! Around here, we call that damning with faint praise," says Middle-aged Man Number Two.

"You do?" says Linny, impressed.

"Fine's not exactly what I meant," Cornelia tries to insert. No one notices.

"He didn't make that up!" the ample woman roars, poking Middle-aged Man Number Two in the chest with her finger, as though he'd been an incorrigible plagiarist for years and she couldn't stand by and watch it a second longer.

Shrewdly seizing the opportunity to turn the conversation away from her sex life and her grammar usage, Cornelia jumps in, "Shakespeare?"

"Pope," corrects, gently, Middle-aged Man Number One, his voice heavy with sympathy, almost sorrowful. She can't read, she can't speak, and she can't have sex, is what he's thinking.

The ample woman flaps two circular slices of sopresseta at Linny and Cornelia. Linny takes hers, breathes its aroma for a second, and then pops it into her mouth. "Suck-up," Cornelia thinks, and she starts to shake her head, but the ample woman's eyebrows shoot up and Cornelia doesn't wait for the emotion—anger or pain, she can't tell which—to travel down the woman's face. She takes; she eats.

"Feel better?" the ample woman asks her.

"Yes. No. I mean I couldn't feel better. I really mean: why would I feel better? Wait, what I'm saying is I'm perfect. I feel perfect!" and now Cornelia is shrill, as you knew she would be, given time. Not shrill by nature, she's been driven to it, you have to admit, by a relentless onslaught of pity and understanding.

"That's it, then, for Martin, I guess," sighs Linny.

Apart from Cornelia, everyone in the store, perhaps everyone on the sidewalk outside the store, perhaps everyone in the entire city nods, knowingly.

"No, that's not it. Of course that's not it!" How did this happen to me? Cornelia thinks. She feels like the subject of her sex life is a puppy or a ferret, something she'd never in her right mind let off its leash, but which is now somehow running amok among total strangers. Pushed to the edge, she throws decorum to the four winds. Her voice blasts through the shop like a foghorn, only higher. "It was the first time! Just because there weren't fireworks the first time doesn't mean there will never be fireworks. We're human; we're adults; we teach each other; we communicate; fireworks don't just go off, wham-bang; fireworks *evolve!*"

Awestruck by the utter, asinine nonsense of this metaphor, everyone is still. Into the stillness, the ample woman drops the word, "Wrong." Then she says it again, "Wrong."

"Oh, jeez, now she'll start in about her sexual history," moans Middle-aged Man Number One.

"I'm not talking about my sexual history, although I could. Fireworks! I've known fireworks. I'm talking about science."

"Science?" says Linny.

"Pheromones," the woman turns to Cornelia, "The chemicals in his body call out. The chemicals in your body answer. It either happens or it doesn't."

On top of being dumb, Cornelia is dumbfounded. The woman turns to Linny.

"She's never heard of pheromones?"

"I've heard of pheromones," whines Cornelia. She is pathetic beyond all imagining.

"Cornelia's not a science person," explains Linny to the ample woman. "Her sister Ollie, she's the scientist in the family. Some kind of star geneticist. Beautiful, too. Tall. And you should see her husband."

The ample woman clasps her hands together and nods, as though this explains a lot, which it probably does, but that's another story and none of her business, goddammit. And, not to put too fine a point on it, but Cornelia would not call five foot six "tall."

"For your information, I got excellent grades in science! All through high school, excellent grades!" the hapless Cornelia bleats.

This is why you don't discuss your sex life in a cheese store in South Philadelphia. Because it can only end one way: with you standing in the middle of the shop, thirty-one years old, head thrown back, screeching about your report card at the top of your lungs.

On the way back to my apartment, Linny and I stopped, as we always did, outside the playground at 11th and Lombard to watch the children through the fence. It was December and heading toward evening, but the kids who were there didn't seem to notice the cold. They ran around with open coats and climbed all over the jungle gym, mittenless. I was wearing leather gloves and holding a paper cup of hot coffee, but, all on their own, my palms remembered the feeling, the burn of the metal monkey bars under them, the numbness moving outward to my fingertips. I watched one kid cry as his mother peeled him off the pole he clung to. He wanted to keep playing; he didn't want to go home, and I remembered that, too.

"Remember that?" said Linny, "That feeling of never wanting to stop even when you were freezing cold? Where do you think that feeling goes?"

She always does that, says the thing I'm thinking. I wanted to tell her about after sledding, how Cam, Toby, Ollie, and I, and sometimes our friends Star and Teo, too, would sit on the mudroom floor soaking wet, taking off our boots and how it wasn't until our feet and hands started to hurt with that bad, coming-back-to-life hurt that we'd realize we'd been cold at all. But I was punishing Linny for the cheese shop, so I just shrugged.

"You can't stay mad at me, Cornelia. You know you never can, so why bother trying?"

I didn't say anything. We kept watching the kids. One boy, three years old or so, in a lime green parka and a ridiculous, multi-colored fleece jester's hat was still swinging. His mother was pushing him, and he was singing, unaccountably but with great brio, "Gonna lay down my sword and shield, down by the riverside, down by the riverside, down by the riverside." I'll take him, I thought.

"I'll take that one," said Linny, pointing to the boy, "But only if the hat comes with him." I looked at her.

"It's not that I can't stay mad at you," I told her, "It's that I can't *get* mad at you. If I could ever get mad at you, I'd definitely be able to stay that way. Just so you know."

We kept walking, "I ain't gonna study war no moooore!" sailing over our heads like a streamer.

It wasn't that the sex was bad. It really wasn't. It's that the evening was so exquisite, so without flaw in every other regard that the sex should have been a revelation; it should have thrown us over the moon. And it didn't, not quite.

When I told Linny this, back in my apartment, she said, "So you're saying that the only thing missing from a night of otherwise perfect, unbelievable sex was perfect, unbelievable sex."

In the allegory of my life, I can never decide if Linny is Snark or Truth.

"That's not what I'm saying at all. You should have seen the dinner he made. The flowers on the table. The way the lights came in through the window. If you could have seen his face when he looked at me. And heard the things he said, not just before, but after. As a matter of fact, after was great. I loved after, and you know how awkward after can be," I talked; then I stopped talking.

In the allegory of my life, if Snark and Truth turned out to be the same character, well, it would not surprise me a bit.

I'm a fan of suggestion, obliquity, discretion, the cut to the morning after, the camera's eye turning upward, outward, to the sky, to the cuckoo clock over the bed, to the rushing river, away. Forget those slick bodies tangled on the floor or grappling on kitchen tables. Sexy is Jimmy Stewart and Donna Reed talking into the same telephone receiver, their anger tipping reluctantly over into desire, the desire as much in the distance separating their two mouths as in their proximity to each other. What I'm saying is: you're not getting details, not detailed details anyway. If you're anything like I am, and, like most people, I assume most people are like I am, this is just fine with you.

That being said and at the risk of your believing me insane or at least supremely weird, I'll tell you how I think of *Date Seven*, how it's parsed out and cataloged in my memory. Bullets, they call them, right? Here are the bullets:

- "Compliment One"
- "Almost *Rear Window*"
- "*Notorious*"
- "Not *Casablanca*"
- "Compliment Two"
- "Food"
- "Sleep/No Sleep"

"Compliment One": it didn't get me into bed, if that's what you're thinking. Not because I'm not susceptible to flattery; I am, at least to the right sort of flattery, and this was very much the right sort. But because, pre-compliment, very pre-compliment, in fact, as soon as Martin asked me to dinner at his apartment three days prior to the night in question, the going to bed part felt inevitable. We both knew it would happen and we both knew that we both knew it would happen, but we didn't mention or even hint at the possibility of its happening, which we both appreciated.

His apartment was perfection, no surprise there. "A bachelor pad," he'd warned me, but its only bachelor-pad quality was its complete consistency. Every piece of furniture from the chaise to the sofa to the dining room chairs and every other item in it—lamps, plates, martini shaker, pepper grinder—was clean, curvaceous, ingeniously put together. My own apartment was uneven, overfull, raggedy in patches, but it grew around me organically, by accretion, like the shell of a chambered nautilus. I loved it and everything in it, loved every specific item with a specific love. But nine-and-a-half people out of ten would certainly prefer Martin's ripped-from-a-magazine decor, its having so obviously lived as a vision in some visionary designer's head before it became an actual living environ. And even I, tiny half-person clinging stubbornly to my funny, messy, personal idea of home, enjoyed the sensation of being a tiny, half-movie star on Martin's elegant set.

Martin made drinks while I stood by a long window overlooking Rittenhouse Square, now aglimmer with Christmas lights, distance turning it into an underwater city. On a table next to the window, an orchid plant with a single white flower glowed.

"I bought the view, really," said Martin. He handed me a cold shimmering martini in a cool shimmering glass. I looked at him as he looked out the window.

"The agent was waxing poetic about moldings and noiseless dishwashers in one of the most amazing displays of eloquence I'd ever heard. Scripted, probably, but it seemed completely extemporaneous. There was a whole stanza, I think, on the parquet floor, beautifully delivered. Hand gestures and everything. But all I did was go from window to window, looking out." His voice was like music, low and warm. An oboe, maybe, or a French horn.

He turned to me, "She hates me, that agent. I've seen her around town a few times over the years, and she snubs me cruelly. You know what I love best about you?" Just like that.

It took a minute for me to say, "What?" because that word "love" was flying around the room like a bird, flashing its wings. I looked at the small luminous face of the orchid for help, but, like all orchids, she was entirely self-involved, enwrapped in her own beauty.

"Your stillnesses. Those listening stillnesses. I don't know anyone who keeps herself so still while other people are talking."

The compliment, the view, the lights, the orchid, the drinks in our hands, Chet Baker quietly singing "Time after Time." It was one of those dropped-from-the-sky silvery moments when you stand there believing that every last thing in the world is delicate, lovely, and precise, including and especially you. I set down my drink and gave the mouth that had just bestowed such fine words upon me a truly sterling kiss.

"Almost *Rear Window*": Grace Kelly can be a lot like an orchid herself, gazing at the world from several gold and white removes away. But she can smolder, too; she can flirt like nobody's business. That's what I like best about *Rear Window*, how flesh-and-blood she gets when she comes on to Jimmy Stewart, the gleam in her eyes when she opens the secret compartment of her Mark Cross bag to reveal the peignoir set and slippers she's brought with her. "Does she ever have plans for you, Mister," say the peignoir set and slippers, with delicious frankness.

As I leaned into Martin with my sterling kiss, we bumped into the orchid's table. The orchid didn't budge, of course, didn't blink an eye, but, at the other end of the table, my handbag went flying onto the floor, spilling out, not its entire contents, but just two items. Martin and I swooped down to retrieve them, almost bumping heads; I got the toothbrush; he got the fresh pair of underwear. I considered going the embarrassed excuses route. Instead, I chose knowing, can-you-handle-this smolder. I smoldered, and Martin—god bless him—smoldered back.

"*Notorious*": The smoldering was interrupted by the chime of the kitchen timer, and my first thought was, "Please, please, please don't let him say 'Saved by the bell!'" because it would have been too-obvious, amateurish, but he didn't of course, and I could tell it didn't even occur to him, which evidently is more than one could say for me. He walked away, turning once to toss me my underwear and flash me a grin, and I returned my workaday version of slippers and peignoir to my handbag, then followed him into the kitchen.

It was duck, glistening darkly and smelling like heaven. Martin stood poking it with the kind of authority I rarely feel while cooking, even though I'm quite a decent cook, which made me want to stand behind him and put my arms around him, so I did. Thanks to my ridiculously high heels and a lifetime of practice in standing on tiptoe, I was able to rest my cheek against his shoulder. His sweater was sage green and the softest sweater I'd ever felt.

"I love men in sweaters," I said.

"I'm a man in a sweater," he said.

"Tell me about the duck," I said, and he turned around in my arms and began to do just that, beginning with the market where he bought the duck and the alleged purity of the duck's diet, thus sparking the *Notorious* segment of the evening. Hitchcock again, I know, but the man knew his way around a love scene. Ingrid and Cary kissing and laughing their way from the balcony to the living room, straight through a telephone call, and all the while talking about dinner, that they would stay in, she would cook a chicken, they'd eat it with their fingers. Kissing him, laughing, she accuses him of not loving her. "When I don't love you, I'll let you know," he says, kissing her. We didn't say anything like this to each other—I threw it in because the line is just so great—and we talked about duck instead of chicken, but the moving from one room to the next, the smiling into each other's mouths, the shadows sliding into all the right places, under cheek-bones, along jaw lines, and just the pleasure of it all, happiness suffusing every glance and touch, we got that spot on, exactly right.

"Not *Casablanca*": "The chief beauty of the duck is that it can wait," Martin told me, mid-kiss, and this is the point at which the camera turns away, maybe running over the sensual lines of the art deco and modernist furniture, taking a peek at the street beneath the window, resting on the duck cooling in its pan, before switching off altogether.

If you've been wondering whether Martin was one of those men who looks so divine in clothes that he is diminished and somehow nakeder than naked without them, he was not.

He had delectable sheets.

We hit that hard-to-hit balance between intensity and kindness, demand and generosity. We really did.

There was not one awkward second, not a single readjustment, no "Ow, my arm's sort of twisted under . . . that's better" business. Our rhythm was as effortless as the ocean's; we waltzed; we tangoed.

And the earth did not shift on its axis. It should have. Clearly, it should have. The stars could not have been more aligned. But, it did not.

I'm not sure why. But just afterward, before either of us had even caught our breaths, I looked at his faultless profile, at his lashes resting on his cheeks, and at the hollow at the base of his throat that is one of my favorite parts of the human anatomy as it is one of everyone's favorite parts of the human anatomy, and, in the presence of all this loveliness, the words that came into my head were these: "Who are you really? And what were you before? And what did you do and what did you think?" Except that when Rick says this to Ilsa in the Paris flashback, you know that they already know everything that matters about each other. You know because you've seen them together in Casablanca, seen Rick's eyes when she walks into the room in her white dress, his dark, broken, longing gaze, and you've seen her tilt her face up to see him, her eyes lit with tears, and you understand that, in spite of Nazis and husbands and distance and leavetakings and history, they are connected to each other in the deepest way and for all eternity.

I wasn't disappointed, exactly. But I lay on Martin's bed and knew in my bones that this night was not ever going to give rise to a moment in the future when Martin and I would stand together, alone and outside of time, with the world going mad around us, and say to each other, "We'll always have Philadelphia." It wasn't that kind of a night.

"Compliment Two": Martin said my face was pretty.

Something you should know about me: I have a pretty face. I do. I'd be lying if I said I didn't.

Although I'm not remotely blond. I get a lot of Mia Farrow circa *Rosemary's Baby*. And Jean Seberg. Jean Seberg is a name thrown around a good deal at the café—you probably guessed that—mainly because the desire to discuss Jean-Luc Godard is simmering just under the surface of everyone's interactions with each other, and they'll give themselves any excuse to let that desire boil over.

That's what people do; they compare people they see every day to famous people. The guy who delivers pastries has Humphrey Bogart's hairline and slightly buck teeth; the girl rollerblading outside the museum is the spitting image of June Allyson in the 1949 version of *Little Women*; your parents' accountant, from a distance, looks so much like Sidney Poitier in the *Lilies of the Field* it takes your breath away. That sort of thing. So any famous woman with a little triangular face and big eyes who, being a famous woman, is way more beautiful than I am, that's what I hear.

Oh, and I've gotten Audrey Hepburn from exactly two men. While there's not a drop of truth in the comparison, I gave them credit for at least knowing on which side their bread was buttered.

So, I'm pretty, pretty enough. The trouble is that my kind of pretty is not the kind I'd have chosen. I've heard all those words: gamine, piquant, waifish, what have you. I've heard elfin; elfin stings. And pixie, *pixie*? A word to the wise: the grown women who want to evoke pointy-eared beings scaling mushrooms and wearing acorn caps for hats are few and far between. We all know what those words truly mean; they mean I'm teetering on the edge of cute. And cute is death. Denigration, death, and decay.

Still, every boyfriend I've ever had has told me I had a nice face. (I dated one misbegotten guy who said, "You're definitely a face girl, Cornelia." Translation, as if you or anybody else would need one: "You've got no body to speak of. Your face was a bone thrown to you at conception, and not every man would appreciate it, but I do.")

But Martin, Martin, Martin. As I lay there thinking the "Not *Casablanca*" thoughts, Martin did something that pushed all of those thoughts not out of but certainly to the back of my mind, to a shadowed little corner where their own mothers wouldn't recognize them.

Martin propped himself up on one elbow and, seriously and with great care, began to run his finger lightly over my face. He did this for a long time, and in his eyes and in his fingertip was reverence, just the sweetest kind of awe. My bones and skin turned golden under his touch.

Finally, he said, "The trouble with your face is that it's ruining me for other faces. It's making me rethink every face I've ever liked."

Then he smiled, and his eyes didn't say, "What a cunning little chin!" His eyes murmured, "Garbo, Gardner, Bacall, they've got nothing on you, Cornelia."

"Food": We talked; we laughed; we ate the duck. It was the last word in ducks. That duck was a marvel.

"Sleep/No Sleep": We went back to bed. Martin held me. He slept. He was the kind of sleeper you knew he would be: serene, dignified, no snoring, no talking, his profile casting its elegant shadow on the wall, the bed, the woman in his arms. I was the woman in his arms, and all night long, I didn't sleep a wink.

LIZ DOLAN

The Lady of Annie B Street is Gone

Ninety-five-year-old Nellie Mulligan,
an amber-eyed munchkin,
outspoke her preacher husband
by fifteen hundred Sundays. Still dead-
heading her portulaca and roasting
green peppers from her garden
until her hard-of-hearing son
whisked her from under the canopy
of copper beech, each planted at the birth
of a child. He sold her helter-skelter house,
the walls still battle-ship green,
their holes stuffed with Wrigley's.
Then he died six months later
leaving Nellie rudderless. Shipped
to a nursing home where she pined
for sea gulls shrieking,
        her starched sails fluttered
        flimsily as silk.

MARIBETH FISCHER

Stillborn

"Nothing hurts as bad as they say it does," she told me later. "And clear, pure memory doesn't hurt at all. What hurts is forgetting."
Josephine Humphreys, *Rich in Love*

A few sundays ago my mother phoned as I was eating dinner in front of the TV, her voice startling me because it wasn't her usual time to call. The minute I picked up the receiver, she said, "I don't want to talk, but I had to phone you, Beth."

"What's wrong?"

"Nothing, nothing at all," she told me. "It's just that I found another book—" She paused. "It's about a mother who leaves." She didn't need to say anything else. I scribbled the title and the author's name on the back of a mail-order catalog, promising to buy the book as soon as I finished with classes the following afternoon.

After hanging up, I sat still for a moment, listening numbly to the voices on the TV and remembering that summer five years before when my mother first left our family to be with a man who was— nothing more than a name and a photograph from her 1959 high school yearbook. I was twenty-two at the time, newly married and living in Iowa. It was a summer of drought, of endless bone-white skies and acres of dying cornfields. I could hardly imagine then, as the sun brutalized the landscape, that grief wasn't simply something to get through, like a bad dream or a dry spell.

I stared down at the new title in my hand. Ever since my mother left, I've been reading novels and short stories about women who leave their families. I know, of course, that the books won't give me the answers, but that's not what I want anymore. I am simply trying to find in fiction what I can not find in real life—understanding.

When I read Richard Ford's short story "Great Falls," my mother had only been gone for three months. It was September and I still believed that she'd be home for Christmas. The story was told from the perspective of an eleven-year-old boy named Joe, who made me think of my younger brother Mark, only a year older. Home in New Jersey, Mark would have started school already and I tried to picture him in the mornings, waking up, realizing—as I did every day—she's gone, and, worse, *she left.*

"And my mother herself—why would she do what she did?" Joe asks at the end of the story. "I have never known the answer to these questions, have never asked anyone their answers. Though possibly it—the answer—is simple: it is just low-life, some coldness in all of us, some helplessness that causes us to misunderstand life when it is pure and plain, makes our existence seem like the border between two nothings, and makes us no more or less than animals who meet on the road—watchful, unforgiving, without patience and desire."

I read that quote ten, fifteen times, the words "low-life" and "coldness" echoing in my head long after I'd put the book away. How I hated what those words suggested; how I still do: that ultimately our most painful decisions are borne *not* of grief or fear, love or regret or joy but, instead, of a terrible selfishness that lies beneath the surface of our lives like a cancer. I hated the implication that it was that simple, that arbitrary, that just as anyone could be struck with illness—so could any of us be struck by this "coldness," this numbing inability to distinguish right from wrong.

There were other books. In one, the mother who left had dark permed hair and long blood-red fingernails. She drank too much whiskey and talked too loudly about the men—and the women—she had loved. In another, the mother was sick, abusing her daughter sexually. And in the novel my mother phoned to tell me about a few Sundays ago—*Father Melancholy's Daughter* by Gail Godwin—the mother who left her family dies before she has a chance to come home, before her daughter can understand.

Last week I read the novel *Rich in Love* by Josephine Humphreys. In this story, the mother leaves so abruptly that when her daughter comes home from school the door of her mother's car is hanging open and her macramé purse, along with a bag of groceries, is still sitting on the front seat, where a container of butter pecan ice cream has melted. Two hundred pages later, the mother returns, her leaving "like a television serial that had gotten so complicated the plot could only be resolved by calling itself a dream, backing up and starting all over again."

I realized, then, that for most people, most women, what my mother did five years ago truly is unimaginable. And yet, I, her oldest daughter, not only have to imagine it, I have to understand it.

Recently I listened to a friend of mine, an artist, talk about how she wants to go to an artists' colony to work on some paintings. But she can't bear to leave her children—in ten years she had never been away from them for more than a few days. Susan has heard my mother's story; she hasn't judged it, and wouldn't judge it, yet I know that she can not imagine doing what my mother has done. I also know, however, that until the day she left, my mother could not have imagined it either.

I wish I could explain to Susan how it happens so quickly. *Nobody* thinks she can do it. Maybe that's why, of all the books I've read, the only insight that rings true for me is the detail about the ice cream melting all over the front seat of the car. I know it really does happen this way, as you are carrying groceries into the house or ironing your son's favorite soccer shirt or standing in front of your closet wondering what to wear. I know the unimaginable becomes imaginable in a moment just that ordinary.

Until the day my mother walked out, I naively thought that it was only a certain kind of woman who would do such a thing; a woman who shouldn't have had children or never really wanted them in the first place; a woman whose daughters spoke of her with contempt and shame. And if she was a good woman and she just happened to have made a mistake, well then, she'd come back, wouldn't she? Just like Meryl Streep in *Kramer vs. Kramer*. She'd come back full of regrets and promises never to leave her son again.

Two weeks before my mother left and flew to Montana with Nick, her former high school sweetheart, my husband and I came back from Iowa to visit. It was then, my first morning back, that my mother confessed to me her longing to leave. Dan, my stepfather, had left for work over an hour before; my younger brother was at school; my husband was asleep in my childhood bed. My mother and I were sitting in the kitchen, picking at a plate of hot blueberry muffins. Rain clattered against the bay windows, which were steamed from the heat of the oven.

"I think I'm in love with someone else," my mother said quietly, staring down at her hands. She spoke the words so quickly that I couldn't understand them at first. They sounded like pig Latin: *mai nai ovelay ithway emeonesay*. I remember feeling frustrated, wanting to shout at her, What are you talking about? Even now I'm not sure if she repeated what she'd said or if the words themselves unscrambled. All I know is that I heard them as an echo, blurred and distorted, as if she'd shouted them across a distance. *I'm in love with someone else.*

Outside everything looked very shiny and very green. Bottle-green. Apple-green. Sea-green. Olive-green—as if my sister and I were still kids and had just gone down a row of Crayolas and scribbled long streaks of that color over and over across the window. Nick, my mother had called him, this man she apparently loved. *Nick.* The name was familiar and I recognized the way she said it, the same way that I could identify songs I hadn't heard in years. Vaguely, I remembered kneeling on the living room floor with my mother when I was still young enough not to be in school. It was raining then too, a slow, silent drizzle like lines of static across an old black-and-white movie. Twenty-eight years old, already divorced from my father, she was showing me her scrapbook and high school yearbook, pointing to a photograph of a thin, dark-eyed boy I didn't recognize. I wondered if this was when I first heard my mother say Nick's name. "This is the boy I dated before I married your father," she might have confessed. Five or six years old, I would have looked at her in amazement, shocked to think of her dating or going to parties, incredulous to realize that once my mother had been young.

Sitting in my mother's kitchen two weeks before she left with Nick, I heard her say that she had practically been engaged to him when she was twenty and that her parents had convinced her to break it off. "They never gave him a chance," she said. She sounded distant as she spoke of it, a cadence of sorrow in her voice that I'd never heard before. I thought of how, when my older brother and I were kids, we used to tie rubber bands around empty shoe boxes and pluck them as if they were guitars. But we could never control their deformed, squeaking twang; we could never make real music. My mother's voice had that same wire-tweaked quiver. I wanted to lay a steady palm against the shuddering cords of her throat.

"I don't mean to make this sound like a soap opera," she said. "It wasn't. It was just the fifties. But we wanted different things then, Beth. I wanted a nice house and good clothes for myself and my children—I don't think there's anything wrong with that either—and my mother kept telling me that I'd never have that with Nick, that Nick would never amount to anything, that if I married him it would be the biggest mistake of my life." She shook her head, brushing the memory away like a strand of hair fallen in front of her eyes. "When I look back, I don't understand it," she whispered. "I was twenty years old then. Why didn't I stand up to my parents?" She spoke so softly that I could barely hear her: "I was afraid." Her face was lacquered with tears; I felt as if I was staring at her through a window. Without looking at me, she continued: "So I ended it. I sent Nick a Christmas card and told him I'd decided to marry your dad. I wanted to write a letter, I wanted to explain, but didn't know how, I didn't know what to say. . . ." She shrugged and tried to smile, as if to show me that she understood how ridiculous this all was, but her face crumpled and she was the color of water stains on old love letters. "What I did to Nick was the cruelest thing I have ever done to another person," my mother said. "And I've never gotten over it."

It was then that she told me that Nick had phoned her one afternoon a few weeks before. It was the first time she had heard from him in over twenty-eight years. He was at his sister's, he said. Her name had come up, and he got to wondering how her life had turned out.

"What did you tell him?" I didn't look at her when I asked, afraid of the truth I might see in her eyes.

Gently, she touched my arm. "I told him I was happy," she said. "And I meant it. I was."

"Then what—"

But she held up her hand to stop me. "Nick told me he had business in Philadelphia, and he wanted to know if I could meet him for lunch—" She glanced at me hesitantly. "I told Dan about it, Maribeth. I honestly didn't think it would be a big deal and certainly I had nothing to hide." She started crying again. "It's not what you might be thinking. The entire lunch Nick and I talked about our kids and afterwards we didn't even hug goodbye. I figured I'd never see him again."

"So *what* happened?"

"I don't know. I love home and should—" She drew in her breath, seemed to hold it in her throat for a moment and then blew the words out like smoke. "I phoned Nick, Maribeth. I told him I'd never stop loving him."

"You did?" I asked incredulously. "You?"

She left abruptly on a Monday morning. For the first time in her life she rode in a taxi alone, then boarded an airplane without her husband or children. She went to Milwaukee, the city where she and Nick had grown up, where they had met and fallen in love. The following morning they flew to Montana, a place my mother had never been. Later, try as I might, I couldn't picture her in such barren, open surround-ings, in "a landscape dominated only by sky" and "punctuated," as she would eventually write, "not by sounds but by stillness." Earlier that spring, however, Nick, a roofing consultant, had been contracted to fix the leaking stone walls of a small church near the town of Hardin, Montana. Stone by stone his crew would take the building apart that summer and then slowly rebuild it. My mother would spend her after-noons in a tiny café, drinking iced tea and trying to concentrate enough to read. Most days, she would tell me, she couldn't get through more than a page.

In Iowa the drought continued. For weeks at a time it seemed this was all anyone talked about. In the afternoons the local pancake house where I waitressed was filled with farmers drinking cup after cup of coffee. There was nothing to do except pray for rain, and hope. Often, driving west along Route 30 toward the next town, I would see women standing on their porches, staring out at the flat expanse of yellow-blue sky, waiting. In July there was talk of busing in a tribe of Sioux Indians from South Dakota to perform a rain dance.

I too spent the summer waiting, first for her letters, then for the sound of her voice over the phone. At night I would sit for hours, watching as the sun set and the Iowa sky darkened, tightening like the skin around a wound. I tried to picture her in Montana, tried to imag-ine her sitting at a dinner table with him, laughing softly as she took a sip of wine. I wondered what he looked like and what about him was special enough that my mother would abandon her life to be with him.

By the autumn my mother and Nick had returned to Milwaukee and were living in a small two-bedroom apartment just off the interstate. Alone, with no friends, no one she could talk to in the long afternoons when Nick was at work, my mother often phoned me. She told me of the different recipes she was trying; she described the books she was reading—Jane Smiley's *The Age of Grief;* Mona Simpson's *Anywhere but Here;* she tried to laugh at herself for feeling such exhilaration the day she passed the Wisconsin driver's test. "I did it," she said, her voice ebullient. "Can you believe it, Beth?"

Quietly, I congratulated her. I knew it didn't matter that my mother had been driving all her life. It was as if she was seventeen, as if she had gotten her license for the first time.

When she phoned me on September fourteenth, however, I knew the minute I heard her voice that everything had changed. "It's me," she whispered when I picked up the phone. She sounded scared.

"Are you alright?" I said.

"I don't know. I was okay when I woke up. I was going to do some reading and I'd taken some spaghetti sauce out of the freezer for dinner—" She began to weep. "All of a sudden the pain just started washing over me, Beth, and I couldn't stop it. I realized it was Dan's birthday yesterday and our anniversary tomorrow and I didn't understand what I was doing here anymore. *Why* am I taking spaghetti sauce out of the freezer, *why* am I not home in my own kitchen?" She was sobbing now. "And that's not all."

She waited for me to remember and, of course, I did: on this day fourteen years ago she had given birth to a stillborn, a seven-pound boy named and baptized Daniel Joseph. In all the years since it had happened, she had spoken of it to me only once before.

I remember feeling frightened for her. There was such unrestrained sorrow in her voice that I thought of water, black ocean water on a moonless night—and how afraid I was to enter it, to wade deeper than my calves.

Outside it was a bright autumn day. A breeze riffled the papers spread out on my coffee table. I heard a bus pull away from the stop outside my apartment. I thought of the other September fourteenth, the day the baby had been born.

It had been a rainy Friday. My sister, brother, and I had come home from school to an empty house and a neighbor waving at us from under a dark umbrella across the street. "Over here, kids!" she called. "Your parents aren't home." The three of us raced across the street, kicking up arcs of rain behind us. My older brother won as always, beating my sister and me to the neighbor's porch. "She's having the baby, isn't she?" His delighted squeal seemed to skip over the puddles like a stone flung sideways across the surface of a pond. My sister and I were also shouting by now: "Is she having the baby?"

The neighbor offered a tenuous smile. "I think I'll let Dan tell you all about that when he gets here," she said.

A few hours later, my stepfather picked us up and took us home. "Your mother had a boy," he told us as he tried to get us to come sit with him on the couch. But we were jumping and screaming in celebration. My brother was yelling to the tune of "Old McDonald"—"B-B-B-O-Y, B-B-B-O-Y, B-B-B-O-Y, Yes I have a Bro-ther!"—until finally my stepfather blurted it out—that the baby was dead.

On the phone now, fourteen years later, I asked, "Is it the baby, Mom?" Is that why you're so upset?" I was upset myself. "Should I call Dan?"

"There's really no point," she whispered. "I've hurt him too much already."

"It's not irreparable," I said. "You can still go home."

For a moment she didn't say anything. I felt how the echo of that word—*home*—hung between us, static in the line so that it seemed we were losing our connection.

"I can't," she said finally. She sounded surprised, as if this wasn't what she had planned on saying. Again she repeated it (testing the words the way I had once tested a snowflake on the tip of my tongue.) "I can't." Her voice was choked with something I couldn't name— panic or resignation perhaps, or maybe simple grief. After she hung up, I remember standing for what seemed a long time with the phone against my ear, coiling the cord around and around my fingers as if, somehow, I could reel my mother closer.

She is driving home from the food store one morning in late September. It is early, only a little past seven, but she has been unable to sleep lately and decided she would get the shopping out of the way. It is cold out. When she came out of the apartment this morning she noticed the windshields of the cars were covered with a layer of frost as thin as parchment paper. Already she wears a winter coat and, as she is setting the grocery bags into the back seat of her car, she sees her breath dissipate into the cold morning sky. In New Jersey it would still be warm, she thinks, she would be having coffee on the side porch, twelve-year-old Mark would be getting dressed for school in the clothes she bought him last spring.

She is almost at the turn-off to her apartment complex when she sees the children waiting at the bus stop, sees the group of women, their mothers, standing in a huddle around them, trying to shield the children from the wind blowing off Lake Michigan. Suddenly she feels ill. She thinks of Mark, of how each morning, after he was dressed and his book bag was packed, he'd come to her room and wake her by laying a warm washcloth on her face, the same way Dan had woken him. She thinks of his face in the window of the school bus, remembers that he was so scared on his first day of kindergarten that he threw up. She is afraid she herself will be sick and pulls the car onto the shoulder of the road. Later she will call me. She will tell me this story.

Still, she will fly home to see Mark twice that autumn and, twice, despite the obvious pain she is feeling, she will return to Milwaukee.

I pictured her that autumn in the various gift shops near her apartment, where she spends afternoons hoping to find in some preprinted

Hallmark card words which might somehow neutralize her family's anger. Too dressed up in the clothes she has no other place to wear, she lingers at the racks of specialty cards: "To A Special Daughter"; "To A Wonderful Son"; "Have I told you I love you lately?"; "How much do I miss you, let me count the days." I wonder if she notices the blue and white posters one aisle over advertising Yom Kippur cards. Does she know this means "Day of Atonement"? Does she know that all she has to do to be forgiven is come home?

My mother and Nick returned to Montana for Thanksgiving, hoping, I imagined, to find again the brief happiness my mother must have felt there earlier that summer. I was convinced, however, that waking to the silence of a hotel, eating Thanksgiving dinner in a restaurant—being without her children on a holiday—would only remind her of all that she had lost. Consequently, I allowed myself to hope: as I stood alone in my own kitchen on Thanksgiving morning, making stuffing the way she had taught me and baking the traditional pies she had always made, I promised myself that soon she would come home. She had to, I thought. How could we get through the holidays without her? And how could she get through them without us?

I pictured her in Montana, lying alone in the queen-sized bed of the Western Inn where they were staying, waiting for Nick to return from the dining room with a pot of coffee and some freshly baked brioche that the concierge set out each morning. I could see her growing impatient and hungry, wondering what was taking so long, could see her wrapping herself in the thin chenille bedspread and walking to the high latticed windows, which reminded her more of Europe, she wrote, than of the "Wild West."

In Iowa, as I set out the china and silver we'd received as wedding gifts, as I served turkey to the friends my husband and I had invited to dinner, as I wrapped leftovers for them to take home, as later that night I sat in the dark eating piece after piece of French silk pie, I pictured my mother standing at this window, her head against the glass, the sunlight falling over her like a white slip. Perhaps this is when she would feel the heaviness in her body, the stillness. Perhaps this is when she would realize that the new life she had wanted so much with Nick had quietly died inside of her. I could see her crying now, could see her moving slowly across the room toward the phone. . . .

The Thanksgiving weekend passed, however, and nothing happened. When I talked to my mother a week later, she admitted that the holiday had been horrible. But it no longer mattered, because whatever "horrible" meant, my mother hadn't called us; she hadn't come home.

"Was her life that bad?" I sobbed to my husband. "Was it so awful that she'd rather be in pain than come back to us?"

When I recall those weeks between Thanksgiving and Christmas, weeks which a poet once referred to as "the unimaginable present," I remember only the confusion and disbelief: she wasn't coming home. Maybe this was why I watched the documentary about stillborns that was on TV that November. I was willing to look anywhere for a clue—some hint—which would help me to understand: *Why?*

I learned that in Australian hospitals, unlike many in the U.S., doctors allow a woman who has had a stillborn to hold her baby after delivery. A nurse will take pictures of the child, sometimes let the mother dress the baby in something special to be buried in. Psychologists say that the greatest regret of the mothers of stillborns is that they never held their child, never got a chance to say goodbye. Their sons or daughters were simply whisked out of sight as if they had never existed.

I hadn't expected the show to upset me. But as I clicked the TV off and watched the screen fade from green to grey to black, I felt as if something was blackening inside me too. I couldn't stop thinking about the dark-haired woman on TV who had given birth to three stillborns. For each she had a photo album filled with pictures of her dead child and of herself as she underwent labor. As she was being interviewed, she had almost frantically flipped through the pages of these albums, ordering the cameraman to focus in on the pictures. At one point she had stopped him, pointing to a favorite photograph and trying to explain why she liked it. She tried not to cry when she spoke, but her voice cracked and she had to turn away. I had been horrified.

Later, however, I realized that this horror was unjustified. Those photographs were all she had. The only proof of the life she had borne, a life which *had* existed, despite what everyone told her. And it struck me that perhaps what was truly horrible was *not* that a woman would save a photo album full of pictures of her dead child, but that she wouldn't; that instead, afraid of being crazy or morbid, she would do what everyone said she should—she would forget.

I remembered the afternoon before my mother's stillborn was delivered. By then he hadn't kicked in almost two days. Already she must have known that he was dead. My sister and I had no idea that anything was wrong, however, and so we spent the afternoon coloring pictures for the baby's room.

My mother lay flat on the four-poster double bed, a heating pad rolled like a washcloth beneath her breasts. Each time we finished a drawing we brought it to show her. As we stood hesitantly near her bed, she would smile, momentarily looking away from my stepfather who sat at the desk near the window, absently rolling a pencil over the wood in harsh, jerking movements. "Thanks, guys," she'd say, holding the picture in front of her face and studying it before she set it carefully on the night stand with all the others. There must have been twenty or thirty of them. My sister and I would have colored all night, I think, if it hadn't been for my stepfather.

Entering the room once again with another drawing, my sister behind me, I saw my mother softly punching her clenched fist against her distended stomach. She froze when she saw us peering in the doorway, our pictures held in front of us like invitations for admittance. She cupped her hand slowly, protectively, to her stomach then. In that split second before my stepfather turned away from us, I thought I noticed a tear on his face. But he snapped his dark eyes away from me before I could be sure. All I could see was his back, a grey shape outlined by a too-bright September sun, which seemed to lie to us about the season.

"It's okay," my mother said, staring not at us but at my stepfather. And then turning her strange quivering smile on my sister and me, she gestured with both arms. "Come here. Let me see what you colored this time," and we scrambled into the room, hopping knees first onto the bed. I remembered her softness, the damp sweaty smell of her thin velour robe, and then the surprisingly sharp grip of my stepfather's fingers clamped tight around my wrist as he jerked me from my mother.

"That's enough," he said. He tried to hold his voice rigid with control but it came out shaky and painfully frazzled.

My mother said, "It's okay, Dan, really."

In their odd watery stares, I saw an entire conversation that I didn't understand.

My stepfather shook his head and then more gently pulled my sister and me from the bed. "I'm sorry, girls. But your mom needs to rest for a while."

My sister and I went back to our room. We began to clean up and, without talking, arrange the crayons into systematic rows of colors.

Midnight blue, navy, ultramarine, cornflower, sky blue. Darkest to lightest. And then another color.

Fourteen years later, the November after my mother had left, it wasn't so easy to find a means of ordering the world. As I paced about my apartment in Iowa, pictures of the Australian woman in my mind, I sensed for the first time that my mother probably wouldn't come home—not because of Nick, not because of the baby who had died, but because somehow, in all the years of forgetting, some part of my mother had died. How dramatic this sounded and yet as I got up from the couch I couldn't help but recall a conversation I'd had with my mother earlier that autumn. She had been seeing a psychologist in an effort to understand how a woman like herself, a woman who had always prided herself on being a good mother, a good wife, could so suddenly leave. The psychologist, she told me, had written under diagnosis "prolonged grief." My mother had laughed at this. "What do you mean?" she had asked. "What do you think I'm grieving for? I was happy."

"So happy that you left," he reminded her quietly.

Absently, I flicked on the stereo. Anne Murray, one of my mother's favorites, was singing "Daydream Believer": "Cheer up, sleepy Jean / Oh, what can it mean. . . ." Through all those conversations when I had asked her to come home, when she had whispered, "I can't, Beth. Please try to understand," she must have known, as I did now, that if she returned we would pretend once again. We would pretend that her leaving had been a whim; we would pretend that she was happy. We would forget—just as we had after the baby died.

She had talked to my sister and me about the stillborn only once, years after the fact. I don't know how the conversation came up or why we were discussing it. I simply remembered her describing how her friends pretended nothing had happened, how they acted as if the baby hadn't been real.

"He would have been so sick," they had told her.

"It's better this way. . . ."

"At least you didn't bring him home and start loving him. . . ."

She told us, too, that when my stepfather reached out to hold the baby in the delivery room, the nurse had stepped back and abruptly pulled him away. "It's better if you don't," the nurse apologized. "There's really no point."

"Dan said he had black hair," my mother had told us. "That's all I know." She had turned to stare outside the window, something she did often when she was upset, as if looking at another landscape was all it took to distance herself from the one she was in.

After a moment, she said, "Nobody understood that the baby was already real to me, that he had a personality even in the womb. At the end of the pregnancy, he used to wake up every night at four in the morning—right on the nose. I'd go into the room Dan had fixed up and sit in the rocking chair and sing to him and rub my belly until he settled down." She had laughed quizzically, the way people do at jokes they don't understand. "I mean, I knew even before he was born that he wasn't going to let me sleep through the night the way you guys did—" She shook her head in wonderment. "To think that I hadn't already started loving him," she said.

I put a pot of water on for tea and went to sit at the table, waiting for it to boil. When I began to cry, my sounds seemingly enormous and out of place in the quiet and darkness, I thought it was for the Australian woman with three dead children, but then it occurred to me that I was crying for my mother, for all that I had never understood. I realized too that I was crying for my own loss. Because all through childhood and adolescence, when I thought I was getting to know my mother, and later, after I was married, when the two of us would sit at the kitchen table for hours, talking and drinking tea—all the time, she had been as distant to me, as unknown to me, as that dark-haired woman on the other side of the world, that woman who, unlike my mother, had understood what it means to grieve.

It's not the stillborn baby I think of so much anymore when September fourteenth interrupts my life like a cold, leaving me achy and tired. It's my mother's wobbly but bright smile as she fixed our lunches before school the morning the baby was born, knowing that he hadn't kicked or moved for more than two days. It is her making sure we each had a quarter to buy a soft pretzel at recess; it's her going to the hospital without the diaper bag packed full of pastel-colored baby clothes. It is my mother carrying a dead baby inside of her and never letting go of that pink crescent of a smile, which, I think of it now, seems almost separate from her face. As if that smile had nothing to do with my mother at all.

ALLISON FUNK

Downstate

In the next-to-smallest
of states. Ten miles from the bay,
twice that to the sea.

For those passing through,
Sussex County's an interlude,
a turn off the highway into soybean and corn,

her Lincoln,
a dot on the map
smaller than the peppermint drop

she'd dissolve on her tongue
walking back to Grandmother Sallie's house
from her Great Aunt May's general store

down the dust road
she waded barefoot,
over the tracks.

To anyone driving through,
through the Depression, the passenger
glimpsing her from a train

as she takes the long way home:
a girl of little consequence,
my mother.

Sixty years later she's taking me
to the clapboard house
her grandfather, a ship's carpenter, built.

She has it by heart—
the parlor with the horsehair sofa, Victrola,
the library table where the photographs stood.

Back there,
she says, pointing to the phantom chicken house,
she'd help pick a bird out for supper—

nothing better with succotash
and the huckleberry pie almost worth the chiggers
that itched after a morning's picking.

Bindweed now
where the truck garden had been,
where clouds formed

from her grandfather's favorite pipe,
the ox head with carved horns.
Of course the house is smaller

than she remembers,
and the present owner won't let her in.
Someone is sleeping, somebody's sick inside.

The shingles worn sandpaper thin,
windows covered with plastic in steamy July,
we'll look elsewhere for her beloved grandmother—

in the cemetery that's all
that is left of downtown.
Here my mother will wander the rows

as if they too are Sussex roads
she's remembering: Uncle Harry,
May and Caddie,

so where's Sallie?
Sweet Sallie smelling of the wintergreen
liniment she rubbed on her joints.

Flushed from her search,
my mother moves away from me
in this small town of the long

and not so recently gone. "Another time,"
I cry, wanting to drive her beyond
the voice she is hearing:

Here Biddy, Biddy
her grandmother calls to the chicks,
calling them to her, the ones she has lost.

ALLISON FUNK

Afterimages

Where have they wintered,
the battered ones?
What compass guides them?

Questions she will ask,
though not until spring,
the girl in a Delaware autumn

who sees herself elsewhere,
shining in the plumage
and primaries of the Tropics.

Dazzled by the Monarchs
dressing the pin oak they've chosen
to roost in behind her house

she'd abandon everything
to follow them into another season
and so she makes her wish—

whither thou goest—
so strong is her longing
to blur off course,

migrate to another coast
to escape the snow that,
foiling her, will fall,

will cover her
in her winter land.
No matter,

she will console herself until spring,
when among last year's leaves
she'll look for a trace of topaz

and the telltale flashes
along the edge of a wing.
Who knows which among the venturing

return, even which generation
passes above shadows
of the girl, the tree

roosted in once? Afterimages,
the girl, the tree
familiar after this much time,

the headiness of flight,
the distance traveled from her,
the girl I come back to.

DANA GARRETT

From the Seventh Floor of the Carvel State Office Building

It was after the plea
    and before the prosecutor
interrupted, began again on how to civilize the wild
youth of the city
                    that the falcon flew by the window.

Its distance:
a lawless point that plotted the prospect
of far-off trees amid streets and buildings:

more green than grey
more place given than made
more bad news for developers—
    the advance of unpoliced spaces—
more sense to cede
to a rule exceeding our guilt and innocence.

VANESSA HALEY

For a Former Student Found at Fleming's Landing After Two Years at the Bottom of the Smyrna River

You dream you are the sunfish
swimming around the empty cabin
of your skull, flitting in
and out of your eye sockets,
curious at what is left:
faint phosphorus
of brainy light,
molecular eddies of thought
lingering in the undertow.
The river swirls.
Blueclaws wave as they
scurry across the silt bottom
where you still sit
inside your car, glittering
bones at home among barnacles
and minnows edged with gold.
Jewel of a girl, star
of the Smyrna River, popular
with eels drifting in benign
black slenderness,
and catfish cleaning house
forever in honor of your visit.
Even the large-mouth bass
adores you,
kisses you all over
as though you are a lover
come home at last.

VANESSA HALEY

George Stubbs's "Plate for the Sixth Anatomical Table of the Muscles, Fascias, Ligaments, Nerves, Arteries, Veins, Glands and Cartilages of a Horse, Viewed in Front, Explained"

At the age of six, he was helping his father in the slaughterhouse,
nudging cows into narrow chutes, their mouths still chewing
the cud; eyes mild, dreamy. They barely flinched
when their throats were slit, *only a fly biting*, standing
docile in blood pooling dark until their knees
buckled under the weight and they felt themselves
collapsing atom by atom, then reassembling
again in fields of sweet clover where white birds
flitted, lit, flitted, lit at the edge of daylight.
Meanwhile, George drew bone after bone
from every angle, detached, skillful beyond his years,
determined to comprehend the skeleton's architecture.
Even before he felt a longing for Mary Spencer,
who became his common-law wife and assistant,
he loved the small muscles that elevated the horse's lips,
the panniculus extending over the thorax,
abdomen and flank, the carved beauty
of each terrible nostril. Layer by layer,
he splayed and peeled back flesh, the horse
suspended on wires from the barn's
thick beams, planks positioned just so
under each hoof to shadow a canter
or leisurely walk through the woods.
Downwind from that abandoned farmhouse
near Lincolnshire, black flies swarmed
but never found the source.

In the drawing labeled table six,
which, in reality, was the beginning,
the horse had just been led by a rope halter
from a farm two miles away. Stubbs
covered its head with a cloth sack,
bled it deftly, then injected soft tallow
into its arteries and veins. *What magnificence,*
he thinks, as he hoists the horse like an enormous
marionette, ropes creaking in the pulleys' grooves,
the animal swaying, hovering above the stone
floor as though it is about to ascend
into heaven on silent-thundering hooves.

GARY HANNA

The Visit

Her walk, her dashes
around the house, her
stops in dusty corners,
the way she brushes
past the organdy drapes,
whispering over the oriental.
The gas flame flickers
in the fireplace that never
worked, dishes quiver,
still on the table.
The years grow slow, like
smoke wandering past
the sunlight, and all at
once, in too soon time,
the house is empty as
glass, and I've grown old
missing the noise.

WENDY INGERSOLL

The Practice of Scales

Every hour comes another student,
uncertain as light on water,
thumbs clinging to Middle C,
fingers splayed like rushes caught in pond ice.
Slow tempo on the scales,
I show them,
then double, triple time, four notes per beat—
the scales are a ladder
    to climb the music—
        college mornings I brought my metronome
to small rooms with old uprights.
Major, minor scales, thirds, sixths, tenths,
hands separate, hands together,
then diving deep into Chopin and
Brahms, embracing Bach.
In the dorm someone said Play—
I plunged into a Prelude,
blanked in the middle,
    couldn't find the missing measure—
        it's okay to lose your place, I tell my students,
if we remembered every tune we ever played,
we'd drown—parallel scales, contrary,
chromatic, natural, harmonic, melodic,
again until you get it right—my students
rise like minnows to the lure
or not, cast for me a glint
of light bending through water.

McKAY JENKINS

"And None Came Back" is a condensed version of the book, *White Death*, which tells the story of one of the deadliest avalanche tragedies in American mountaineering history. It recounts a climb that claimed the lives of five young men trying to make the first winter ascent of the highest peak in Montana's Glacier National Park, and the dangerous and high-profile effort to save them. The book is also an exploration of the mysteries and folklore of mountain wilderness; the fascinating science of snow and ice; and a meditation on man's relationship with risk in the face of dangerous weather and terrain. It traces the country's obsession with so called "extreme" winter sports, from World War II's remarkable 10th Mountain Division, the country's first unit of high-altitude soldiers, to the current generation of media- and market-savvy adventure entrepreneurs.

And None Came Back

Some years ago, on the day after Christmas, five climbers walked into Bob Frauson's ranger station in St. Mary, on the eastern side of Glacier National Park. The young men, all local boys, were prepared for a serious winter expedition, their packs heavy with skis, crampons, and ice axes. They also came equipped with a deep knowledge of the Glacier backcountry and extensive avalanche training at the hands of some of the West's finest mountaineers. But their plan was audacious even by their own standards: an ascent of the north face of Mount Cleveland, one of the country's biggest vertical walls at four thousand feet. It was the winter of 1969, and the face had never been climbed.

For months, the boys had enjoyed one of the mildest climbing seasons in memory: warm, clear weather that had lasted deep into autumn. But despite that fall's run of good weather, winter conditions are notoriously unpredictable in Glacier's mountains, nowhere more so than on its highest peak, 10,448-foot Mount Cleveland. What the team needed to know was not Frauson's opinion about its north face— they had been studying that for years. They needed to know about its snowpack.

In Bob Frauson, they could not have encountered a more competent adviser. A large man with bright eyes and generous jowls, Frauson was a World War II combat veteran who had served with the Army's Tenth Mountain Division; in 1944, he'd celebrated his 21st birthday on a reconnaissance mission to the base of the German stronghold in the Italian Apennines known as Riva Ridge. Recognized nationally as an expert in winter mountaineering, he had spent the years since in the northern Rockies and knew the moods of winter weather as well as anyone alive. When he trained new rangers, Frauson made no bones about the dangers of high-mountain rescue, or high-mountain play. He would show his young charges a body bag and tell them, "This is how you'll come back if you go out climbing where you're not supposed to."

Montana was filled with expert mountaineers like Frauson, many of them Tenth Mountain vets, and their protégés. The five boys who knocked on his door—Jerry Kanzler, Clare Pogreba, Ray Martin, Mark Levitan, and James Anderson—were only in their late teens and early twenties, but they had rambled around Glacier since they could walk. Jerry Kanzler, 18, and his older brother, Jim, had been raised climbing here with their father, Hal, an Okinawa vet with a passion for wildlife photography. Park rangers knew the Kanzlers to be among the most talented climbers in the region.

Their friends Ray Martin and Clare Pogreba had founded the climbing club at Montana Tech. They were known as Mutt and Jeff to family, friends, and professors alike: Ray, who worked summers in Alaska fighting fires, was a gangly six-foot-six with a grin as broad as his face. Clare was a stocky five-foot-two, with a sloping, Eastern European nose; his head came to just under his friend's armpit. Clare had taken to flooding sections of ramp inside the college football stadium to construct a long sheet of ice, and he'd inch his way up it using crampons and ice axes.

At twenty-two years old, Martin and Pogreba were the oldest, and the leaders in spirit if not necessarily in ability; even they considered Jerry Kanzler to be a superior mountaineer. Not long before the Mount Cleveland trip, the Kanzlers had gone off to Oregon and Washington to climb some of the highest mountains in the Northwest—Mount Rainier, Mount Hood, Mount St. Helens, and Mount Adams—all in a week. Jerry's grace on rock faces left his companions awestruck. Peter Lev, a skiing and climbing instructor at Montana State who would go on to become a co-owner of the world-renowned

Exum Mountain Guides, considered Jerry the best mountaineer he'd taught.

James Anderson and Mark Levitan were not nearly the technical climbers their friends were, but they were nonetheless comfortable on high peaks. Levitan, 20, was the bookish son of a Tenth Mountain Division battalion surgeon who had been the division's only officer taken prisoner of war. Father and son had scaled the Grand Teton. At Montana State, Mark had also enrolled in Peter Lev's ski mountaineering class, and it was there that he befriended fellow intellectual James Anderson. By the time of the Mount Cleveland expedition, Anderson, 18, had already climbed the comparatively gentle west face twice, although during the summer. The sheer wall of the north face, especially in winter, would present challenges of a different order.

The team was missing its most accomplished climber, Jerry Kanzler's brother, Jim. Recently married and responsible for a young son, he had accepted a job as a ski patroller at Bridger Bowl. But if anyone could do the north face, this group could; together they'd pioneered routes up peaks from Bozeman to the Canadian border, including a first ascent of Glacier's Citadel Spire, with its daunting 350-foot pinnacle. Pogreba and Martin had completed a two-week course in avalanche safety in the Tetons. Before they graduated, before jobs and families and Vietnam, they wanted to scale Mount Cleveland.

What happened to these climbers left an indelible mark on an entire generation of outdoorsmen. Prepared and informed, suspended between an older corps of relatively few and highly skilled experts and today's army of backcountry skiers and climbers, they stood on the eve of a new era of American adventuring. Their story is no less relevant today than it was in 1969.

Compared to the peaks of Colorado, Glacier National Park's mountains are, in height at least, modest. But there are no discernible foothills here. You come up the Flathead Valley from the south, or across the plains from the east, and there it is: a mighty fortress of mountains, rising without preamble from the flatland, beckoning and forbidding your approach. In winter, because they trap clouds moving in either direction, the mountains of Glacier are blanketed by incredible amounts of snow; along the Continental Divide, annual snowfall can reach one thousand inches—more than eighty feet. Much of it falls on Mount Cleveland. But in 1969, no one would know just how much snow covered its upper reaches until it was too late.

Looming over the north-central section of the park, Cleveland's summit affords unmatched views—the Glacier peaks to the south, Alberta and British Columbia to the north, Idaho to the west, a hundred miles of prairie to the east. Because it is inaccessible, miles and mountains away from any road, Cleveland cannot be driven to and climbed in a day. In winter there are no rangers nearby, no tourists. There is only the wind, blowing over the ridges.

The winter of 1969 had already seen some big avalanches up high on Mount Cleveland, some snapping trees as they came rumbling down. "That mountain doesn't give a damn about anyone," Canadian naturalist Kurt Seel once told a local paper. "In the summertime, rocks roll constantly. In the wintertime, it's the wind and snow. That mountain is alive all the time."

At the St. Mary ranger station, Frauson drove that point home. For some time, the boys told him, people had been telling them the expedition was foolhardy. But Frauson figured his role was to advise, not to scold. He warned them about the mountain's severe weather patterns and impressed upon them the extreme difficulty of rescue should they run into trouble. Mount Cleveland was particularly prone to avalanches, he cautioned, sometimes ten or fifteen a day. Rocky-faced and rising well above timberline, the peak is virtually bare at its upper reaches. No trees means no anchors for the vast fields of snow.

Moreover, Frauson emphasized, the north face had recently been glazed over by an ice storm; it was "an escalator of moving snow." He argued that it would be more prudent to try the comparatively easy route along the southwest ridge. Though precipitous on both sides, it would steer them clear of the rock—and snowslides so prevalent on the north face. They would also avoid the center of the west face, which presented serious dangers of its own. Its geometry—a "parabolic mirror," Frauson called it—made it exceedingly dangerous avalanche terrain after even the slightest accumulation of snow. Climbing a bowl is like climbing half a funnel, the wider end above catching snow until it can no longer hold it all. Once the strain becomes too great, the snow dumps down the bowl from all sides. By the time the funnel narrows, the snow is running very fast and very deep.

The boys assured Frauson that they would use extreme caution, but the mission was still a go. They told him not to worry unless they had failed to report back by noon on Friday, January 2. As they left, he wrote in his station logbook: "Five boys checked out to climb Cleveland on six-day expedition."

Hiking or skiing in avalanche country is like walking in a valley inhabited by grizzly bears: Your senses become more alert. You become aware of tiny sounds—every creak of a tree limb, every snap of a twig. When each footstep on a steep slope is potentially your last, you tend to pay attention to where you put your feet. Time slows down. Your actions matter.

Once a slab of dense snow becomes sufficiently unstable, it can begin to slide downhill with almost unimaginable force. Small avalanches can carry impact pressures of up to one thousand pounds per square foot, enough to completely demolish a wood-frame house; larger slides, with twenty thousand pounds per square foot, can crush a concrete building. Researchers have estimated that an average powder-cloud avalanche of one hundred and sixty thousand tons can generate twenty million horsepower, about 2,857 times that of an Amtrak locomotive. Getting caught in an avalanche is like trying to stand on a breaking wave. It both violently tumbles you forward and sucks you under.

In January 1951, after a two-day blizzard dropped thirty-eight inches of snow on Alta, Utah, avalanche expert Monty Atwater was checking the slopes before turning skiers loose. At a steep, concave chute his ski patrol partner triggered an avalanche, and Atwater fell through the cascading snow until his skis hit the hard base of snow underneath. "I was knee deep in boiling snow, then waist deep, then neck deep," he wrote in his 1968 memoir, *The Avalanche Hunters*. "Very fast and very suddenly I made two forward somersaults, like a pair of pants in a dryer. At the end of each revolution the avalanche smashed me hard against the base. It was like a man swinging a sack full of ice against a rock to break it into smaller pieces.

"My principal sensation was one of wild excitement," he wrote. "Under the snow there was utter darkness instead of that radiance of sun and snow which is never so bright as directly after a storm. It was a churning, twisting darkness in which I was wrestled about as if by a million hands. I began to black out, a darkness that comes from within. Suddenly I was on the surface again, in sunlight. I spat a wad of snow out of my mouth and took a deep breath. . . . The next time I surfaced I got two breaths. It happened several times: on top, take a breath, swim for the shore; underneath, cover up, curl into a ball. This seemed to go on for a long time, and I was beginning to black out again. Then I felt the snow cataract begin to slow down and squeeze. . . . I gave a tremendous heave, and the avalanche spat me onto the surface like a seed out of a grapefruit."

There are, in fact, several ways to die in an avalanche. A third of the fatalities are caused by trauma to the head and neck sustained during the fall, from smashing bones on rocks buried in the snow or from the contortions inflicted on a body by cascading snow.

The rest are due to suffocation. Even with a small air pocket, the warmth of a victim's breath can seal the snow around his mouth much as perspiration seals the inside of an igloo or a snow cave. Within minutes, a virtual mask of ice forms around the face, cutting off any flow of air.

Few experiences are more terrifying. "Try as I did, it was absolutely impossible to expel the snow from my mouth," a survivor named Bill Flanagan told avalanche researchers Betsy Armstrong and Knox Williams. "The ball of snow simply packed harder each time I tried to gulp air around it." When he finally came to a rest, the ice ball in his mouth "was so big and hard that I was unable to get it out from behind my teeth. I was able to crush it bit by bit with my front teeth and finally reduced it to a size I could at last spit out."

With so little oxygen available under snow, avalanche survival depends critically on the efforts of survivors to dig out their compatriots. There just isn't time to wait for rescuers. And when all the members of an expedition get buried, the chances for survival are very slim.

The Mount Cleveland team camped the first night at St. Mary. The next day, Saturday, December 27, they made their way across the Canadian border to Waterton Townsite, a humble collection of uniform white wooden buildings that served as headquarters for Waterton Lakes National Park. Here they checked in with the Royal Canadian Mounted Police and hired a local named Alf Baker to ferry them back across the border by motorboat to Glacier's Goat Haunt ranger station. Eight miles away, at the other end of Waterton Lake, Mount Cleveland dominated the southern horizon. That day, the temperature would never rise above the high teens, and as the boys scanned the gray skies and the snow-dusted slopes, their enthusiasm for the trip must have been tempered by the cold. Although there were only a few inches of snow on the shore of the lake and on the lower slopes, how much had accumulated at higher altitudes was impossible to guess.

They docked at 11:00 AM. Jim Anderson was the first ashore. Spinning around, he snapped a photograph of Clare Pogreba, in an orange slicker and baggy pants, pulling the aluminum boat ashore as Jerry Kanzler handed out wooden snowshoes. (Under his balaclava, Kanzler wore a full beard, but his thin mustache gave away his youth.) Protruding off the bow were three sets of metal ski poles, their baskets pointing outward like a bunch of flowers. Ray Martin knelt on the dock, arranging backpacks and long wooden skis.

These first moments of organization were hasty, the boys stamping the cold out of their feet and rubbing their hands. Once they had hauled out their gear, Alf Baker motored away, the flag on his little boat's bow snapping in the winter breeze. Perhaps because they were hiking off-season, with no rangers to check their progress, the boys did not sign the Goat Haunt registration book. They did not plan to get lost.

An hour or two later Anderson snapped another photo, this one looking back toward Waterton Lake. From this vantage point, perhaps five hundred vertical feet above the lake, the boys could see that despite the relatively light snowfall thus far in the season, there was in fact considerably more snow above the tree line than below. More snow than they had planned on seeing, period.

Removing his pack while arriving at a break in the woods, Pogreba gave Martin his camera. Whether the boys were still skiing is impossible to tell from the photo. Kanzler and Pogreba were both wearing high lace-up leather boots; although they'd packed snowshoes, the snow was not deep enough, here under the trees, to merit their use. Levitan had a heavy coil of climbing rope strapped to his green pack. Kanzler carried a double load, his own orange pack strapped atop his father's old green Kelty like a koala cub clinging to the back of its parent.

Rather than following Camp Creek to the west face, the boys followed another line—along Cleveland Creek—to the north face instead. They were apparently still planning to make some first-ascent history.

By the end of the day, after a four-mile walk, they reached the bottom of the north face and set up a base camp. What they saw could not have been inviting: Snow clouds covered the mountain's summit, and loose powder avalanches were scrubbing the north face clean as quickly as the snow built up. Out of reach of any avalanches, the boys decided to build three snow caves in case the weather turned much colder. There, beneath the frigid stone of the north face, they spent the night.

The next day Sunday, the 28th, with snow still falling up high on the mountain, they discussed their options. The north face would demand their most exquisite technical climbing skills, skills that two of the team, James Anderson and Mark Levitan, did not possess. The chill of the rock would be unforgiving, the footing slick, and the handholds, where they existed at all, unreliable. A far more tenable route would be up the base of the northwest ridge and out onto the west face. Ropes would have to be fastened not to climbing protection, but to each other in case someone slipped on the ice.

Their decisions were not casually made. With the weather threatening to turn, the boys knew they should get up and down the mountain without delay. Step by step, they checked for settling and cracking snow underfoot, to gauge the tension in the snowpack. Their cheeks picked up any shifts in the wind, determining which angles in the mountain would be covered in deeper, windblown snow. They listened as their footsteps fell for sounds of sudden settling, the ominous *whoomph* of a weak layer of invisible depth hoar, buried like ball bearings deep in the snowpack, giving way under their weight.

Meanwhile, Bob Frauson began checking the skies. He drove to a vantage point near Cardston, Canada, to look at Mount Cleveland. Even from a distance, he could see the unmistakable plumes of avalanches cascading "all over."

Three days later, on New Year's Eve, Bud Anderson, James's older brother, flew a single-engine plane over the mountain, hoping to check the boys' progress. He spied what looked like tracks along the lower reaches of the west face, which he thought odd, given the boys' itinerary. As he looked closer, though, he caught his breath. The tracks ended at the unmistakable edge of a massive fresh avalanche, about halfway up the mountain. Strangely, Anderson also thought he saw tracks leading away from the debris and convinced himself that the team had continued on its way.

From the air, however, Anderson could see that the snow on Cleveland was deeper than anyone had suspected after such a mild autumn. Given the way the weather had played out in the late fall and early winter—warm temperatures, then light snow, followed by cold temperatures—the snowpack had become a textbook example of the formation of depth hoar.

Since the boys had told their families not to worry until January 2, Bud Anderson spent New Year's Day at home in Bozeman. Early the next morning, he and Canadian warden (the equivalent of a ranger in the United States) Jack Christiansen took a boat to Goat Haunt for what they expected to be the triumphant return of the group. There was no one waiting at the dock. Hiking around the ranger station, the pair came across some ski tracks climbing up through the timber toward the north face. Following the tracks, they found abandoned skis and snowshoes about a mile and a half from the lake, near timber-line. It appeared that the boys had decided to attempt the north face after all, and that they were still on the mountain. Meanwhile, Frauson and the other Glacier rangers had grown worried too, and when Anderson called shortly after 9:00 AM, a search swung into full gear, complete with planes and helicopters.

On January 3, two teams of rescuers, including Bud Anderson, gathered at Waterton Townsite, packing climbing skis, ice axes, probe poles, and ropes. Over the next few days they would be joined by several dozen of the best mountaineers in North America, some of them friends and mentors of the missing climbers. Volunteers (including well-known cousins George and Mike Lowe) began arriving from the Tetons to the south, Canadian alpine specialists from Jasper and Banff to the north. The search suddenly became one of the most complex and dangerous in the region's history. And the weather up high was deteriorating, as winds kicked up to twenty-five knots and the wind-chill dropped to minus forty-four. The cloud cover hung so thick that it entirely occluded the upper half of the mountain.

But following the ski tracks toward the mountain, at about 10:30 that morning, the searchers discovered something haunting: remains of a fire, coals still smoldering near the base of the north face, about a half-mile above the abandoned gear. The boys' base camp. Around the fire the searchers found two backpacks, four aluminum-framed cargo packs, two tents, a cache of food, and an array of gear: helmets, stove, carabiners, pitons, webbing, socks, foam pads, sleeping bags, two hundred feet of avalanche cord, and a can of exposed color film.

Leading away from the camp were not one but two sets of footprints, the first heading to the north face, the other to the west face. Had the boys split up? Divided as they were in the level of their mountaineering skills, the searchers figured, perhaps they had separated to attack the mountain from two angles. But wherever they'd gone, the weather would be making it difficult to survive for long. If the boys had somehow managed to hunker down in snow caves to ride out the cold, their food supplies would almost certainly be gone by now.

When he heard about his younger brother's disappearance, Jim Kanzler bolted for Mount Cleveland from Bozeman, bringing with him Peter Lev, the climbing instructor, and Pat Callis, a chemistry professor from Montana State who was also one of the decade's most celebrated climbers. In 1963 Callis and his partner Dan Davis had made the first ascent of the north face of Mount Robson, one of the great

challenges in the Canadian Rockies; along with Lev, he had become a
mentor of the missing boys.

The afternoon of January 4, as even more winter rescue personnel
streamed into Waterton, Jim Kanzler produced two photographs of
the north face of Mount Cleveland, taken by his brother two years
before. He marked the photos with the routes that the boys had discussed, and the search team began formulating its plan. Supplies were
already stretched thin—only three tents, for example, remained for
the new arrivals, which could severely limit a rescue effort that required a full day's walk simply to get back and forth from Goat Haunt
to the mountain. But with a Pacific front on the way, the field leader,
American ranger Willie Colony, decided to move everyone by boat
from Waterton to Goat Haunt, along with gasoline lanterns, stoves,
tents, shovels, and cooking gear. Ice was already forming on the lake,
and soon all supplies would have to be moved by helicopter or snow-
mobile, or on people's backs. Bob Frauson remained behind to direct
the search.

Early on January 5, the search party organized into five groups. A
team of Canadian wardens attempted a climbing reconnaissance of the
north face. Three other Canadians set off onto the northwest ridge.
Three American rangers looked again at the lower portion of the west
side, while the last group took binoculars to the southwest ridge of
Goat Haunt Mountain to scout for avalanche activity on Cleveland's
north face. The last group—Lev, Callis, and Kanzler—was told to
climb the bowl on the west face. With the main search party concentrated on the north face, this was the safest place for them, Colony and
Frauson thought, out of the way of the professional search team—and
out of the way, had the boys fallen or frozen or been buried by an
avalanche, of the most likely disposition of their bodies.

The plan, the rangers said, was for the three friends to go fast and
light, with no sleeping bags, stoves, or any other overnight gear. They
were to work their way around to the upper end of the west face and
then descend to its base by nightfall, where they would be met with
tents, sleeping bags, and dinner. But Callis rejected this plan. They
weren't familiar with the terrain, he argued, and no one could predict
what sort of hardships or bad weather might be encountered. Climbing with no overnight gear meant that if they did get stuck on the
mountain, they would be in for serious trouble.

Still, Callis, Lev, and Jim Kanzler represented the finest technical
climbing skill that northwestern Montana had to offer, and they were
intensely motivated. They had taught their friends most of what they

knew about mountaineering, and while the other searchers were looking for five lost boys, these three were searching for their closest companions. After some hard debate, they decided to take full backpacks,
with sleeping bags, a stove, a shovel, and two days' worth of food.
They did not take a tent. If they were to spend the night on the mountain, they would dig a snow cave. On the way up the west face, looking
for the little brother with whom he'd climbed so many peaks, Jim
Kanzler cried.

After four hours, Canadian warden Peter Fuhrmann had climbed part-
way up the chute of Mount Cleveland's north face without finding
tracks. Over on the northwest ridge, the other Canadians did see a few
tracks and what appeared to be human urine marks. Meanwhile, on
the west face, the day grew late for Kanzler, Lev, and Callis. Working
their way up the bowl from the northwest ridge, they searched into
the early evening, climbing up past a scree field and then up a ramp to
the left of a ledge that in summer supported a waterfall. Physically and
emotionally wrung out, they peered into the diminishing light, looking for the tiniest protrusion from the snow cover, for anything that
might turn out to be the tip of an ice ax, the end of a climbing rope, a
piece of discarded clothing. Initially there was little snow—just a few
inches of light powder under their feet. But then they encountered
something that left them with a sense of horror: a series of "crown
faces," or fracture lines, two to three feet deep, that extended all the
way across the bowl. A massive slab avalanche had broken off above
them, causing the entire bowl to release. Kanzler, Callis, and Lev
could now see why there had been so little snow on the way up. Everything in the bowl—nearly a half-mile across—had slid down the
mountain.
    After radioing down to Goat Haunt, the three dug a snow cave and
spent a long night on the mountain. In the morning they began to
search the avalanche path. Finally, frustrated by hours of fruitless
combing, Callis was walking down the west face when suddenly, in the
surface debris of the avalanche, he saw a small backpack. In that moment, the entire search changed. The main party had been concentrating on the wrong side of the mountain. At least some of the boys had
been here, on the west face.
    The Callis team reconstructed what could have happened. Although
it was possible that the boys had triggered the slide on their way
down—perhaps by glissading down the slope—the avalanche had
probably released on their way up. Most likely they had crunched

through to a layer of depth hoar and sent a fracture line running up-hill. Eventually it would have reached a weak spot in the terrain—a dip in the face, a rock outcropping—and broken off completely. All this would have happened in an instant, without their ever seeing it.

Years later, an accomplished technical climber named Terry Kennedy, with whom Jim Kanzler had made a number of first ascents, would offer an analysis of what might have happened to the boys on the west face. "They follow a gully onto the ridge," wrote Kennedy, "ascend it a ways, then begin a long but easy traverse to the middle of the west face under several thousand feet of cliffs. The logical thing is to keep traversing to the center of the face and do the standard route. They go. The snow becomes deeper.

"They look up and what do they see? Answer: dry cliffs. At some point the series of short cliffs disappears and they find themselves on even easier terrain that only warrants plodding through it. Maybe they recognize soft slab and maybe they don't. . . . The day is probably waning quickly just a week after the solstice and they are going to have to keep the pace stiff to get up and down by nightfall. Up they go, breathing hard, their attention on the summit, not the plates of snow fracturing underfoot."

If the boys on the west face had somehow heard the avalanche bearing down, they might have tried to leap on top of it before it bowled them over. Or perhaps they tried to run out of its track but found the flow moving too quickly. Once they were knocked down, they likely tried to grab their ice axes and self-arrest. Perhaps they tried swimming out of the slide, furiously waving and kicking to thrust themselves out of the surging snow. Or barrel-rolled sideways, in an effort to move faster than the snow and get out of its teeth. Nothing they did, it now appeared, had allowed them to escape.

Avalanche rescue depends critically on the speed of the search team's response. Only one in five victims has been saved by an organized rescue team; out of the 140 found on American slopes by teams of probers since 1950, 121 were already dead.

So it was with little hope that the searchers helicoptered to the west face. Where the arms of the avalanche converged, lines of probers jammed poles through the snow, expecting at any moment to hit something solid—another pack, a boot, a body. Progress was agonizingly slow. In some places, the avalanche debris was too hard to penetrate. They tried a magnetometer, and it sounded once, but intensive digging revealed only flecks of metal in a stone.

Finally a prober broke through and struck something soft. Digging, the team discovered a buried parka and, in its pocket, something even more promising—a camera with film in it and an additional roll of exposed black-and-white film. All of the rolls were flown off to be developed; they arrived back at five o'clock the next morning. The color film found at the camp merely chronicled the boat trip across Waterton Lake. Virtually all of the black-and-whites, however, were taken as the team approached the north face. Some of the images were sharp enough to show the upper mountain covered by a heavy blanket of snow, indicating that conditions were considerably worse than when rescuers went in.

The images were, in their innocence, unbearably poignant, as if apparitions of the climbers themselves stood before the rangers, offering clues to their route but little hope for their safe return. Here was a photo of Jerry Kanzler and Clare Pogreba, best of friends, sitting in Alf Baker's boat and staring off into the middle distance. Here was Ray Martin, on the dock, smiling his goofy smile and standing half again as tall as his companions.

On January 7, with fresh avalanches still plummeting down the west face and winds gusting up to fifty miles per hour, the searchers returned to Goat Haunt and packed up the boys' base camp. Back at Waterton Townsite, Bob Frauson called a supplier for one more set of equipment: five body bags, to be delivered in unmarked boxes.

It would be another five months—after the spring thaw had broken up the snowpack—until the search resumed. With grizzly bears emerging from their dens and beginning to congregate below a waterfall on the west face, their noses leading them in the direction of decay, rangers once again climbed up the bowl. On May 23, 1970, a couple of rangers, exploring on foot, make a remarkable discovery. There, lying on the chunky wet snow, was another camera, flung from its case, lens pointed at the sky. It had clearly been wrenched free from a climber's neck or from the pocket of a backpack. The case, lying nearby, had James Anderson's name on it. The last picture on the roll showed all five boys standing together at about eight thousand feet on the west face.

Like spring buds sprouting from winter hibernation, more gear began to pop to the surface. On June 7, a wool knit cap on the main avalanche path. Three days later, a rucksack. A week of nothing, and then a plastic bag containing flashlight batteries.

Two weeks later, five rangers ascended the west face in intermittent rain and snow. At 9:00 AM on June 29, at about 6,800 feet, they climbed up the side of a waterfall that, frozen-over in winter, had now begun to drain the western bowl. Above the waterfall, the snow—although solid and deep—had been hollowed out by running meltwater. Thirsty from the climb, Jack Christiansen bent down to get a drink and caught the unmistakable whiff of decomposition.

Carefully, nervously, the men shone a flashlight up under the meltwater cave and peered into the darkness. The sound of running water, inside the tunnel, was loud; a full-fledged stream ran right past the men. Peering deep inside the cave, the rangers made out a head and a pair of arms hanging down from the six-foot snowpack. There, attached to a red Perlon rope, was the body of Ray Martin.

As searchers followed the rope from Martin's waist to its terrible end deep in the snow, they discovered four more bodies. All were found in states of violently arrested tumble. It took several days of relentless digging, but once the bodies were removed from their encasement, the cause of death became grotesquely clear. The boys had not lived long enough to suffocate. They had been killed by the fall, carried half a mile down the slope and some 1,500 vertical feet by a vast, tumbling wall of snow. Ruby Martin would recall that her son Ray "was six-foot-six-and-a-half, but when they found him he was six-foot-13 because of a broken back and neck."

The searchers set about identifying the bodies and putting them into the body bags that Bob Frauson had ordered. The last thing they did was take pictures of the dead boys. Strangely, none of the photographs came out.

JAMES KEEGAN

Mule

You looked up, bent near the haunch, when
I named that animal I'd never seen.
"And how did you know it's a mule?"
And like the eager boy at school I was
I answered, "It's too big for a donkey—
big like a horse. But the ears are wrong.
And the face slopes down kind of stupid."

What you knew of mules you knew
by driving nails into their hooves
the way your father showed you to.
What I knew (since precious few
came clopping through Queens) I knew
from books or TV, or did you
sometime whisper it to me?

If you had, we had both forgotten.
That day, you looked like I should not
have known, like we learn the names
of beasts by taking hold alone.
You cupped your hand above the hoof
and bent the foreleg back to show
the soft frog hid inside the hoof's hard ring.

You placed my index finger on
the spongy edge. A sharp stone
could lodge there, you said, and infect.
If so, you'd have to crack the hoof
and drain the foul stuff off
to save the beast from going lame.
It was a fact, a hands-on thing you knew.

And to this day it is more true
to me than a thousand other facts
I've learned by rote and stored away.
A hidden place. A hurt. Hard work to heal.
Nothing I can do feels as real
as that—a stone, a hoof, a nail.
I tap at words to drive the point of them

toward hurt, toward some release,
my hid frog ringed by the bone facts
of what I've done and haven't done.
Some days the mule in me's too lame
to step. Too brute to name his pain.
I hear you then, "Hold the beast close, boy.
Tap steady. Tap even. Tap home."

AMANDA KIMBALL

Levittown, 1951

She thinks of the men with the tree drill
as she waits for her husband,

how they came down the street,
putting one hole in each yard.

She thinks of the precision, how uncomplicated it was
as she adjusts the folded bed sheet
catching blood between her legs.

The day after they'd moved in,
she'd watched them for almost half of an hour

first the drill man
followed by the man with the tree,
the truck with the fill dirt.

Standing at the picture window, fingertips to her flat belly
the weight of another pregnancy
pulling at her shoulders—

a prayer to St. Anthony
in her mind before she could erase it,
find me the joy in this.

And now, as her husband
pulls into the driveway,
holds his hat to his head as he tries to
avoid the mud from the seeded yard—

the blood, seeping past the sheet,
sticking to her legs,

she marvels at how those men
had gone all the way down the street
with no struggle against the tedium,
the filthiness of the work

how they had performed their tasks
with such order,
such a dream of perfection.

e. jean lanyon

some metals tarnish

we took for granted solid brass handles
would be made forever; brass rings
would always be on the merry-go-round.
we were taught the permanence of solid things,
encouraged to dream of tomorrow.

brass could always be polished
with salt and vinegar, lacquered
to stay bright, resemble gold.

in 1941 saturday cinema newsreels,
flashed round mouths of babies
screaming in bombed ruins.
our fathers were taken away.
our mothers dressed like men,
wore heavy hairnets, drove trucks,
riveted ships.

we were fingerprinted, given i.d. tags,
taught to crouch in corners during bombings,
practiced silence in blackouts,
learned the words "closed for the duration."

in windows blue stars turned gold,
our mothers wept at night.
someone boarded-up the merry-go-round.
pennies were made of lead.
the bottoms of bullets were brass.

EMILY LLOYD

Jane Eyre, Unbanned

—upon hearing of a bill to ban books with gay characters in Alabama libraries

You think of Mr. Rochester, mad wives
in attics, Jane herself, as plain as flan.
You don't remember Helen Burns, Jane's friend

from school. Reader, I married her. I pressed
my eighth-grade self between those pages like
a flower, left for later hands. Helen.

"I like to have you near me," she would cough,
romantically consumptive, after Jane
sneaked to her sick-bed. "Are you warm, darling?"

We'll always find ourselves inside the book,
no matter what the book, no matter how
little we're given. I was twelve; gay meant

nothing to me. I only knew I'd go
to Lowood Institution, rise at dawn,
bare knuckles to the switch, choke down the gruel,

pray to the bell, if this meant I could hold
another girl all night, if I could clasp—
this even if she died there while I slept,
this even if I died there in my sleep.

ALEXANDER LONG

Unfinished Love Poem

—for James Wright

Like I've been saying
All along, I'm not sure
Where they've gone
Off to. Why can't I think
Of that place as full
Of lovers secretly kissing
In unmodified light?
This afternoon's rain settles
Along my jaw.
I hope my bus is late.
Three beers by noon,
And now I go to chop
The rows of onions
For my bosses who mark
Up the booze for us all.
We keep coming back.
This is the life I've got.
I make salads from hearts
Of iceberg picked by migrants
Who curse and bless
This country, state, and town;
Their corner with the motel
Whose windows acquire a sheen
Over them as they drink
Five-dollar Cuervo
And spit it into their hands
To slick back their hair,

Desiring the unattainable
Strippers who pass through
Once a month. Oh Sweet
Jesus, I keep imagining
The regulars and the lawyers drunk
Again, sliding off their chairs.
What I really like
About the clearest days
Isn't the light itself.
At the trolley stop in Sharon Hill,
Where I grew up and most can't
Leave, I'd stand there
With the two bums,
Big Bob and Chicken Man.
For being desolate, they dressed
Nice. They stank, though,
And sniffed glue every chance
They could. Otherwise,
They no longer seemed to desire a thing,
Not even the other's shadow
On the hottest afternoons, flirting
With oblivion, waving to it
As it floated by quiveringly
Over their ears,
White and light as milkweed.
Trying to think of them again,
In their polyester suits
And dress shirts
Buttoned all the way up
To their scruffed wattles,
Whose collars resembled a hit pigeon
I saw once by the curb—
Its wings lifting slightly
As another A. Duie Pyle rig
From Pittsburgh barreled through
Sharon Hill, where I grew up,
Without stopping until it hit
The limits of West Philly—
I can see they have
Completed that agenda the dead
Stars have laid out, and I don't know

Where they are now. So it is
This bus stop
We all end up at,
Telephone wires swaying
Between oceans, the sun
Hovering right there, between
Our fingers, with all its busted light.
I've heard it called a lot
Of things, not one of them
Accurate. The pines
And maples dripping with rain,
For example, have their Latin
Names that make them
Seem larger, which I can remember
Well enough most days,
Which I love.

BONNIE MacDOUGAL

In the opening scene of the novel, *Out of Order*, a lavish party in Greenville, Delaware, celebrating newlyweds Doug Alexander and Campbell Smith turns into a night of betrayal and tragedy when Cam hears Senator Ramsey announce that "Doug Alexander is the Party's next choice for this November's election to the United States House of Representatives" and a phone call announces that the senator's thirteen-year-old son has been kidnapped. Even as the senator—Doug's mentor—asks Cam to track down his son, she questions why her husband told her nothing of his plans, and why this father seems less interested in his son than scandal. She soon learns that everyone has something to hide, and as the kidnapping unravels, and a series of murders looms closer, she is forced to face her own past—and the lie she has lived with for years.

Out of Order

They moved in a pack, six young males, fit and feral, loping flank to flank with an ice fog swirling at their feet and clouds of hot steam puffing from their mouths. Berms of cindered gray snow rose up on both sides of the road, and they ran between them in perfect unspoken formation, as if cued by some pheromone only they could sniff.

Cam was alone on the narrow country lane, and she slowed as one of the pack suddenly broke formation and surged toward her. He lifted something as he ran, a long ellipse that gleamed to a high polish in the moonlight, and swung it down into the curbside mailbox with a splintering crash.

She flipped on her high beams. Six boys and a baseball bat stood frozen on the road before her, a tableau vivant of teenage vandalism, until a second later the headlights scattered them like a laser blast.

"Kids," she muttered.

She was already late, and her nerves were strung tight. She'd spent the last two hours in a frenzy of dressing and undressing, pinning up her hair and tearing it down again, carefully applying makeup only to frantically rub it all off, until at last Doug had mumbled that it might be bad form to arrive late to a party in their own honor. Cam was afraid it was even worse form to arrive separately, but finally she'd insisted that he go on ahead.

Now, watching as the boys dived into the bushes and rolled out of sight, she was glad she had. If Doug saw what she just had, he would have felt duty-bound to stop and do something. It was his nature: if he could do something, he did it. And more to the point, if he knew something, he spoke it. Doug would never have remained silent about the boy who'd just broken the spine of someone's mailbox—the same boy who should have been passing canapes at the party tonight: Trey Ramsay, thirteen-year-old son of their host, United States Senator Ashton Ramsay.

But keeping secrets was an old habit for Cam. She did with this information what she did with most: she filed it away.

She drove on, but a moment later her headlights shone on something else: a dark van was pulled over to the side of the road, and a man stood beside it with a cell phone to his ear. Calling the police, she supposed, and felt some relief that the matter was out of her hands. He was wearing jeans and a ski jacket, respectable enough attire for a Friday night in the suburbs of Wilmington. But there was something in his stance, a dark edge to the way he turned away as she approached. Her eyes flicked up to the mirror as she passed him. For a moment he looked as fit and feral as that wolfpack; for a moment she wondered if he weren't more dangerous than they were.

But only for a moment. She was on the brink of a new life, and no spoiled delinquent or mysterious stranger was going to keep her from it. She kept driving.

A cold February moon shone down on the unbroken snow of the open fields and the hundred-year-old hedgerows that marked off the boundaries of the old Greenville estates. This was the château country of northern Delaware, a region settled two hundred years before by a tribe of Franco-Americans who came to establish a utopian colony but ended up manufacturing gunpowder instead. Today, the DuPont Company was an abiding presence throughout Delaware. If only six degrees of separation existed between any two people on earth, then only one or two existed between DuPont and any son or daughter of Delaware. Cam smiled as it occurred to her that she was part of that family now, too, a daughter-in-law of Delaware.

The lights were blazing at the end of the Ramsays' driveway, and she turned through the gate stanchions and drove around a circle of snowcapped shrubs to the front steps of the house. It was a decaying old manor of dingy white stucco and faded black shutters, but tonight Cam thought it shone like a palace. Tonight the Ramsays were honoring the newlyweds before what she expected to be the ionosphere of Delaware society.

A valet parker trotted around the side of the house, and madly she shrugged out of her Gore-Tex parka and tossed it in the seat behind her. Her dress was a strapless ball gown of velvet and satin that cost her two months' salary. There was nothing left in the budget for an evening coat after that.

"Evening, miss," the boy said and opened her door.

She hesitated a second, the span of a heart skip and a quick convulsive shiver, then stepped out bare-shouldered into the cold night air.

Twin pillars flanked the front door, each one carved like a headstone with the letter V—for victory, Senator Ramsay would have claimed, but first it was for Vaughn. Margo Vaughn Ramsay was the one with the money, and this was her ancestral home. Cam pressed the bell and prepared her smile, and an instant later Margo threw the door open.

"Campbell, darling!" she cried, and scanned the street a moment before she pulled her inside. "You're here at last!"

Margo was wearing yards of green and gold brocade cut something like a kimono, and her steel-gray hair was gathered up in a topknot and shot through with a lethal-looking ivory rod. The first time Cam met her, she'd worn Mao-style silk pajamas, a curious look for Christmas Day, but later Doug explained: Margo spent her childhood in the Far East with her State Department father, and she continued to maintain an affection for all things Asian.

"Mrs. Ramsay, I'm so sorry I'm late—"

"Nonsense. No one's late but Ash." Margo's black eyebrows arched up over flinty gray eyes and high-cut cheekbones. "The train. Again."

Doug had also explained this: the Senator kept a monk's cell on Capitol Hill and commuted home by Metroliner on the weekends. The Tuesday-to-Thursday Club was the derogatory term for such legislators, although, according to Doug, Ramsay adhered strictly to a Monday-through-Friday schedule.

"Everyone!" Margo called. "It's Campbell! At last!"

A buzz of voices rose up, and as the bodies began to spill out into the center hall, Cam felt a stab of her old insecurity. The men were all in tuxedos, and the women in ash-blonde pageboys and severe black gowns, while there she stood in a dazzling white ball gown with her hair tumbling long and loose down her back. Once again she'd dressed wrong, once again she was out of place. But quickly she reminded herself she was the bride and the guest of honor here tonight; this time it was proper to stand out.

A pianist was playing Gershwin in the living room to the left, and a babble of voices still came from the library to the right, while here in the hall, a swarm of guests pressed in close around her. "A pleasure, young lady," someone said. "A pleasure."

"Best wishes to you both!"

A wiry woman seized Cam by both hands. "Oh, I've been so anxious to meet you!" she cried.

"Campbell, Maggie Heller," Margo said.

"Doug's told us so much about you!" the woman gushed. She was overanimated and overthin, as if a hypercharged metabolism was burning off calories faster than she could stuff them into her mouth. "And you know we all adore him, and we wish you all the best!"

"And here's someone you must meet." Margo pulled her free from Maggie Heller and steered her in the other direction, toward a man with pocked skin and deep vertical creases through the hollows of his cheeks. "Norman Finn."

"Congratulations!" he said, stepping forward with the stench of tobacco smoldering from his tuxedo.

Cam shook his hand briefly, repelled by the reek of cigarettes and by that word—*congratulations*—that always struck her as double-edged. "How do you do, Mr. Finn?"

"No, just Finn. Everybody calls me Finn."

"Finn," she repeated doubtfully, then gave a start as a man behind her leaned in too close. She turned to find a video camera zooming in on her face. Strange, she thought, turning away; the society pages could only use stills. Margo continued to pull her along, and Cam continued to clasp hands and murmur greetings as the faces whirled past and the pianist played "'S Wonderful."

"What a wonderful occasion!" the next woman said. "We only wish you'd had your wedding here."

"Yes, why were we cheated out of a wedding?" someone else asked.

Cam smiled and explained. Since she had no family and Doug's mother couldn't travel, they'd kept it a simple affair, a civil ceremony in Florida with only Doug's mother and aunt as witnesses, followed by a honeymoon on St. Bart's.

"I'm sure it was all lovely," Margo said. "But Ash and I decided: if we couldn't have a Delaware wedding, we'd at least have a Delaware wedding reception!"

"Good thing, too," said the pock-faced man, Norman Finn, just Finn. "Gives us a chance to look you over."

Cam gave him an uncertain glance. She didn't know what he meant, nor even what he was doing here. There was something disquieting about him, an undercurrent of crude power, as if he were a plantation overseer or a casino boss.

"Campbell," said the overeager woman, Maggie Heller. "That's such a lovely name!"

"Thank you." A second later Cam winced—wrong response— though appropriate enough if they knew the truth.

"You're a lawyer in Philadelphia?"

"Yes. With Jackson, Rieders and Clark."

Finn announced to the crowd, "That's the outfit that acquired Doug's firm last year."

Cam's lips curved in a coy denial. "Oh, not acquired, Mr. Finn. Our firm *merged* with Doug's."

"I'd say it's a merger, now." he said with a coarse laugh.

"Are you planning to sit for the Delaware bar?" another man asked.

"I already did, last summer. Passed, too!" she added pertly.

"What's your specialty?"

"Oh. I'm just an associate," she said airily. "I do whatever they tell me to do."

"But what department are you in?" the man pressed her.

Her smile dimmed. "Family law," she said after a beat.

"Ahh." He gave a too-knowing nod. "We called that domestic relations in our firm. Until one of our clients thought that meant her husband was having an affair with the maid!"

"I remember that case, Owen," put in a man behind him. "And damned if she wasn't right!"

Cam gave a strained smile through the crowd's laughter.

"No, wait a minute," Finn said. "Doug told us you're an asset-finder."

"Yes," she said, brightening. "I do a lot of that. Executing on judgments, and tracing assets the defendant might have stashed away."

"Oh, I see the connection," a woman remarked dryly. "Since nobody conceals assets better than a man heading for divorce court."

"Damn, is that what asset-finding means?" Finn said. "Here I was hoping it meant Campbell could help us with our fund-raising."

She gave him a confused look as another round of laughter broke out. He stepped closer and brought a vapor of cigarette stench with him. "Margo, let me take over the introductions here. I got some folks Campbell needs to meet."

"By all means, Finn." Margo relinquished Cam's arm and turned at once to work the crowd. "Why, there you are!" she cried. "How long has it been? Oh, I know—the train! Again!"

More names and faces scrolled past Cam as Finn pulled her along through the hall. *Owen Willoughby; Webb Black; Carl Baldini—you know, Baldini Construction?; Chubb Heller—you met his wife, Maggie, already, didn't you; Ron March—as in the U.S. Attorney Ronald March?— that's right; John Simon, because every party needs a friendly banker.* Cam nodded and smiled and felt a ripple of unease. None of these names was familiar to her, though she'd been following the Wilmington society pages for months. She tried to tune into the snippets of conversation around her. It was the usual party banter that month—the latest movies at the multiplex, the latest White House sex scandal, the latest showdown with Saddam Hussein. A sharper exchange sounded behind her. *Numbers look good. You see that poll yesterday? Yeah, but without the cash, what can he do . . . ?* Margo's voice sounded distantly, its pitch dropping in Doppler effect as she moved to the back of the house. "Yes, Jesse's waiting at the station for him. Trey . . . ? I don't know—he must still be upstairs. He's probably trying to find something to wear. He's been growing out of everything! He's all wrists and ankles these days!"

Finn veered off course and pulled Cam through a cluster of people to reach an old man slumped in a wheelchair. "Jonathan, this is Doug's bride," he announced loudly. "Campbell, meet Jonathan Fletcher."

At last, a name she'd expected to hear tonight. Jonathan Fletcher was a member of Delaware aristocracy, a third- or fourth-generation millionaire. "How do you do, Mr. Fletcher?"

The old man looked up with a squint under woolly white eyebrows and said nothing.

"Campbell—" spoke a woman behind the wheelchair. "Is that a family name?"

"Yes." Cam watched peripherally as Margo picked up the telephone on a console table by the stairs. "It was my mother's maiden name."

"Sounds Scotch," the old man said in a deep rumble that shivered the loose flaps of his jowls.

Cam lip-read as Margo spoke into the phone across the hall: ". . . wondering if you've seen Trey anywhere tonight . . . ?" "Hundred proof," Cam quipped.

"You don't look Scotch," Fletcher said with a suspicious growl. "More Irish maybe."

She tossed her head and sent her hair cascading down her back. "Aahh, go on with ye," she said in a brogue that brought a loud burst of laughter from the crowd.

The alert pianist made a quick segue into "They All Laughed."

Twenty feet away Margo hung up the phone. The bones showed in her face for a second before her flesh slackened into a smile once more.

"Where do you hail from, Campbell?" someone asked.

"Pennsylvania. Lancaster County."

"Oh, but tell the rest!" Margo charged across the room so fast that the gold threads sparked in her gown. "Campbell was raised by her grandmother after her parents died in the Philippines. Can you imagine?—they were missionaries there."

Jonathan Fletcher's shaggy eyebrows rose. "Died how?"

"In a Muslim massacre," Cam said. When everyone's faces froze in horror, she added, "But this was almost thirty years ago. I was only a baby."

Finn bent down close to Fletcher's ear. "That's eighteen-carat stuff, you know."

The old man nodded and finally pulled his rheumy eyes from Cam to demand of Margo, "Where's that husband of yours?"

"I told you, Jonathan. The train—"

"Where's that husband of mine?" Cam said, almost as querulously as the old man.

She won another laugh from the crowd as Finn pointed her toward the library.

It was a dark-paneled, heavily draped room furnished in a jarring blend of Chesterfield sofas and Japanese silk screens, a dim and dreary room during her previous visits here. But tonight a fire crackled on the hearth, lamps shone from tabletops and wall sconces, and Doug Alexander glowed incandescently in the center of it all.

On any objective tally of looks, he would tot up as average bordering on nondescript. Everything about him could be summed up as medium: medium brown hair, medium brown eyes, medium height, medium build, albeit with a slight professorial stoop to his shoulders. But there was something about him that lit up a room, and he was lighting this one up now. From the piano came the strains of one of their favorite songs, "Someone to Watch Over Me." Doug's head came up, and when he spotted Cam in the doorway, he sent her a signal with his eyebrows—You okay?—and she sent one back to him with a smile—Fine, wonderful!

Standing there, gazing at him, she was. She'd been a loner all her life, but she was half of a couple now, part of a unit, united, and she never had to be alone again.

An arm suddenly slipped around her waist and a voice spoke in her ear. "Watch out, babe. You almost look besotted."

"I got news for you, Nathan," she retorted, pivoting in a swirl of white satin. "I am besotted." She rose up on tiptoe to hug the tall black man, then stepped back to regard him with a suspicious squint. "What in the world are you doing here?"

"Me?" He feigned affront as he straightened his red bow tie. "I was about to ask you."

But that was exactly her point. Nathan Vance was as much a nobody as she was. That was the basis of their friendship. They'd drifted to-gether in law school the way misfits always do—Cam a poor white orphan girl, and Nathan the son of a family that was black in color only. "No, really," she insisted. "How'd you ever get invited here?"

"Okay, one, I went to school with you." He ticked off the points on his fingers. "Two, I used to work in Philadelphia with you. Three, now I work in Wilmington with Doug. And finally, four, I'm the only one in the world who can claim friendship with both the bride and groom. Thus, I respectfully submit, no one deserves to be here more than me."

It came to her then, the source of all her unease tonight. This was no gathering of Wilmington society. There was no one here from the Beaux Arts Ball committee or the Winterthur point-to-point races or the symphony board. She looked back to the library to see a strange man clapping Doug on the shoulder as another whiff of conversation came her way. *See that trade policy paper he did? A lot of prime stuff in there.*

Nathan's gaze went past her and his shoulders went straight, and Cam turned to see Norman Finn bearing down on them.

"Oh, Finn," she said. "I'd like you to meet my friend, Nathan Vance—"

"Hell, I know Nathan. How's business, young man?"

"Fine, sir. Good to see you tonight."

Lawyers, Cam thought as they shook hands. Of course, they must all be lawyers. It was a logical enough guest list for a party in honor of the marriage of two lawyers, hosted by a former attorney general of the state. But she caught another fragment of conversation: *Yeah, regis-*

trations are up, but the fund-raising levels—Her bare shoulders shivered as a blast of frigid air shot through the hall, and she turned around as Senator James Ashton Ramsay burst through the front door, larger than life. "Margo!" he roared as the crowd turned his way "When's dinner? I'm starved!"

A cheer went up, and Cam squeezed back against the wall as the rest of the crowd pressed forward, everyone clamoring for an up-close and personal view of the senator. He was an imposing figure, tall and barrel-chested, with a hawkish nose and a flowing mane of yellow-white hair that lent him his nickname: the Lion of New Castle County. He peeled off his overcoat and tossed it over a bamboo-backed chair, then pitched himself into the throng.

"Hello, Finn! Owen, Sarah, good to see you! Maggie, my girl, how are you? Ron! How're you doing?"

"Welcome home, Senator!" Finn shouted.

The other guests picked up the cry, as if Ramsay didn't appear in the same place every Friday night. "Welcome home, Senator! Welcome home!"

"Good to see you!" he boomed to them all in return. "Thanks for coming!"

At last Cam understood. These were what Doug called the Party people—by whom he meant not people who liked to party, but rather the people who worked for the Party. She should have realized. The Party was close to a religion for Doug: he tithed, attended regular services, and took an awful lot on faith.

He was working his way toward her through the crowd, and she cut ahead to meet him. "Honey?" she called.

"Hold on," he said, smiling, and brushed past her.

"There's my boy!" Ramsay yelled and held an arm out to Doug. A path parted, and another cheer went up as the two men pounded each other's shoulders.

The front door opened again and another chilly blast of air came in, this time admitting an unnatural blonde in a lustrous black mink coat.

"Ahh, here's Meredith now." Ramsay pulled the woman front and center before him. "Everyone—I want you to meet Meredith Winters. I coaxed her up from Washington for the weekend, so you folks be sure and show her a good time."

Jesse Lombard, the senator's longtime factotum, slipped in the door behind them and was there to catch the woman's mink as she poured it off.

"Who is she?" Cam whispered to Nathan as Jesse unobtrusively bore the coats up the stairs.

"Political strategist. Used to read the news in San Francisco. Now she's running Sutherland's campaign in Maryland."

"Wow." Phil Sutherland was a name even a political agnostic like Cam could recognize. He'd been the commander of the armored division in Desert Storm, author of a bestselling autobiography, host of a hugely popular radio talk show, and founder of a Baltimore inner-city mentoring project so successful it was now the model for a dozen similar efforts across the country. His bid for the Senate was the most closely watched race in the country.

"But isn't it kind of early for Ramsay to be interviewing campaign consultants?" Cam asked. "It's more than four years before he has to run again."

Nathan only looked at her.

"Margo!" Ramsay bellowed. "Where are you? And would somebody please put a glass of something in my hand so I can make a toast here?"

On cue, four white-gloved waiters materialized from out of the kitchen and came through the crowd bearing trays laden with flutes of champagne. Margo appeared on their heels and swept to her husband's side. He kissed her with a resounding smack, then snatched a glass off the nearest tray.

"All right, attention, everybody," he said. When the buzzing didn't dwindle, he went to the staircase and climbed up a few steps. The piano music cut off, but there were another few moments of excited humming as the crowd jostled into a semicircle around the base of the stairs. The man with the video camera positioned himself carefully in the front line and kept the tape rolling.

"Good evening, friends," the Senator said as silence finally fell. "I'm glad to see you all here tonight on this wonderful occasion, and I'm proud, too, and I'll tell you why. You all know Doug Alexander. Some of you also knew his father, Gordon Alexander, a man I was lucky enough to call my best friend. We lost Gordon too soon. Way too soon. And when Dorothy got sick and Doug was only a half-grown boy, there he was, facing adversity that most of us couldn't cope with as adults. But he never let it get him down. He took good care of Dorothy. No mother could've asked for a better son. His teachers loved him, his coaches couldn't do without him, and as for me, if I didn't see him at my dinner table every Sunday, I didn't call it a good week.

"Doug grew up into the kind of man who never gave second best and never settled for it, either. He got himself through the best schools, he was hired by the best law firm in town—Sorry, Owen," he said to a man who gave a gracious shrug. "Yours is good, too, but I have to speak my mind here—and he's done nothing but first-class work since he passed the bar. There hasn't been a major real estate development deal in the state that Doug hasn't been a part of. This new waterfront development, every industrialization project that got off the ground in the last decade—they all had Doug Alexander working feverishly behind the scenes to make it happen. The people of this state owe an awful lot to him. And I don't have to tell the people in this room how much the Party owes to him. He's been a good and loyal member and a tireless worker for our candidates.

"But there's always been a missing element to this young man. And it's made Margo and me despair about him more than once."

A few of the guests exchanged uncertain glances.

"But you see, it was the way he was made," Ramsay went on. "He wouldn't settle for second best in a wife, either."

A burst of relieved laughter sounded as Cam's face began to burn.

"But guess what, folks? It turned out he didn't have to! It took him a while to find her, but he got himself a dilly." He peered down into the crowd. "Whoa, hold on. We're missing the bride here. Campbell, where are you?"

"Go on up," Nathan hissed in her ear.

A smattering of applause sounded as she was propelled through the crowd to Doug's side at the foot of the stairs.

"There she is," Ramsay declared, pointing. "You can all see for yourselves her obvious attractions, but folks, I'm here to tell you that she's also smart and sassy and she's gonna keep this boy on his toes for the rest of his life!"

Doug gave her hand a squeeze as the guests laughed and applauded.

"We couldn't be prouder of Doug Alexander if he were our own son," Ramsay said. "But we also know that our proudest day still lies ahead. For tonight it's my honor and privilege to announce to you— and I thank you, Norman Finn, for letting me be the one to announce it—that Doug Alexander is the Party's choice for this November's election to the United States House of Representatives!"

Cam almost buckled at the knees. Doug's hand slipped free, and she looked up through swimming eyes to watch him shaking hands and beaming a thousand-watt smile through the crowd. Ramsay pulled him up beside him on the stairs and threw an arm around his shoulders.

"Friends, I give you Doug Alexander!" He held his glass high. "Our next United States Representative!"

"Doug Alexander!" the crowd roared.

Cam's fingers clenched on the stem of her glass as the guests tossed back their champagne.

"Better get up there with him," a voice said out of a cloud of floral perfume. Cam turned and looked into the sharp features of the blonde woman, Meredith Winters. "Go on," she said, and pried the glass out of Cam's hand. "These photo ops don't come cheap."

Cam stumbled toward the stairs, and when Doug reached a hand down, she grabbed it and held on like a woman overboard.

He made a speech, and even in the ice fog swirling around Cam, she could tell that he'd written and rehearsed it in advance. He was lavish in his thanks to the senator, whom he'd come to regard as a second father. No one could have grown up with a finer role model than Ash Ramsay. He was warmly appreciative of Margo, who'd never failed to make him feel welcome in her home. He was deeply moved and honored by the trust and confidence the Party was showing in him tonight. He singled out Norman Finn and thanked him for the many opportunities to be involved in the Party's work, to make a real difference in the lives of Delawareans. Nothing could make him prouder than to continue that work in Washington.

"As most of you know," he said, "my number one priority is full employment for the people of Delaware. And by full, I don't mean moving names off the unemployment roll and onto the McDonald's payroll. I mean real jobs, with real benefits. Jobs that require the best of your abilities. The kind of job you can spend your life in and raise a family on."

He paused to give a disarming smile. "But much as I'm for full employment, there's one citizen of Delaware who's been employed too long and too far beyond his abilities. And sadly, I think it's time for him to get on the unemployment roll. And the man I'm talking about is . . ."

He raised his arms like an orchestra conductor, and the entire crowd shouted out in unison: "Hadley Hayes!"

Doug waited with a grin until the laughter and applause died down, then said softly: "You know, I thought the happiest day of my life was the day this incredible woman here beside me consented to become my wife. But then I realized I was wrong, because the happiest day of my life came two weeks ago Wednesday when she looked up at me and said 'I do.'"

Cam looked up at him now, astounded that the man who barely stammered through his marriage proposal was broadcasting his feelings to a houseful of strangers.

"But now, with my wife here beside me, and all of my friends here before me, I realize I was wrong both times, and that the happiest days are those that lie ahead of us—as we win this race and march on to Washington!"

Nathan Vance brought his hands together in a rhythmic, hollow clap, and it caught and swelled into a deafening round of applause. Doug turned to Cam and kissed her, long and lustily, while the cheers echoed through the narrow hallway and roared inside her head.

Outside and a mile away a long, loose line of boys was ambling aimlessly down Sentry Bridge Road. The adrenaline rush of the mailbox-bashing was over, and now they were laughing and stumbling and sticking their legs out to try to trip each other. At the head of the line, Jon Shippen dug his hand in his pocket and turned around with a grin to show the rest. "All right, Ship!" went up the cheer when they saw what he had: a joint pilfered from his brother's stash. He lit it and took a drag, and the sickly sweet odor rose up and swirled through the smell of wood smoke that already hung heavy in the crisp night air.

Trey breathed it all in as he waited for the joint to reach him at the back of the pack. This was his favorite time, after the spree, when all of his senses came alive. Everything seemed sharper to him now. There was an edge to the light that let him see the things he usually missed: the faint quivering of the pine needles; the road slush crystallizing into ice as the nighttime temperature plunged; the hundred different shades of black in the sky. If he could paint this night, he'd use greens so deep and dark they'd blend to black. He'd call it—what else?—*Greenville Night*.

Jason had the bat, and he was dragging it in the snow behind him, leaving a track like an animal with a wounded leg. He passed it over to Trey when the joint reached him. It was down to half an inch by then, and he had to hold it with the precision of a watchmaker to get it to his lips. Trey dragged the bat the same way Jason had and looked behind at the trail it left. For fifty feet, he imagined, a crippled animal had been following them through the night. His gaze drifted upward, to the car that was rolling slowly behind them with its headlights off.

"Shit," he hissed and grabbed Jason by the arm.

Abruptly the headlights flashed on, the siren screeched awake, and the lights started spinning on the roof.

The boys in front of him took off, and Trey dove over the berm and rolled across the snow, then scrambled on all fours through the undergrowth of the hedges. He tore through to the other side, jumped to his feet, and went into a flat-out run across the field. He heard Jason huffing behind him and slowed a second to let him catch up, then side by side they ran on, their boots crunching loudly through the snow until they reached another hedgerow. On elbows and bellies they inched forward through a tangle of branches. Trey raked his hair back out of his face and peered through to the other side. Martins Mill Road lay below them, deserted.

"We lost 'em," Jason said with a panting laugh.

Trey scanned the road. The sirens were still wailing distantly, but there were no cop cars here. He rolled to his side and looked back the way they'd come. The tracks they'd left in the snow looked like a line of black ants marching over white sand dunes.

Jason flopped onto his back, fished a cigarette out of his pocket and lit it. "Want one?" he asked, dragging deep.

Trey didn't answer. The sirens cut off abruptly and he crawled forward for another look at the road. To the right, where Martins Mill crossed Sentry Bridge, he could see the dim outline of a car. It was waiting there, halfway between him and home, which meant he'd have to go back the way he came, across the field, pick up Sentry Bridge down below, then circle around Chaboullaird and come out farther down on Martins Mill.

He was up on his haunches, ready to start the run back, when a quick beam of light swept over their footprints in the field.

Trey wheeled one way and Jason the other. As Trey burst through the hedges, the headlights flashed on from the cop car at the corner. He spun left and galloped along the shoulder of the road, but it was no use. The snow was dragging at his feet, and the sirens were closing in behind him.

"Hey! Over here!"

Trey's head swiveled left. A man stood beside a van parked in a driveway. The side door was open, and the man was waving him in.

Trey didn't stop to question. He tore up the driveway and dove into the van, and the door slid shut with a crash behind him. He was in a cargo compartment, and there was a wire mesh screen separating it from the seats in the front. A minute later the driver's door opened and closed, and the man ducked his head down low behind the wheel. He didn't speak, and neither did Trey.

The sirens crescendoed to their highest pitch, and for a few seconds the flashing lights of the cop car reflected in a dancing array of red and blue against the sheet metal interior of the van. Trey crouched down low on the floor, until at last the lights passed by and slowly the sound of the siren faded away in the distance.

"Whew." Trey came up on his knees on the carpeted floor. "Thanks, man. I owe you one." He reached for the handle on the sliding door. "Wanna pop the locks?"

The man turned the ignition, and the engine started with a low growl.

"Hey!" Trey didn't know whether he should say more. The neighbors were always going out of their way to do favors for his family; the guy was probably just giving him a lift home.

But when the van backed out of the driveway, the wheels cut the wrong way. "Hey!" Trey lunged for the rear doors, but they were locked, too.

He scrambled forward and yelled through the wire mesh. "Hey! Do you know who my father is?"

The man looked back over his shoulder and locked eyes with Trey. "Yeah," he said. "I do."

H. A. MAXSON

Slug

My daughter lifts the dog bowl up
and looks from it to me and back,
and her face asks what wrote its history
here in this shining concavity in luminous
loops and crosshatchings that shimmer
when she tilts it to catch the last of sun.

I see it then, a slug
no bigger than a sliver, a nick
in the reflected light.
Its trail, wanderings of a night
and day, a confusion of dead ends
from lip down slick aluminum walls
to the center of this cup collecting light.

Minutes more it might have burned alive.
So I point him out, gray back and fish-white
belly clinging its ooze to the shine.
My daughter unwrinkles her nose
and stares down like a tiny god and tilts
the bowl filling with her own small shadow.

JANE McCAFFERTY

Delivered

After driving lost in winter rain, after a wrong exit and a blind man at a gas station pressing her trembling palm with a cold coin that looked like the moon, after her black boots riding the gas pedal and brakes simultaneously, after the song *Bones, sinking like stones, all that we hoped for* playing again and again in the grey world of the car, after boundless tears that have left her eyes swollen, she pulls into the city of Baltimore, this woman who is not quite young anymore, this woman in the long black coat whose dark hair flies behind her in bitter February wind, this woman who wished as a child to live with a large dog in a cave like the hermit in a book she read under an oak in '72 when the boy next door was home from Nam without one of his legs. He would sit looking down at her from his bedroom window. She remembers this now, getting out of the car, the song still with her, and the strangeness of having a life courses through her blood. It takes her breath away as the face of the vet in the high window splinters in her mind.

Like the ice on the sidewalk breaking. Her legs are shaky. But they carry her along. She is looking down now, her boots immeasurably sad and distant because they belong to her old self, her old life, and yet are moving her innocently forward toward the hotel which she will discover contains a mall on the first floor, escalators rising like silver teeth under gargantuan chandeliers and leading logically to the second floor, where she sees it: the conference of writers milling about in huge rooms filled with tables of books that rise up like cities that too easily collapse, books that might begin to look forlorn if the woman who is not quite young anymore stops to consider how many of them will never be read, or will be read hastily—for she is of this time where the writers outnumber the readers, where anxiety rules each singular student of the centuries who yearns to read every fine book written and unwritten, and knows she will die before she reads a tiny fraction of these books, die without faith that heaven will be filled with books or faith in anything beyond the dissolution of body into earth, which makes the hands sweat in voracious gratitude when turning the pages of those books that momentarily face down despair.

She surveys the towering cities of tomes, stumbles.

Return To A Room Lit by A Glass of Milk.

A book title, yes, but today seems the best set of directions she's ever come across.

In her throat a random memory of her husband with dark eyes shining falls like a warm star down into her chest and explodes.

Here, pausing near the top of the elevator, where streams of humans rise, some of them smiling and laughing, many of them engaged in animated conversation, here as she surveys the humans interacting, it seems utterly unreal that two days ago her husband turned to her in the winter dark of a parked Honda and said, in so many tortured words, that the ending of their love story had somehow mysteriously rolled into his heart like a tank. Unreal that he is not standing beside her, her shelter, her reason, her barrier, her filter, the person who understands her humor!

When he announced this to her, that he was leaving after their fifteen years together—announced through his pain—she'd cried out, in a stranger's voice, from the hidden depths of her being, "*I'm sorry, I'm so sorry!*"

"No, no, don't say that!" he begged her. "Please don't apologize! You have *nothing* to be sorry for!"

But she could not stop apologizing. Surely she had done something to deserve this pain. In fact, she *almost* had words for what she'd done, she almost knew, even there, at the beginning of the most radical heartbreak of her life, what she'd been guilty of all along.

("Go to that Baltimore thing," he'd insisted, a week before he told her the big news. "It will be good for you. You need to get *out there*." He was revealing an old, recently ripened anger, it seemed, at how long ago she'd somehow stopped going anywhere significant without him. At how she'd abandoned her self. (That girl was on an old train, leaning hard against the window, taking notes.)

When had she begun to dream of being miniature? If she could only be miniature, she'd told her husband, she would live in his pocket. (A joke they shared, yes, but fueled with too much desire and weird desperation.) That would be perfect, he'd said in the old days, laughing, I would love you to live in my pocket; my job might be endurable then;

we would never be apart. Eventually you could become microscopic and sail down the rivers of my veins.

This conversation was held repeatedly throughout the years of their long and passionately twisted marriage. It was held in the farmhouse where a sullen llama named Burton looked in through the blue curtained window each morning, waking them. In the walk-up where an old Indian, professor emeritus in another galaxy, had served them vodka in sippy cups, lecturing them on the triumphs of the Chinese scientific tradition. It was held in the rowhouse next to the eccentric evangelical who said upon meeting them that winter of '99, *Just call me Fat-Ass Wanda.* It was held in the apartment when their giant bald landlord surrounded their yard with mountains of cans and newspapers and called his dog loudly at five in the morning: *Here, Be Be Rebozo!* while they lay in bed laughing that someone would name their dog Be Be Rebozo, trying to recall who the hell Be Be Rebozo *was*, some dude from Watergate, right?

Had she been more intelligent about love, she would have known that such a ritualized conversation might be a sign that something was not quite right. *One should not desire to be miniature.* One should never long to live in their husband's pocket, or anyone's pocket for that matter. One should stand up straight and be counted, rely on self, develop "good boundaries" and grow. We can assume most experts would agree that this desire to *shrink*, (to nearly, let's face it, *disappear*) is surely a sign that one's mental health might need a little tune-up?

She stands now by a glass window and breathes. The Baltimore sky begins to snow, little puzzle pieces floating down to earth. A low voice behind her says, "We're supposed to get more than a foot by tonight," and a wave of sickening fear goes through her. Snowed in! But I want to go *home!* (But where is home now?) In the street below a child walks along, holding his mother's hand. Why is this simple scene so compelling? The child skips a little, to keep up with the mother. The mother wears a green coat, no hat, no gloves. The child wears dark mittens, a pointed hood tied under his chin.

If her husband stood beside her at the window, she'd turn to him and say, *Look.* If it were a year ago, he would peer down and he would know, wouldn't he? that the ordinary sight of the mother and child walking down the street in the Baltimore snow was enough mystery to last a lifetime. The imagination could rest in moments like these; there was no work to do. You didn't have to look down and think, *maybe the mother is a recovering addict and the boy stays up late talking with her at their kitchen table, the radio tuned into a talk show, the tremulous voices of the loneliest callers teaching the boy about reaching out in the dark.*

Don't imagine the mother's worn blue robe, her smoking, the bulb on the ceiling, the boy's airplane pajamas a size too small, how he falls half asleep in his desk at school dreaming of his father in Baghdad, pencil clutched in his sweaty fist.

Don't start thinking now of some future self tumbling alone in a bed, fevered in autumn.

Let it be; let the world be for once. And breathe, and breathe again. And these breaths will deliver you, moment by moment, she tells herself, into more breaths.

Thank you. Thank you, breath. It seems you're all I have. Thank you.

"And what happened," she tells her husband on her cell phone, her eyes filled with snow-fall, "Is that despite all my seriously misguided efforts, I just didn't know how to *love.* Managing my fear of losing you was a full-time job. So maybe I called that job love, and now I'm unemployed, and I gotta somehow go down there and collect some unemployment, but I'm also in awe. That's what I've discovered in the very depths of my heart. Awe. It's what lives at the bottom of everyone's heart and the world just covers it up little by little. Which is to *say* I think you'd like the new me. I think you should give me another chance. Now that I can *see.* One more chance.

And by the way, when I close my eyes here, you're seated in the center of my heart infused with this perfect golden light."

But the connection is lost. Who knows what he heard. She calls again. Hand trembling. Body trembling. The phone rings and rings. She leaves the window and pulls her coat tightly around her. Walks by a herd of poets, nods, do they know how necessary they are, those poets? How futile, how fortunate, how caged? Shake the bars. Save them from mutilating irony and fire-stealing fame, she prays, taking the silver elevator teeth down to ground level and wandering out onto the sidewalk.

She tries to call home again and again, walking quickly now, part of the street crowd, snow like stitches trying to sew up the endless grey air. He's not answering. He's not answering.

He's not answering.

She walks on this dusky street and thinks of him brushing his teeth in another city, broad-shouldered elegant man standing alone in the purple bathroom with its leaky faucet and the water-stained print of El Greco's *Saint John of The Cross* framed on the wall.

He's not answering.

His wristwatch on the sill next to Robert Conquest's *Reflections on a Ravaged Century*. A mass card from her father's funeral on the bathroom mirror. A toy boat in the tub from when she cared for the neighbor's foster child.

He's not answering.

How can he not answer?

An old woman bends in half coughing, then springs up violently, arches her neck back to the sky, and laughs. Orange patent leather shoes. Hideous orange high-heeled patent leather shoes, like she's going to a dance where nobody will dance. Arms crossed, they will lean against the wall, eyes turned toward heaven, mouths open and filled with brown leaves.

Or: the woman will dance alone in a room with stone walls, a dirt floor, the sky for a ceiling, God as lover.

Remember that old song? Randy Newman. *Oh, Baltimore, ain't it hard, just livin'*.

Can't dance to it.

She continues down the street, taking small steps in her boots, tasting the darkening air. She knows with certainty that her husband is turning toward the window where pine branches brush the glass now, and thinking not of her, but of his new life without her: the return of the numinous! How deliciously strange it will all be! He presses his forehead against the glass.

Probably there is another woman. (A friend quoting a book said in 97 percent of cases there is.)

For one moment she knows that all is proceeding according to some magnificently cruel and beautiful, divine plan—and that if there is another woman, she may have to be thanked.

Do not forget to breathe. A man on the corner, ordinary business guy in wire-frame glasses, is looking at his expensive watch. He's one of these Esquire-readers trying hard to be the good half liberal, half neocon, but she sees beyond her judgment to where his heart beats. Out of dire need for sudden contact she clutches his arm and says, "May I please have the time?" And he meets her eyes to tell her it's just after seven o'clock. "Thank you," she says, but somehow he correctly hears that she means, "My impossibly precious fellow human, I salute your solitude and your life. Your eyes, they shine like the sun!" And he continues to look at her, stunned, a little confused at his own sense of gratitude: why is he grateful to this urgent, unraveling stranger?

Because she's on the other side of fear. Because her face is finally so naked.

Because a naked face is rare.

Nothing left to lose. Breathing deeply. Walking in snow. Pieces of light.

Almost ecstatic with this wrenching and perfectly decimating pain.

She's like a bunch of ashes someone's thrown from a plane.

Baltimore beauty rising up around her as she falls. Streets of humans. Windows. Everyone trying so hard! (Were they always trying so hard and she just didn't notice, were they always this piercingly beautiful?) Lost dog dodging traffic. Eyes. Broken bottle. Shadows. Weeping child. Lone blue glove. Gum wrapper. Someone picks up a coin. A voice cries, wait, come back, please, *wait!*

She stops, stands still and opens her arms, or are her arms opening her?

Some would call it madness. Just as most would say the idea of her apologizing to her husband was a sign of her sickness and, well, low self-esteem, kiddo. "He left you with no explanation and no warning and *you* apologized to *him?*," her friend will say, then remind her that she's still basically the fucked up little Catholic kid counting her venial sins, wishing she could just be Mary and get it over with.

They really did a number on you.

And another friend will cry out, *You forgive everyone but yourself.*

And that may have been true at one time, on some level, but not anymore. She's joined the crowd. She knows in this moment she deserves the same forgiveness as the rest of the world; and the recognition itself is a merging. Her limbs and face are on fire. Her arms stay open.

This moment in Baltimore, Maryland, in the bitter winter, on the street, in the snow, under a snow-moon, where *anyone*, anyone at all, could come forward and be deeply embraced, wrapped up in her coat if they needed it, and held—this, she knows, face lifted now to night sky and eyes closing in ecstasy, *this* is the love she should've offered all along.

FRANETTA McMILLIAN

Martin Luther King at 75

Five years ago his wife
finally left him.
The TV muckrakers uncovered
one affair too many.
Occasionally, he still gets letters
and photographs from young girls
claiming to be his long lost daughters.
He always answers
and politely informs
the young women
he has no money.
He is not rich—only famous.

But these days he's barely that anymore.
When he goes into the schools
the kids only know him
as that guy on the PBS special
they show every spring.
When he speaks of peace and justice
the kids all laugh.
It's a different world, old man,
they tell him.
Full of bling-bling and planes
crashing into buildings.
There will be no peace.
The really young ones
always ask to see the scar.
Sometimes he lifts his shirt;
sometimes he doesn't.

The bullets that almost killed him
still pain him.
Just another inch to the left
and he would have been a goner.
But after five hours on the operating table
and countless years in therapy,
he still walks with a limp
and wakes up some nights
with his blood on fire.

It's a cold night in Atlanta.
According to the perky blonde
weather girl it's the coldest night
they've had in fifty years.
He's out on the porch
in his shirtsleeves staring at the city lights.
Happy birthday to me, he thinks
and closes his eyes.
Soon he can almost taste
the crowd and the sweat on his palms.
"I have a dream," he whispers
and truly, that was the happiest day of his life—
that one time when he
could feel the hand of God.

DEVON MILLER-DUGGAN

Elvis Is an Angel Now

—for Fleda Brown

With every step he takes, Astroturf appears beneath his feet.
When not in use, his wings fold in
Upon themselves, like fans, sort of, but really just
Exactly in the shape his capes fell into
When he leaned down to touch the desperate hand of one
Who loved him so, who brought him flowers, her devotion,
All her prayers, who bears his name imbedded in her skin
And hears his voice and blessing every time the thunder
Rolls across the velvet black of night. And now he has
No need of jewels, of studs, embroideries to pull the faithful eyes
Across his manly shoulders, or on down toward his belt,
Buckled rightly huge across the center of his hips, where his
Procreation flared, or down to where bells swayed 'round his ankles—
No, now his raiment glows in light and dark and heavens ring
And sigh along with every mystic note he sings, and every note
He sings is plump with grace, grace, grace, and
Where he breathes, the faithful swear the air smells all of butter.

DOUGLAS MOREA

Winkle

—on hearing that old NYC subway cars are to be dumped
into the ocean off Indian River Inlet, Delaware

I fell asleep
while riding to work on the New York City subway
and did not wake up for
thirty years.
And when I did open my eyes I saw that I
had none and, slumped in my fiberglass seat in rotted cloth
lay what remained
of my bones.

I think
I've missed my stop and lost my job, I thought, as a little
fish swam into my hollow skull
through one eye-hole and
out the other.

How
churningly bright and black, how rancorously
humming and hammering had been the commute and now
this:
twilight
sixteen miles off the Delaware shore;
artificial reef, deliberate junk train-wreck shelter habitat oasis
hunkered in desert of yawning
submarine sand.

The Silence
clears Its throat in my direction—was I
thinking too loud?
Sorry . . .

TRACY STEVEN PEALE, SR.

Route 82, Above the Brandywine

The sunlight gleams like tinfoil,
    workable parchment,

as tiny swells wend into gray rock and ebb,
    dragonflies searching this brackish wellspring

for crevices deprived of northern moss and wetness.
    Amid the rushes

Wild-geese downdraft while
    finches flitter and twist,

redirecting their attention
    from seed to passing car—

    me, inquisitive,

like loose stones
    scattered on mulchy banks,

silent as the sound of clouds
    slipping into a cobalt blue sky.

DRURY PIFER

Fruitcakes and Fiction

After my pop got drunk and was killed on French Street, Al Johnson said I'd best move in with him if I was willing to work, being as I was a just a kid. He'd learned the bread business from DiFonza who made the best Italian bread in Wilmington on Union Street. Trouble was Al didn't like hauling his big ass out of bed at four a.m. So he quit doing bread and invented his "Famous Brandy Saturated Fruitcake," which made him a success but no millionaire. I traveled with Sam three years before I quit. I had my reasons.

He advertised his fruitcake all year driving around in his truck and talking to people, but he only busted butt in November. Come October, he'd lay in flour, dried fruit, and stuff. Then we'd bake night and day for three weeks after which we put the cakes up to age. Those we delivered was baked a year before on account of aging was the big secret. He delivered everything himself on account of he didn't trust the P.O. which he said was an arm of the government.

The year before he took me in, he'd bought him a new truck and splashed AL JOHNSON'S BRANDY SATURATED RUMCAKE all over the sides of the van in red and green on yellow. After mixing the batches, my job was stacking aged cakes in long pine boxes on the truck that looked, I swear, like coffins. In the space between these boxes Al fixed himself a nice little living space, a sort of home away from home. He had a heater and an armchair.

He hired him a driver too, a runty little guy, Sam Pok. Al called Sam "my Jap," it didn't matter he came from Guatemala. Me, he called "the drunk's kid."

Sam baked his fruitcakes in Dover, Delaware, and made deliveries all the way up to the Oranges in N.J.,and down to Florida, not that I ever laid eyes on an everglade or alligator. All I got was real familiar with the highway. Riding in the van with Al was better than sitting up in the cab with Sam Pok who never quit yakking. His yammering could drive anyone bats. At first I thought working for Al was a good deal on account of he took me out of school. I had a sleeping bag I'd lay on and Al sat in his big arm chair and when we drove into towns we'd unload and deliver. The smell of fruitcake was so strong I'd get high and I thought that was cool too.

I liked nosing around towns I'd never seen before and evenings we'd hole up in a motel that had strips of paper on the toilet seat to tell you it was sanitized. Sometimes I felt so good I'd sing and Al would tell me to can it because if he wanted music he'd have brought a radio.

I said it was the brandy in the cakes made me sing.

"Brandy, B.S.," he said. "Government won't let me use no alcohol. I gotta use that stuff they invented by torturing monkeys. Chemicals. Tastes same as the real McCoy and knocks down my base cost thirty-seven percent."

I said it was dishonest palming off monkey chemicals on customers. "Hell, they could read the label if they weren't so dang lazy," Al said. "Truth is, kid, there's not one man in a million cares a plug nickel about any difference between fact and fiction. All they want is what makes 'em feel good. Divorce rate proves that."

I told Al that before my old man bought the farm, he told me fact is stranger than fiction. Al said that was bull. Lies was better than facts and a hell of a lot more persuasive too. The government proved that. And all you had to do was compare a woman all gussied up to the plain thing to catch his drift. I said I'd still vote for real over paint.

"Kid, you've got a lot to learn," Al said. "You're one of them hard-heads has to see it before he believes it, so I'll show you." He grabs the intercom and tells Sam Pok to pick up the next hitchhiker and send him around to the back of the van. I asked him what he was going to do and he said, "Depends on the monkey we get."

Maybe ten minutes later Sam stops for our monkey. He's an old guy, gimpy, squint-eyed and smells like a pile of dirty rags. He's wearing this beat up officer's coat faded to gray with gold epaulets tarnished snot green. From the mud on his butt and boots he looks like he's slept in a swamp. His duffel bag is patched with duct tape and Al sitting in that big leather chair makes him nervous. But he plays it cool and says, "Howdy boys. Name's McAllister," winking at me because I'm the kid. Al just looks at him and I keep quiet too.

Sitting on the duffel bag, McAllister works off his boots. It's not easy. Reminds me of my old man pulling the skin off a chicken. He had a bandage all bloody on his left foot and a yellow sock all holes on the right. I felt sorry for him but Al expected me to pay attention and keep my trap shut.

Pretty soon the old guy's nose starts twitching. "Damn!" he says. "What's that dadblamed stink?"

"Same as what it smells like," Al says.

"Enough to make a man hongry."

"Could do that," says Al. "Depends on the man."

McAllister stands up and studies the boxes stacked up along the walls of the van. "Whooie, that is one mighty powerful smell coming outta there," he says, working his nostrils. "What's that it says on the side, fruitcake? What's that?"

"Can't believe everything you read," Al says. "What's your line of work?" McAllister says he's second mate on a ship out of Newport News.

"That's a lot of hooie," Al says. But he says it while he's blowing his nose so only I can understand him. I offer the old guy what's left of my salami sandwich from breakfast and he wolfs it in one bite. "Ain't had nothing to my gut since yesterday. But I gotta tell you, boys, that's one powerful smell coming out of these here cake boxes. Could be a broke bottle of liquor in there." The old boy takes to sniffing along the seams of a box and he's getting himself all worked up. "Man that is powerful cake," he says. "You boys thought of taking a look see? Can't do no harm."

"If I was you, Sailor," says Al. "I'd leave sleeping dogs lay."

"Smells damn good all the same," McAllister says. "What kinda cake's gonna smell like that? Could be it's going bad. Could be, we help ourselves, we're doing some folks a favor before it gets ruin't."

"Doubt that, Corporal," says Al.

"I figure it wouldn't hurt no one, we open just one of them boxes," McAllister says. "I always carry a crowbar in my duffel. Comes in handy."

"Nothing like a crowbar," says Al.

McAllister scratches in his beard and knocks on the box with his knuckles. "Say, these here cakes don't belong to you, do they?" he says.

"Can't say they do," says Al.

"I take it you boys ain't hongry then? "'Cause my stomach's been raising cain even before yesterday."

"I just follow regulations, Sergeant," says Al. "You're a seafaring man. You know how the government works."

"Government?" McAllister backs away from the boxes and stares at Al. "You with the feds?"

"Couldn't say if I was," says Al.

"Lookie, bub, all I said was I'm a damn sight hongry," says McAllister. "There's no regulations cover that."

"Maybe not, but you gotta admit planes crash," Al says.

"Planes?" McAllister is scratching his armpits, neck, and beard. He looks at me, hoping I'll help him out. I keep my cake hole shut.

"You think the government wants people to know the facts?" Al says.

"What facts?" McAllister is squinting at me again. So I look real serious and puff out my lips.

"If God meant us to fly I figure he'd given us wings," said Al. "You know what goes up breaks up sooner or later."

"I'm talking about them cakes," McAllister says.

"Me too," says Al, and he pats the box behind him. "You want to ask yourself, Lieutenant, what happens to folk in planes sooner or later."

McAllister looks spooked. His eyes show white. "In these here boxes?" he says.

"You got a nose. Trust it, Captain," Al says. "Take a good, stiff sniff. Believe what your proboscis tells you."

"Hang on now," says McAllister. "You're not telling me you got a lot of dead folks in these here?" He snatches off his cap and rubs his nose with it good and hard.

"You said that, not me, Commander," says Al, patting the box real gentle. "If the government didn't say it, you want me to say it? You won't catch me saying it."

McAllister works over his nose and chews on his lips some. Then he goes back to scratching his nicotine-yellow beard. Al starts laying out lunch. Sliced ham, Swiss cheese, rye and brown bread, thigh off a roast chicken, and a bottle of Italian red. "You're welcome to tuck in, Commodore," he says. But old McAllister's face has gone green, reminds me of the walls in the hospital where I saw my dad laying dead.

"Calling them cake don't seem right," he says.

"Since when was the government ever right?" Al asks.

"That's for damn sure," McAllister mutters and jerks his thumb at me. "Only how come you got this punk kid riding along with them boxes?"

"He's a good looking boy. He gives mothers and young wives comfort in their hour of need," Al says, spreading mustard on his ham. McAllister sits down on his duffel and starts rocking, holding his stomach. "You sure you don't want a bite, Admiral?" Al says.

"That smell's something awful powerful," McAllister says, muffling up his face in a messy old scarf. "You got one strong stomach, bub."

"A man can get used to most anything," says Al. "I was you, I'd try a banana to bind your stomach." He offered a banana.

McAllister squeezes his nostrils and coughs. "That don't make you puke?" he cries. "Hellfire, it's worse'n a dead cat under a boiler."

"It's nature's way," says Al. "Right, kid?"

"Yep," I say. But it's a lie and I don't feel good about it.

"Thing I always like," says Al, "When you get back outside the truck, man, the air smells like real air. It's like you're breathing for the first time. Like you're new borne. Ask the kid."

"How many of them you got in here?" McAllister asks, running his eye along the boxes.

"Hard to say," says Al. "The ingredients are pretty well chopped up. The government has us measure everything by weight until we get enough for one item. Then we mix in the preservatives. This lot now, they could last two years in a cool place."

"Mother of God," McAllister cries, putting his head between his knees.

"When I get to feeling bad I just tell myself it's nothing but a lot of fruitcake," Al says. "Works every time. Five hundred pounds pecans, two hundred pounds dried apricot, forty pounds seeded kumquat, candied orange rubbed with lemon peel, candied pineapple, candied cherries, coconut—"

McAllister stumbles up and begins dragging his duffel bag to the sliding door. If he'd have got it up I swear he would have hit the pavement and we're making seventy miles an hour.

I grabbed the old coot and Al told Sam Pok to slow down and pull over. When we got the door rolled up, old McAllister tumbled down on a grassy strip and just lay there sucking wind. I wanted to tell him, hey, it's just fruitcake. But Al says it's always best to leave a man with a good story to tell. Nothing kills a good story faster than the truth. "Nothing will kill good company faster than throwing around a bunch of facts," is what he told me.

So we left poor old McAllister looking like a dead dog in the grass by the Dover bypass. After an hour had passed, Al asked me if I still thought truth was stronger than fiction. I had to admit he had a point. But him making a monkey out of old McAllister finished me with Al Johnson. Maybe I am just a dumb kid, but lies are still lies no matter how they grab you. I still believe in the truth even if you never know if it's a lie.

FRANCIS POOLE

Lost Springs

It's a circular spring
surrounded by limestone ledges
that you can dive from
or lie down on to get warm
after you crawl out shivering.

Once you are chastened by
the arrhythmic chill of the plunge
go under and swim down
to the shallow sandy bottom
until you reach the drop off

and a submerged cypress,
its gargantuan body
draped with moss and eel grass,
one gnarled root in the shape
of a deformed foot
wedged in the cleft of a rock.

When you approach the immense trunk
rub your hand back and forth along
the muscular ridges of its back
as you would in calming
any creature hopelessly trapped,
not yet prepared for
what's to come.

LYNN PRUETT

Shouting Nazarene

Aching for coffee on a morning when her breath tasted of stale beer and second-hand smoke, Andrea walked down Pleasant Street toward a diner that harbored homeless people. It was her favorite eatery in Northampton, an anomaly amid shops that sold Ecuadorian textiles, jewelry from the Far East, exotic ice cream, blintzes, enchiladas, and gnocchi.

Anticipating the BLT that would get her through the grind of the day, she'd barely noticed the slight, bald man who walked beside her. He was wearing overalls and smelled like cow manure. She picked up her pace, aware she could become nauseated, particularly recalling the night before with a semistranger, another disappointment in her quest for a man who would return her passion. One who would understand, when, on the dance floor she turned a dip into a backbend, it was about her, not about him or his chance to preview for his pals the one-night stand he was about to enjoy.

The old man caught her by the arm. He grunted a word she could not understand. He had no teeth and gummed out another word, then gestured at her chest. He waved a five dollar bill in her face and touched his fly.

Andrea lashed out. She felt a hard crack as her forearm met his skull. "My father is a minister, for Chrissake!" she shouted at the heap on the sidewalk.

How had he known what throbbed under her skin? Her jeans were ragged, her T-shirt dingy. She had on work boots crisscrossed with dyes. Yet he had sensed it, like they all did, this compulsion she could not turn off or satisfy. She dashed away from the diner, up the hill, then down the narrow alley to the dark brick burrow where Epithet Press was housed.

Inside already at work were Earl and Lloyd and Regina. The press was small and eclectic, owned by a wealthy Hampshire College drop-out. They made paper and organic inks and brought out small broadsides of sentiments copied from Victorian tombstones. Andrea watched Earl and Lloyd struggle to unload a crate of charred princess wood. She'd transform it into ink, perhaps a shade of orange swirled with red like the yolk of a bloody egg.

Oh what did she want? All right. Someone athletic, physical, in shape—say it, yes it mattered. A man who listened as much as he talked. Tall, dark, and handsome, yes, handsome would be nice for a change. But truly, she couldn't take a handsome man seriously nor could she deal well with blonds; they seemed insubstantial. Not a hairy one either. Maybe she was too picky. Maybe her problem was her.

That day instead of going to lunch at the diner, she stayed in and listened to Regina, an anorexic, wretch and flush in the washroom. It was creepy how familiar the throaty sounds of forced air and water were. Andrea realized Regina's passion was not the food, but the expulsion of it. And what of her own? To make love whenever the feeling arose, no matter the circumstance, to open up to the feeling and let it, the greatest experience on this earth, happen. That was her passion and her shame. Yet, in her heart she believed that this passion was good, a gift from God, even though everyone else all her life had made her think otherwise.

Andrea imagined her own past being flushed away. No more one-nighters. She'd save herself for a man who could appreciate her sensuality, approve it, stroke it, and not be afraid of its power. A man she chose, one who would have to know her before her need for sexual expression took the relationship toward a tawdry end. God, I am desperate, she thought, as she clacked out a personal ad on the antique typewriter.

FEMALE #357386

I am so tired of playing games. It seems the men you meet in bars are just full of bull. I am in my early 20s and pride myself on being fit. I dress well and enjoy dinner, dancing, and the usual forms of entertainment. I am looking for a sincere man who can appreciate me and wants to be appreciated too.

She mailed it and went to the diner and bought two BLTs to go. "You must watch me eat," she told Regina. "This is how it's done. Bite, chew, swallow, digest, yum. Now you try it." She unwrapped the second BLT and talked Regina through the whole sandwich and took her into the ink room and taught her how to mix ochre and titanium and kept her there all afternoon.

Andrea received only one letter after posting the ad. She felt ripped off. Maybe her ad made too much of herself. Maybe the only available guys lived in bars. She cleaned her fingers, inky from the color of purple inspired by the great circles under Regina's eyes, and delicately unsealed the envelope. Grimacing, she read the letter.

My dear:
I have not been in a bar since I was a child, which I suppose is a bad beginning. But truth will out. I was in the bar to collect my father who fixed jukeboxes in the city of New Orleans. There, you have learned of my humble beginnings and where I spent my youth.
Although I do not frequent bars, I do appreciate restaurants that provide a dance floor. I prefer to dance to a pit band in dim light, with slow sensual sounds moving softly around.
A mystical blue light shading the room cool, and yet, a fire smoldering beneath the blue. Ah yes.
Describe to me how you dance.
Richard

A bit perplexing, Andrea thought. She didn't know anyone who spoke like that. Maybe Richard was an artist. Maybe she was out of her league. She waited another week but received no more replies to the ad. She was getting moody, doodling at work, thinking of blue nights, of being cool and smoldering at the same time, of a long slow burn. That was appealing, so much more appealing than the wham-bam-who-gives-a-damn experience she'd been having lately. She found a run of miscut vanilla-scented paper in the dumpster, selected a clean page, and wrote in violet:

Dear Richard:
It's hard for me to describe a dance because I don't think like that. I just dance. If the music's hot, I'm hot, if it's slow, I'm getting a drink of club soda. I never thought of music as hot and blue at the same time. I've been trying to imagine what that feels like, the way you dance. I can see the lights turning things blue and the music sort of under everything, but what does that feel like?
When I dance, I get into the music and it goes right through me, like the drum beat is my heart. I shimmer like the tremor of an earthquake.
Your friend
Dear friend:
Is that a religious affiliation? Friend?

Richard McCorvey felt that the correspondence with #357386 was a mistake. Friend seemed a bit uneducated. The way she danced was cliché, mocking his perhaps overeager literary outburst in the initial letter? He'd answered her ad because it was the only one that mentioned dancing, or so he allowed himself to think. The scent of the paper and the strange violet ink, a backdrop for the almost childish chitchat, was mysterious in the way he'd found the actual Dead Sea scrolls mysterious. His curiosity then, too, had been about the hand that had moved across the page. Brown, surely, as his was and possessed of such confidence. Friend's hand was strong, the lines clean and straight, the letters distinct, but the color—purple!—suggested a boldness he found distressing.

What to do? In the springtime an old man feeling not old at all? He put on red sweats and jogged up the road leading to the infernal cow farms that twenty years ago seemed doomed to the voracity of subdivisions. The hint of moist earth and sharp young grass filled his nose. In his early manhood, in the Deep South, if he, a black man, had jogged along a road, he would have been considered suspicious. But up north, he was expected to be athletic and it hadn't been bad. In the early 70s, teaching at UMass felt like true liberation from childhood restraints. Gates fell, laws died. Everyone whooped it up. He could have sex without thought of matrimony—and with white girls.

Forbidden as strange fruit, he'd been very appealing to the wealthier students who crossed town from the private women's colleges to hear him say *Pentateuch* and *Deuteronomy* in his thunderous voice. The young women may have dressed slovenly in jeans, body suits, and hiking boots, but the brand labels were upscale. They drove expensive cars and took skiing trips to Stowe and Sugarloaf and Vail, and occasionally invited him to Lake George for a clandestine weekend. After a few confrontations with outraged white fathers, he declined those invitations because there was nothing about love in any of them.

His pace slowed to a walk. Though he ought to sprint up the long hill, he couldn't make himself speed into the glare of twin silos. He blinked against the two monstrous barns and equally monstrous white farmhouses facing off at the crossroads. From these pristine buildings would rise the odor of cows. It was only a matter of days before the nefarious cloud would roll west toward his house and loll there until the fall. He'd never gotten used to the smell of manure or the sound of lowing. After he retired next year he could move, but first he wanted to find a wife.

He'd prefer a woman who was like Doris, his wife who'd died of cancer when they were both twenty-nine. For him the word "wife" conjured a supple being, a woman with a girlish laugh and thick hair.

Though he could never say it out loud, he craved this incorrect thing—a young wife.

How they danced, he and Doris. The shimmy and shake of southern gospel hotter than any rock and roll, Hallelujah the most come-on word in English when Doris let it roll from her luscious lips, her mood choosing which syllable got the accent. He remembered them all, the "HA" times and the "lu-JAH" times.

Her death had sent him whirling into education. Too hurt to minister to people's souls, he'd taken The Word to their minds. He had analyzed the Biblical texts, broken the books down into small, comfortable, digestible words. He had become a popular teacher.

Richard walked home, breathing through his mouth to no avail. Already the air was tinged with cow. Overhead the leaves had fleshed out and darkened to a less-searing shade of green. It was time in the correspondence to ask some questions point-blank.

Andrea was put off by the religious questions but she figured she'd answer them and shake him loose. Already she was planning a better ad for next month, one that lied but got more responses.

Dear Richard:

I am a PK. Preacher's kid. I know that's boring news for you. A PK who isn't rebelling by hanging out in bars or joining the army. Native of Dover, Delaware, Methodist for generations. Personally I think religion is overdone but you asked so there it is.

Richard was thrilled by the news. They shared denomination, but more than that she was the daughter of a minister's wife. She would be familiar with, not shocked by, that station. He liked this way of dating, a safe exchange of questions, which seemed more honest than a face-to-face encounter. He reread her letter. She wasn't rebelling against her parents, or so she said. What was she doing?

Dear Richard:

I know you must be getting more interested in me and I suppose that's the point. But when you write letters full of APB questions, I don't like them as much as when you write about yourself.

So here's the info:

College: over and done with. Job: satisfactory. I make inks and set type at a small press. Share a house with several roommates. Never been married, not sure if I want to be yet.

Now some questions for you: the same as you asked me but put them at the

bottom of the letter. In the letter, answer the question: What do you collect? Then I'll tell you what I collect.
    Andrea

Her name was Andrea, a name that yielded few new clues and kept her face a mystery. But more disconcerting was her request. Richard didn't collect anything. Necessity dictated his budget. He hoarded food in case he was snowed in. Cans of every vegetable, meat, and noodle combination were stacked in shelves in the basement bedroom. Dental floss, Scope, seven green towels, jars of lotion, three sets of fresh flannel sheets, these things he'd collected after his first Massachusetts winter. There were a few Minutemen game programs in the guest room. He followed the UMass basketball teams, first when Julius Erving was a star, then through the loss-laden 80s and now into the top ten 90s. It got him through the miserably long winters. In the garage he found stacks of the bumper stickers he'd had printed back when he couldn't stand one more student asking if Tennessee was on the coast or if people in the South really had worms. The stickers said, "Provincialism is Global." Students passed out hundreds, and he'd enjoyed some notoriety and popularity. But then in a cataclysm of diversity hiring, which Richard likened to the path of a pinball, sometimes wildly out of control, sometimes sputtering down the hole pointless, REAL Africans became the rage, then Caribbean-Africans with studies of cultures rarely found in North American shores. Anything to avoid self-examination, he thought. Perhaps now he felt unhip, or lame, or whatever word would be current for his students. He poked around his house for several days thinking how he was going to lose this correspondence because he didn't collect anything.

Andrea didn't collect anything either. She just put that in the letter and figured she could forget about it. But the question gnawed at her while she mixed colors for the inks. Bent over pots of ash, she added secret drops of peppermint oil for her own olfactory health. She loved to squeeze sodden lumps of paper pulp but that was a habit not a collection. She took home errors and false starts, malformed papers, some thick and pebbly, others creamy, all somehow delicious, flecked with wild grasses and frets of leaves. Scraps, they weren't a real collection. What did she collect? One-night stands. She couldn't write that. Besides you never had anything but memories and what was special about those memories? If you collected memories that simply meant you were human.

Dear Andrea:
   I have a doctorate. I work at the university. I own my own home.

Facts that told nothing yet how important they seemed when defining yourself. Impatiently, Richard erased the sentences and dashed off.

   Please join me for dinner April 11 at Chanticleer's, 8:00 P.M. I will wear a white carnation in my lapel. I have a doctorate. I work at the university. I own my own home.
   RSVP: Richard

Andrea paged through the dresses in her closet. She hadn't worn a dress since Christmas Eve service at Wesley United Methodist, her father's church. She hadn't worn one on a date since her Caesar Rodney High School prom. Which to choose? Richard was a man who knew of simultaneous hot and cold and yet he obsessed on religion. Perhaps a religion professor? She sighed as her eyes narrowed on the dark corner of the closet.

More importantly, how did she feel?

Careless. Eight guys who couldn't spell had answered her second personal, in which she claimed to be a retired airline stewardess from Sweden in need of English lessons and long walks on the beach. She closed her eyes and flung her hand into the closet. It brushed a patch of velvet.

She closed her fingers around the soft shoulder of a velvet dress. She'd always worn velvet to the Christmas Eve service back home in Dover, green when her mother dressed her, red during the teenage years, and finally, when she hit twenty-one, black. An hour before worship, Andrea would climb to the balcony and take a seat at the very edge of the railing. Below, the sanctuary glistened.

Candles threw light on the slick green holly sprays resting beneath the stained glass windows. The curved wooden pews, like large wide sleighs, shone, freshly polished. Anthems rolled from the organ while the congregation slowly filled the church. Most people were dressed up, their hair shiny and clean, the men in suits, the women and girls adorned in red, green, and gold.

In the balcony things were different. Latecomers, fresh from parties, congregated there, adults giggled without shame, and every year old Mr. Adams fell from a rickety chair set up for the overflow. Andrea preferred to sit with the sinners, as she called them.

After the prayers and sermon and carols, the electric lights were

dimmed and everyone held still. The sanctuary blazed with candle-
light, the doublets mounted on the end of every pew flickering like hot
white flowers. A huge candelabra burned on the altar and twin advent
wreaths glowed near the pulpits. In the hush of expectation, Andrea's
father moved like a dark angel and lit the fifth candle. Christ was born.
From the back of the church, beneath the balcony, a lone bell ringer
swung the deepest bell, sending up twelve low golden notes that
lodged in Andrea's chest and buoyed her to the outside with the other
worshippers, quiet but for the tramp of their feet on the snow. Warm
with the bell tones, she waited for her parents in the parking lot and
relished the cold air and the white snow muting church bells around
Dover as they proclaimed Christmas.

Touching the velvet, she had a glimmer of what Richard meant in
his first letter of being warm and cold and blue at once.

She wore black hose and slight heels, and the black velvet v-neck
dress with its flared red skirt. Her dark hair, fresh-cut, was short and
sleek, her lips dark red. Chanticleer's restaurant suggested Richard
was going to spend some nice money. She let herself dream against her
past experiences. The man who'd fit, he'd be a bit taller and wearing
something hip but subtle, a suit was not too much to hope for. After
all he owned a home, had a doctorate, and worked at UMass. If he was
all flared out in color, she'd eat and leave. That might work for pea-
cocks but not for humans. His interest and the way he wrote still mys-
tified her. Religion mattered but so did music and mood. Someone
spiritual but not New Age?

She stared at her chic self and thought of her daily attire, jeans, wor-
kboots, ancient T-shirts. What the hell was this all about? Good food.
Conversation. Solving a mystery. To her red lips and made-up eyes
she said, *I will talk. Or else he will talk all the time and it will all be about
him, not us. I promise I will talk about*—she paused. *If he's a religion professor*, she smiled at herself, dipping her chin and looking low out of
the tops of her eyes, *I will talk about sin.*

Chanticleer's was busy, well-lit, and warm. It was expensive, the
food trendy, its specialties seafood and steak. In the basement, there
was a dance floor and a bar, offering the possibility of touch.

"I'm to meet a gentleman with a white carnation," Andrea said to
the host who smiled and led her around the corner and down a corridor to a table for two.

The man who rose was black. And old. And wearing a white carnation.

The host swept back her chair.

Andrea's smile grew brighter as she held out her hand. This must be a joke, she thought, a big fat joke that Richard's playing on me. Well, she decided, her grin luminous, if this is a test, then I will test him. Richard was probably a weirdo who answered personals for the sheer joy of humiliating lonely people. He was probably seated nearby, watching.

"I'm—"she began.

"Andrea," said the man, pronouncing it On-dray-yuh.

"Yes," she slid into the chair. The man returned to his seat. It was difficult to guess his age other than to say over forty, perhaps even over fifty. His hair was gray and cut close to his head and, though there were a few wrinkles around his eyes and mouth, the rest of his rich brown face was smooth.

"I have taken the liberty of ordering a Chablis," he said.

"Good," said Andrea.

He smiled. "Followed by red snapper from the Gulf."

"Nice," she said.

"I do not eat steak," said Richard. "It helps the local economy."

"Whatever." At least she'd be well-fed. Her eyes darted to the next table which was occupied by two fat old ladies. The one behind Richard was encased in a wild green and white number that formed a backdrop for his sober gray suit but picked up tiny green squares in his tie. There was no reason to suspect the real Richard of being male, she thought. And yet, he had to be.

The wine arrived. They drank without a toast.

"Are you a religion professor?"

"A professor of religion, yes."

She took a deep breath. "Good. Then you can explain sin. I was raised a Methodist, but it was like we float above sin." She took a gulp then tried again. "I mean, it was so easy to be a Methodist. If you made a mistake, you prayed right to God and knew you were forgiven. My friends who were Catholics wrestled with guilt all the time. Everything they did they had to tell the priest. It made every single thing they did important." She stopped but the man said nothing. A very clever imposter so far. She continued. "You're from the South, right?"

"Alabama originally," he said.

"John Wesley," she said. "Tell me about John Wesley."

"Why?"

"He got the Methodists all stirred up about sin but it's kind of passé now. I want to hear about sin, the power of sin." She poured herself a second glass of wine.

Richard smiled while Andrea talked. She seemed so young and so needy. He felt like her parson or professor rather than her date. It was a good thing to have arranged this meeting and put an end to the whole thing. Relief, not regret as he had expected, rose as she talked naively on. His patience would run out before the probable conversations they'd have. He considered living every day as if it was new and took a bracing gulp of wine. Just this morning he had answered a personal for a Christian African-American woman looking for "like man." He imagined her to be a bit plump, over forty, with nice hair, a woman proud but not loud, a woman who would be both wife and minister's wife.

As the speed of Andrea's speech increased, Richard subtly glanced at his watch.

"Andrea, the question of sin, the question of cultural diversity, different manifestations of belief are all interesting and worthy of discussion. You ought to make an appointment during my office hours if you want to talk of those things," Richard said. She would never make a minister's wife in those clothes. Her arms were firm as only a young woman's are. A black woman's face defied age. White women used creams and surgery to present more youth than was natural. Yet if he saw a woman's upper arms he could guess with accuracy her age. "You look lovely."

She blushed. "Thank you." This was going all wrong.

"Your questions are about passion, not sin." His eyes met hers, but his tone was dry.

The exchange of passion for sin was a trick she recognized. She expected the next ten minutes to be devoted to definitions, to fine lines. When her father spoke of passion, he meant Christ's passion for his Holy Father. Talk about ethereal. Her father preached on passion during Lent and traded his white vestment for a purple one.

Richard's drone meant he wasn't interested in her. Yes, this man was Richard. She felt him slipping into the familiar waters of religio-babble. Coming up for air at regular intervals like a whale, then plunging down through the deep green sea, his cheeks full but expressing only a few round bubbles at a time, he spoke truths, gems on land, bubbles at sea, dull, similar, transparent.

Ministers all wanted the same thing, a smooth wife, pretty or not, respectable and clean, a woman women would like and men would not covet. Her mother once said, in an uncharacteristic moment, "It's easier to be Miss America than to be married to a minister."

Andrea gazed down the v-neck at the curves of her breasts, her white breasts. She felt ashamed, totally ashamed of herself. Richard was looking for a potential wife and he'd gotten a tart. Her cheeks burned. No wonder he fell into the sea of words; no wonder he kept his eyes underwater.

She smiled and nodded and gave him a flat, bright look to encourage him to keep talking. Poor lonely man, she thought. No one around here was into religion like he was. "I guess it's hard for you to meet women in the Valley."

He paused, as if slapped, in midsentence, then picked up his knife and fork and cut the salad leaves into pieces too small to chew.

Slowly the burn crept from her face to her neck and shoulders and moved down her arms to her fingertips, a crimson tide that colored her exposed skin like a birthmark. It's not what I meant, she thought, but she could not say it. I meant religion, not being black. She kept her eyes low, on his tie as his utensils shredded the bright green sorrel and dark spinach.

When he spoke again, he sounded like he was talking about someone very far away, like his voice had gone out of his voice.

"There aren't many African-American women here," he said. "Most are professors. I've spent delightful, rigorous evenings debating great questions with them. But as a Christian minister, I represent patriarchy and an acceptance of the dominant white culture, which renders me unsuitable as a partner."

It's not what I meant, she thought. The silence pressed on her as slowly as the ancient printing press anticipating fresh paper. She drank her wine quickly, hoping a buzz might rescue her. But that was what she always did if things got uncomfortable with men and she knew where that would lead. She needed air, fresh air, something light to remove this familiar sense of entrapment, of eating and drinking to occupy the mouth so it wouldn't utter the very things pressing to get out. This meal reminded her of dinners at her parents, the air heavy with the unsaid. She swallowed the lettuce limp with honey-mustard. At home they never had honey-mustard dressing. It was always something that came in a Wishbone bottle, French or Ranch.

She dropped her fork. Damn it. This is a nice date and I did not know he was old or black or looking for a wife. This is my date, too.

"You are doing this all wrong," she said. "You are looking to the future instead of right now. You are making plans and thinking I'm not right for you. Screw that. This is our evening."

A smile touched Richard's lips. Despite her heart-shaped velvet bodice and absurdly chic red lips, this woman was struggling for something more profound. She's flubbed her line and was facing up to it. That was honesty and he liked it. She cupped the bowl of the wineglass with her hand and lifted it to her lips with ease, the gesture so relaxed and confident and gauche, he almost laughed. This girl was a gift, he understood. A beacon, a flame throwing light into the dark little world he'd constructed for himself. Professor, minister, what about human? He held up his glass of wine. "To tonight and the excellence of company."

"That's more like it," Andrea clinked his glass. The future, the next hour, she kept at bay. Instead she looked steadily at him and marveled at his face and the fact that he actually listened to what she said.

Abandoning religion, they ate the red snapper. Richard spoke of Mobile and New Orleans. Andrea described her work, how her fingers were often dented with letters as the type was old and the ink biodegradable. Richard laid open his light-colored palm and said his grandmother was proud he'd never had a callus. She'd insisted on it, actually.

Andrea said, "I loved the calluses I got from playing field hockey in high school. But these," she showed the thickened caps of her fingertips, "look like deformities."

Embarrassed, she ran her eye down the dessert menu.

"Andrea, would you like to dance?" Richard offered his smooth hand.

Andrea led the way down the carpeted stairs to the dark room reserved for dancing. They were enveloped by a yellow fog born of cigarette smoke and erratic lighting. Through the fog came a folk song and a pair of dancers with joints as loose as puppets. Richard steered Andrea clear of them, and dropped two dollars into the jukebox.

"Wow," Andrea said, reading the titles. "They've got everything from Verdi to Twisted Sister, Sun-Ra, Patti LaBelle, Holly Near, Sinatra."

"The Pioneer Valley," said Richard as he picked all jazz.

A couple of janitors smoked near the jukebox. Andrea felt their eyes. She moved closer to Richard, to the feeling of Richard.

They danced close, without touching, to soft jazz. The lights turned blue. They were too close not to touch.

"Richard, what do you collect?"

"Confessions," he murmured, pleased and struck with his answer. "I collect confessions."

Andrea thought, confessions are other people's memories and I collect memories. I will give him a confession. "Well," she whispered. "I always wanted to be a Shouting Nazarene."

"Lord have mercy," said Richard. "Lord, Lord, Lord." He held her as if to waltz but their steps were very small and soft.

"Once my family went to Nashville for the General Conference. I wandered away in the middle of downtown and found an old tiny church. The congregation had their hands in the air and they were shouting."

"Do it here," he said. "Become a Shouting Nazarene."

Andrea stepped away from him. The next song came on, bright with brass and swing motion. She stood still, letting the rhythm of the music enter her blood.

"Do it do it do it," Richard chanted.

Andrea spun in the smoky blue air. She flung her arms above her head and shook them; she shimmered and shouted, "Thank you, Jesus, Thank you, Jesus," but only Richard could make out her words in the din, the formation of those syllables so alien and so familiar.

"Aaaah. Aaaah. Aaaah," said Richard clapping. He was her drum, her beat, her guide, her getgo.

She turned blue in the light, her face and wonderfully long slim bare arms, blue in the light.

Andrea felt like a top spun on a golden thread that ran from her upraised hands to her pattering feet; it was a wonderful unknown feeling, joy.

Her face gleamed blue, pure and unspoiled, the face of a child, thought Richard, and he began to feel a warm glow inside. It wasn't all words, all text, all lecture. He could touch people with the pure gospel, joy and love.

"My dear, my dear," he said as the song ended.

She slid her hand in his and they escaped the floor as it was assaulted with flashing laser beams and the first sneering chords of White Snake.

They were confronted at the steps by two janitors, blowing smoke, the type of guys Andrea usually left bars with. A cigarette pack in the chest pocket, dark hair, thick jaw, and heavy nasal accent. A drunken leer.

"Where are you two going?" the closer one shouted, his damp face shoved forward like a snorting bull.

Andrea expected Richard to drop her hand. She loosened her fingers but he held firm. Both janitors stood on the same step and rolled their broom handles from one thick fist to the other.

Richard sighed. No matter where he lived, it was always this. "If I carried a broom like a weapon and didn't give a damn about myself and others, I might see people the way you do. But I was raised better. Now move, the beautiful lady would like to get by."

"Excuse us." Andrea stepped between the men, pulling Richard along.

"You are so wonderful," she glowed. "Thank you."

A lump rose in Richard's throat. He tried to swallow it but it wouldn't go down. Silly phrases to diffuse the emotion he felt in response to Andrea's tears and joy died on his tongue, and he was glad.

MAGGIE ROWE

Wexford Boy

My grandfather joined the I.R.A.
As a boy in the Wexford hills
defying the English with prayer and guns.
At eighteen he dried gunpowder at the family fire
knowing no better, and in a moment
caught enough scars there
to prove the worth of any man.

The prison camp in Cork could not restrain
those Catholic and Protestant boys
who dug themselves out with a spoon
went barefoot over the wire
walked home across the hungry mountains
expecting to be shot.

When Independence came
and the shadows of the soldiers
lived on only in pubs
he lost himself in the memories
away from his ill-paid working on roads
and his children stepped in fear of him.

But the road-worker's house had a garden
and there his cabbages were round and loved
and his leeks, and his rows of berries
and when his English grandchildren came
he sat them on his trousered knee
peeling the scars from apples for them.

GIBBONS RUARK

A Vacant Lot

One night where there is nothing now but air
I paused with one hand on the banister
And listened to a film aficionado's
Careless laughter sentence poetry to death.

It's twenty gone years and a few poems later,
The house demolished, the film man vanished,
The friend who introduced us to him dead.

I side with one old master who loves to tell
His film-buff friends that film is *like* an art form,
And yet my eyes keep panning the empty air
Above the rubble, as if, if I could run

The film back far enough, I might still start
For home down the darkened street from the newsstand
And turn a corner to the house still standing,

A faint light showing in an upstairs window.
Is someone reading late? Or is it the night
Our newborn lies burning up with fever,
And all the doctor can say is plunge her

In cold water, wrap her up and hold her,
Hold her, strip her down and plunge her in again
Until it breaks and she is weak but cooling?

Is it the night they call about my father
And I lay the mismatched funeral suit
In the back seat with the cigarettes and whiskey
And drive off knowing nothing but Death and South?

Somewhere a tree limb scrapes at a gutter.
The wind blows. Late trucks rattle the windows.
Never you mind, I say out loud to the girls

Away at school, There's nothing there to hurt you.
The sky is thickening over a vacant lot,
And when I leave there is a hard rain drumming
With the sound of someone up in the small hours,

Thirsty, his palm still warm from a sick child's
Forehead, running the spigot in the kitchen
Full force till the water's cold enough to drink.

GIBBONS RUARK

Waiting for You with the Swallows

I was waiting for you
Where the four lanes wander
Into a city street,
Listening to the freight
Train's whistle and thunder
Come racketing through,

And I saw beyond black
Empty branches the light
Turn swiftly to a flurry
Of wingbeats in a hurry
For nowhere but the flight
From steeple-top and back

To steeple-top again.
I thought of how the quick
Hair shadows your lit face
Till laughter in your voice
Awoke and brought me back
And you stepped from the train.

I was waiting for you
Not a little too long
To learn what swallows said
Darkening overhead:
When we had time, we sang.
After we sang, we flew.

ELISSA SCHAPPELL

The Green Fairy

The night sky was breathing, rising and falling in time with the sound of the ocean beating on the coastline below the rocky cliffs of Zambujeira do Mar. Bright glowing halos burned around each silver star. This ring-effect was what my husband Rob and I had been transfixed by at the bar in the center of the small fishing village, how all of the electric bulbs seemed to radiate golden auras. The edges of the tables, the bar, the faces of the other patrons, all seemed to be emanating light. It was like being inside a painting. Not just any painting, a van Gogh painting. It felt like you could see the hand of God in everything. Now, outside, the tops of the trees were as elongated as candle flames, the planets appeared as distant pinwheels; it was van Gogh's Starry Night. Courtesy of the absinthe we'd drunk hours before in a little bar the locals frequented.

The absinthe was why we were crawling on our hands and knees up the steep dusty street to the cottage we'd rented for what we imagined would be six months, or perhaps a year.

We'd recently dropped out of our lives in New York City—abandoning the square world of publishing—to escape to the Alentejo region of Portugal, an impoverished area populated with cork trees and lemon groves. It was rumored that members of the RAF were hiding out on the farms that bordered our fishing village, which also rented out spartan rooms to artists and travelers. We'd come to write—not magazine or newspaper pieces—but novels and poems. Great Novels. Great Poems. We were intrigued by the somewhat adolescent theory espoused by the poet and *enfant terrible* Arthur Rimbaud (when he himself was hardly out of diapers) that to make truly visionary art one had to destroy any and all repressive attitudes that might prevent you from tapping deep into this fertile consciousness. For Rimbaud, imbibing absinthe was the blazing wrecking ball that indeed demolished his inhibitions and set fire to his brain. This made sense.

I wanted to have visions. I was prepared to behave badly. I wanted my life to burn with an intensity others would find blinding. I wanted to have the sort of adventures that would be the stuff of legend. I wanted my life to be romantic and decadent, and slightly, lightly, debauched.

As naive and ridiculous as it might seem, drinking absinthe seemed a good start. As Rimbaud said, "Knowing pilgrims, seek repose / By the emerald pillars of Absinthe."

Absinthe was *the* liquor of choice among Bohemians, artists, and writers during the late-nineteenth and early-twentieth centuries. The Green Fairy played muse to such painters as Picasso and Manet, inspiring them to paint portraits of absinthe drinkers (Degas's drinker is a particularly marvelous study in degradation), but, more importantly, it literally influenced their vision, mixing dream-state with reality.

Some art historians attribute the birth of Cubism to Picasso and Braque painting under the influence. Van Gogh's work at Arles appears strongly affected by vision warped by regular infusions of absinthe. (One hopes that the pain of severing his ear to make a gift to a prostitute was somewhat diminished by the narcotizing effects of absinthe.) Toulouse-Lautrec carried a toot of the stuff in his hollow walking staff. His fondness for *la Fée Verte* (he painted posters glorifying her powers) rivaled his lust for cancan dancers.

The commingling of art and life as an absinthe drinker is crystallized in the work of Oscar Wilde as well as in the poetry of Charles Baudelaire, and Rimbaud's lover and dueling partner Paul Verlaine—who, despite viciously denouncing absinthe on his death bed, stashed bottles of it beneath his pillows.

In America the moribund Edgar Allan Poe regularly wrestled with the devil absinthe—and lost, while Ernest Hemingway became enamored with her in Spain, fortifying himself with absinthe before running with the bulls at Pamplona. Hemingway's absinthe cocktail of choice was a Death in the Afternoon. As he writes in the voice of Jake Barnes in *The Sun Also Rises*, "The absinthe made everything seem better. I drank it without sugar in the dripping glass, and it was pleasantly bitter. . . . I poured the water directly into it and stirred it instead of letting it drip. Bill put in a lump of ice. I stirred the ice around with a spoon in the brownish, cloudy mixture. . . . I was very drunk. I was drunker than I ever remembered having been."

When absinthe was outlawed in America, Hemingway traveled to Europe to stock up.

Absinthe's proof hovers around 68 percent, which is commensurate with a quality vodka or gin. Its ingredients include star anise, anise seed, hyssop, angelica root, calamus root, fennel, coriander, licorice root, lemon balm, and dittany, but its essential ingredient is the neurotoxin thujone, which when taken in excess is lethal. It is thujone, distilled from the herb wormwood, that provides the hallucinatory effects. Its influence on the rods and cones creates a distortion, a fracturing of images and light. Wormwood (*Artimesia absinthium*) appears in the Bible a dozen times, including the Revelation of St. John: "And the third part of the waters became wormwood, and many men died of the waters because they became bitter." Wormwood is the plant that was said to be growing along the path *out* of the Garden of Eden.

The word absinthe is derived from the Greek *absinthion*, meaning "undrinkable." In Russian the word for absinthe is "chernobyl."

I hadn't realized that absinthe was legal in Portugal, and wouldn't have known it had I not, our second week in town, had the good fortune to be in a bar where I spotted the dark green bottle. Its neck was wrapped in twinkly blue foil, the label proclaiming in Portuguese, "Absinto." At first I was sure I was mistaken.

I nudged Rob—he raised an eyebrow. He was in.

"Absinthe?" I asked the bar's owner.

It was.

"Are you sure you want to try?" she asked me politely. Very few American tourists loitered in this village, and thus many locals weren't sure what to make of us. We'd only discover later that the majority of the tourists, mostly German and Italian, had access to absinthe in Spain and Czechoslovakia and parts of Switzerland, and so they entertained little interest in it. Or perhaps they were just smarter.

"Absolutely," I'd said. After all, it was cocktail time. It was still light out—it wasn't as if I'd take a sip and go off, barking mad.

I'd seen the accoutrements of absinthe-drinking in paintings. The glass swimming with the grass-green elixir, the cube of white sugar poised for destruction atop the silver slotted spoon, a flagon of water at the ready. Somewhat to my dismay the owner did not procure any of these but mixed a finger or so of emerald-colored absinthe with fresh-squeezed passion fruit juice. I was slightly disappointed, but still intrigued.

The green absinthe infused with the pulpy, reddish orange juice had turned the drink an unsavory, and rather distressing, brownish color. I brought it to my lips, my nose crinkling at the sharp licorice smell, and sipped. Despite the sour-sweet flavor of passion fruit, a bitter anis-

ette with heady top notes of ethanol rode over my tongue, its finish
not unlike that of a vintage Robitussin. One sip should have been
enough, and yet somehow it wasn't. Even as the fiery licorice flavor
burned in the back of my throat, I took another sip, and then another.
Feeling my muscles coming loose from the moorings of my joints, I
began to feel languid and curious what would come next.

After Rob and I finished our cocktails, we headed down to the cliffs
where we often stood to watch the sunset. It was a lovely warm evening—the sky even more beautiful than usual—so we went down to
the tide pools to gaze at the pink and pale orange anemones, iridescent
limpets, and blue-black mussels. Gerard Manley Hopkins had been so
enamored with sea anemones he'd worn one as a hat; pink and lavender with coral tipped tentacles, now wasn't that an absolute stroke of
genius? Had I possessed at that moment the will to bend at the waist,
I, too, would have been pleased to wear a sea anemone like a hat.

As the sky darkened, fading from a deep velvety violet into indigo,
we clambered back up the rocks and returned to the bar. There we
each enjoyed two more absinthes, this time with only water. This
cocktail was a spectral iridescent green. Lovely to look at, but without
the fructose and clouding effect of juice, this drink even more closely
resembled some sort of oblivion-inducing potion, an enticing poison.
The taste was strongly alcoholic (imagine licorice-flavored lighter
fluid), with none of the pretense of such gentle-on-the-palate anise-
flavored aperitifs such as Pernod or Ricard. This was not an aperitif,
not a drink to start the evening, this drink was the evening.

Hours later, as we crawled slowly and most happily toward our cottage, the sky hanging low over our heads like a tent, I imagined we
were part of a parade of jeweled elephants, each holding the tip of the
tail of the elephant in front of him in his mouth.

The next morning, fearing a crushing headache and a stomach
knotted with pain, I awoke reluctantly, only to find, strangely, that I
was not in the grips of any sort of conventional hangover. No, I felt as
though I'd been struck in the spine by a delicate forked tongue of
lightning. I had the strangest sensation that my left leg had, in the
night, withered and gone numb. I sat up slowly, and, trying to get out
of bed, realized I was unable to stand. After a few ballerina point-and-
flexes, the feeling began to return and I was able to hobble to the loo.
"Well," I thought, "I won't be doing that again."

For the rest of the day, I felt fine, though I had no energy at all.
Certainly I had no brain to write—no burning visions lingered from
the night before. I didn't feel possessed by the muse. Instead, my hus-

band and I lolled on the beach as though anesthetized, intermittently taken by naps. Possessing neither the energy to walk to the water nor the strength to swim—the riptide created whirlpools that had drowned far stronger swimmers than I, even when my nervous system was tip-top—I opted to stand underneath a bracingly cold natural spring that crashed down the rocks. By four o'clock I felt restored. As the cocktail hour loomed, I looked at Rob. It was decided.

By six we were drinking absinthe again, this time at a café. (Absinthe became so popular in Parisian cafés during the nineteenth century that the cocktail hour was christened the *"l'Heure Verte,"* the Green Hour.)

This time eager to play barstool alchemist, we ordered our absinthe straight up with a water side. Deprived of the proper slotted spoon, we resorted to simply dropping the sugar cubes right into the bright verdant liquor and pouring in the cold water. With the first splash, the cloudy transformation from sparkling emerald into a jade opalescence began. The Portuguese called this effect "pigeoning," the French, the very apt "louche."

We sat and sipped our viridescent libation. The sugar helped enormously, accenting the inherent sweetness of the anise. It was bracing and medicinal, and divine. A powerful elixir. I had the sense that something big was about to happen.

An obsession was born.

We began imbibing every day. We would drink absinthe after a late afternoon repast of petite sea snails steamed in their shells and eaten off a pin. Then we would go down to the ocean at sunset and watch the sky change from a piercing blue, to violet, to a dark and vibrating azure. We lay on our backs and watched the swifts diving from the cliffs and the cranes returning to their nests atop the atolls, their huge white bodies leaving contrails against a silky-looking backdrop of fiery rose and orange.

We stared into the tide pools, we talked about what work we were going to do the next day. I looked for a new hat. Later, we might continue drinking at our favorite bar, but most likely we'd go home and play cards with our friend, a painter who was likewise hooked, and listen to American music.

Our favorite absinthe was the local-made white absinthe, which came in a brown stone bottle with a ceramic stopper. Oftentimes the bottle had a famous image—Degas's ruined absinthe drinker, a sloe-eyed Lautrec showgirl—decoupaged on the front. This might have discouraged the casual cocktailer, but not us.

Under the influence of water this white absinthe did not become a greeny opalescent, but a shimmering white, milky and luminous as a deep-sea pearl. White absinthe elicited the strongest hallucinatory effects; it was the most narcotic, and the rarest. These earthenware bottles of *absinto blanco* became our grail. They were incredibly hard to find. Years later, we returned to Portugal and toured the Neto Costa absinthe distillery—the only sanctioned Portuguese producer of absinthe—and bought a case of green absinthe, but it was not the same. Sadly, after journeying all over Lisbon and out into the Portuguese countryside, chasing down leads on white absinthe bootleggers, we were left standing, quite alone, and quite without white absinthe, in the middle of a cow pasture.

Once we had tasted white absinthe, we bought up every bottle we could find, traveling by bike to small towns near us and then via a wreck of a rental car into Lisbon on our quest. No dive was too scary or possible lead too ridiculous to follow. We begged bottles from stores and restaurants—in one case the manager had to be convinced to go and get a ladder out of the basement in order to reach the highest shelf behind the bar, bringing down a pristine bottle furry with dust. We cajoled bartenders into selling us their half-drunk bottles.

Drinking white absinthe was wonderful. I cannot compare it to anything I have had since, though I imagine distilled opium might come close. Over time I came to prefer my absinthe as I had had it the first time, with fresh passion fruit juice and a small handful of crushed ice.

I became addicted to the way this cocktail melted my bones and softened my muscles into uselessness, like an unseen hand traveling up my spine, massaging the cords in my neck, stretching out my legs. It made me want to recline on a fainting couch, though, save that, the beach, a chaise longue, or the top of a cliff would do. Drinking absinthe created the most desirous, languorous effect, and, unlike other alcohols it did not cause me to become overly chatty or mean; it didn't make me weepy or encourage me to unburden myself on strangers. There would be no midnight confessions, no hurled tumblers, no slamming of doors, and no dancing on tables. There was only a delicious torpor. For awhile.

It wasn't until nearly two months had passed that I began to understand what Oscar Wilde meant when he wrote, *"After the first glass you see things as you wish they were. After the second, you see things as they are not. Finally you see things as they really are, and that is the most horrible thing in the world."*

I started to see rings of light during the day, and sometimes my eyes burned as though I had cataracts, but I couldn't look away from the sun. I could lay for hours unmoving, lost in the troughs of my thoughts, overcome, unable to speak. Sometimes I felt strange flutterings in my head, what felt like a moth trapped between my brain and my skull, but I didn't blame the absinthe. I sank deep into a depression. I seemed unable to articulate my thoughts, and often imagined a large golden rope spinning in the sky over my head. Lying on the roof of our cottage, arms and legs out, I felt pinned to the earth. I couldn't imagine ever moving again.

Still, come cocktail time, I would drag myself upright, and put on a dress, and go out. I longed for absinthe. Draughts of beer didn't satisfy, wine tasted sour and flat. When we traveled to places where absinthe wasn't available—Paris, Pamplona—I missed it so much I packed a bottle, though we often killed this after only a day or two. It wasn't so much that I wanted the taste of it (though I do confess to an abiding fondness for bitter herbal elixirs such as Chartreuse), I didn't even necessarily *want* to drink it, but I *needed* to. I was deep under the spell of the green fairy.

After another month I most certainly became unwell. I didn't care if we traveled—we never made it to Morocco. And during the day while my husband and a friend went out and rode their bikes along the coastline—coming back with great stories of towns with chapels that had the bones of saints in glass vitrines, a village with a raven chained in the main square—I stayed indoors. The most I did was walk along the cliffs, or go into town for lemons and cheese. Some days I sat torporously at my typewriter and stared into space. I read Jane Bowles and Virginia Woolf, and dreamed letters I never managed to write home.

I did not realize then that thujone could inspire seizures in people who had preexisting epileptic conditions. Anyway, although I'd had seizures as a child, I didn't consider myself epileptic. The few times throughout my life when I'd experienced olfactory hallucinations—a pleasant scent of oranges—I hadn't thought much of it, assuming everyone, occasionally, had those. Now, however, the neurological effects of the absinthe—the auras, the olfactory hallucinations (this time they were not sweet, but offensive, smoked meat, the smell of rotting pumpkins, human shit), the moments where I became "stuck," unable to move or speak for some period of time—coupled with depression, were conspiring to cause what would be a nervous breakdown I would not recover from for years.

I didn't connect the absinthe drinking with the breakdown, but months later, after we returned home from Europe (our suitcase full of bottles of absinthe), it began to dawn on me. Educating myself about my type of epilepsy—temporal lobe—I discovered van Gogh was epileptic, and that absinthe exacerbated this disorder. *Sure*, I told myself, *blame the absinthe; what about the fact the guy snorted turpentine and ate paint?* Still, as much as I didn't want to admit it—it made some sense. The absinthe didn't cause the breakdown, but it didn't help it either. It ignited the spark. I didn't reveal this fact to anyone for a long time. Why should I? I wanted to drink absinthe, and I didn't want anyone—doctor, friend, or husband—suggesting I shouldn't.

Back home Rob and I learned to guard our stash jealously. Guests who poured themselves tumblers full of our *absinto* were not invited back. We shared only with a select few, slowly creating converts. A lovely result of this was that these new absinthistes would travel abroad and bring bottles back home for us. Since that time in Portugal, fourteen years ago, I have tasted many other varieties of absinthe—the Spanish and Czech varieties, and a few American knock offs—but none compares to the hallucinatory effects achieved with the white bootleg absinthe we drank in Zambujeira do Mar, so many summers ago.

Even now, knowing I should not drink it, knowing it could cause me terrible harm, sometimes when I am given a new bottle, I take a taste. Holding out hope that perhaps I will discover an absinthe that brings about the same magical transformation I experienced for a short time that summer, but this time only for one night. Were I to be put in front of a firing squad I would refuse the last meal, the cigarette, for one kiss of absinthe. Given a choice, I will take my absinthe in a glass of champagne, in part because the taste is divine, but also because the name—"Death in the Afternoon"—reminds me that it is best that I have just one.

If only to preserve my stash.

RECIPES
Death in the Afternoon
Veuve Cliquot, or whatever champagne you fancy
Absinthe

Hemingway gave the directions as thus: "Pour one jigger absinthe into a champagne glass. Add iced champagne until it attains the proper opalescent milkiness. Drink three to five of these slowly."

Momisette

The Momisette, which translates into "little mummy," was popular during the twenties, the era of the great archaeological digs in Egypt. This recipe calls for quite a bit of absinthe. You might adjust the recipe so as not to cause excessive damage to the nervous ganglia, and find yourself, upon waking, wrapped in bandages and semi-embalmed.

    3 shots of absinthe
    ½ shot of orgeat (almond syrup)
    Cold water
    Ice cubes

Combine the absinthe and orgeat in an old-fashioned glass then add ice and water to taste.

ELISSA SCHAPPELL

That Sort of Woman

"Mrs. Dalloway said she would buy the flowers herself."

I remember reading this line in college, and thinking, "Oh wow, big deal." Judging from the margin notes I wrote in my copy of Mrs. Dalloway at the time, *Lesbian? Incredibly modern form for the time! War is hell.* I didn't exactly immerse myself in the text. I wasn't interested in a book about class, and I was impatient with the drifting point of view, and anyway, I thought, I know the sort of woman Mrs. Dalloway was. That was it, I knew what sort of woman Mrs. Dalloway was and she didn't interest me one whit. At nineteen Mrs. Dalloway seemed to me to be the very picture of a sort of woman I grew up with, the sort of woman who I imagined occupied her hours with Junior League business, flower arranging, and all manner of gossip. The sort of woman who would swear until her teeth turned black that everything was fine, just fine as they smiled at their husband's business associates and their wives, smiled at the neighbors, while balling up her own desires like a dirty napkin, all for the good of the family. The sort of woman who would, as Clarissa Dalloway does, lament the tragedy of decorum that allows a suicide to be openly discussed at a party. I vowed that I would never be such a frivolous, ridiculous woman. In my mind women like Mrs. Dalloway had never suffered, had no private lives and no secrets.

The only part I liked, really liked, was the shell-shocked Septimus Smith fleeing the doctor he is sure is going to institutionalize him, throwing himself out the window of his home, impaling himself on an iron fence. In my own adolescent and grandiose bouts of self-pity and depression I could imagine doing the same thing.

In the summer of 1991 my husband and I rented a cottage in a tiny fishing village in the Alentejo region of Portugal. We'd gone there in the hopes of writing the elusive Great American Novel. Among the books I packed was Mrs. Dalloway. I hadn't meant to pack it. I meant to pack The Waves. It had, through some act of fate, just ended up in my belongings.

When we first arrived in Portugal I hadn't time to read much, or for that matter, write as we spent the better part of our time exploring the coves along the beach, and driving through the Portuguese countryside, the cork trees and lemon groves. After about a week a friend came to visit. It came to pass that during the day he and my husband would leave early in the morning and go off and ride bikes together, disappearing for hours to return home sunburned and full of stories, the town with the chapel made completely of bones, a village that had a raven chained in the middle of the square. I was jealous of the time they spent together. They seemed to talk endlessly and effortlessly with each other, about art and politics and music while I found myself resentful and sullen, sniping at my husband, the two of us falling into long periods of silence.

Come with us, they'd say sometimes, but I didn't. It wasn't just that I wasn't much of a rider, I knew they'd have more fun without me, they were asking me to be nice—which I couldn't bear—and anyway I was going to write my book. I sat and I typed. I got up and went to the market. I bought bread and I bought cheese and I made pots of fish soup. I washed our clothes in the sink and hung them to dry outside on the line. I waited for the men to return. Was this what being a wife was?

Back in America I was a wife, sure, but I was wife with friends, I was a writer, and a daughter, and a sister, and a friend, and of course a wife, but in Portugal what was I?

I was nothing. I was supposed to be a writer, but I wasn't writing anything worth a scratch, I was a daughter and a sister, but I couldn't see my family or speak to them much. I was supposed to be a friend, but after a month I began wearying of our friend's constant companionship and wanted him to leave.

I missed having big raucous dinner parties at our house. Parties fueled by cheap red wine and pot, parties that went on into the night with people sleeping over on couches and on the floor, waking at noon and staying for pancakes. I missed feeling necessary in my friends' lives. I was not necessary to anyone, in any way here. Not even my husband it seemed. I missed my friends, missed my family. My life was dull. Some afternoons I walked up along the cliffs and brought back eucalyptus and yellow flowers. I cut flowers from the garden outside our cottage, verbena, wild ginger, and the uncultivated pink roses, with their small hair-like thorns soft and red at the tip, their blossoms flat, uncomplicated and full open.

I sat at the kitchen table and wrote badly for long hours, listening over and over again to tapes of music friends had made me. I sat on the roof of our house and tried to read, I wanted something easy, something light, nothing that would challenge me to feel anything, so I picked up Mrs. Dalloway, annoyed that I had brought the wrong book. I opened it prepared to feel superior to dull old Mrs. Dalloway with her arms full of sweet peas, and her mending, I was prepared to feel very good about my life indeed.

From page one Mrs. Dalloway unnerved me. Yes Clarissa was picking out flowers, didn't I pick flowers too? Didn't I take great comfort in them? As I read on, I came upon rose after rose, what did it mean? Hadn't I just that morning seeing a new rose blooming at our gate finding it terribly symbolic of how no matter how beautiful a thing is it doesn't last?

Clarissa's husband, Richard Dalloway, disturbed me too. Not that he was a bad sort, he wasn't. That was the problem, he was good and solid and kind. He loved Clarissa, he did, but he didn't seem to know his wife at all, and that terrified me. Did my husband, good, solid and kind know me? I had been his wife for almost two years, and yet there were times when I found myself thinking of another man, a man I'd loved in college, hadn't he known me far better? Hadn't he adored me in the same sort of bright and burning way it seemed Peter Walsh adored Clarissa?

That man was younger than me, and he was naive, and I knew that we would not make a good match in the long run, but maybe we would have. Surely he wouldn't have left me day after day to go exploring with his friend. I had made a mistake marrying my husband whose reserve made it seem sometimes as though he didn't love me one bit. A man I'd fallen in love with in part because he'd never give his whole self to me, he'd never give me all that I wanted, he'd keep me curious and off guard. I wondered if he, like Richard Dalloway, ever looked at me and thought of saying I love you, but then didn't.

Clarissa had chosen Richard because in the most fundamental way he made sense.

Had I chosen my husband because he made sense? With no money, no ambition to make money or take care of me, to only write and experience everything the world had to offer him, hadn't he been, perhaps, a bad choice? Or the very best choice?

As I re-read Mrs. Dalloway, this time, freshly, as a wife, I wondered what toll wifedom had inflicted on me. Was I like Sally who went from the cigar-smoking free-spirit nymph traipsing naked down the hall to retrieve her bath sponge to a dowager whose "voice was wrung of its old ravishing richness; her eyes not aglow as they used to be," was I being turned into some kind of *creature?*

When had it happened that I became the creature that waited at the door, waiting for the men to escort me out into the world? I was ashamed of myself.

As I continued to read, I found myself pulled into Mrs. Dalloway, the rhythmic language and sinewy transitions insinuating themselves into my consciousness. I had until that time never felt so infiltrated and inhabited by language, unnerved by the way Woolf moved like a breath from one character's point of view to another, a woman stopping to ask for directions, a child running into the legs of a stranger, each passing the touch of consciousness from character to character.

Reading the words, and hearing the voices wasn't unlike the experience I had sometimes of simultaneously holding many thoughts in my head at one time, of not being able to listen to just one singular voice for any length of time. It was a condition that had gotten worse since I arrived in Portugal. It was a condition that had gotten worse, though I didn't connect the two at the time, since I started drinking the local-made absinthe.

The allure of absinthe was threefold. One, its history, so many of the great writers and painters that I admired from Verlaine and Wilde to van Gogh and Picasso adored absinthe. Two, it was illegal in the United States. Three, better than any other alcohol I know it created in me that most appealing state of languidness, dissolving muscle and mind so that I didn't really care what happened, or didn't happen to me. So while I enjoyed the way it made colors appear brighter and created halos around anything bright, the way absinthe made the night sky itself seem to breathe like a giant beast crouched over me, I became hooked on it because it allowed me to escape, the way that reading allowed me to escape.

I couldn't imagine Clarissa Dalloway ever drinking the way I did, though if she were to drink, absinthe might be just the thing. Unlike the effect of other alcohols I didn't get mean or weepy, I didn't want to dance on tables and rarely did I say the wrong thing when I had been imbibing absinthe, all indispensable attributes in a cocktail.

What I did not realize at the time was that the thujon in the absinthe was exacerbating a seizure disorder I'd had since I was a child, but which I had given no thought to, thinking that everybody occasionally smelled things that weren't there, everyone occasionally got "stuck" into a position they couldn't seem to get out of. I took to spending long hours in bed just staring at a pattern of light shifting on the wall. My husband stood over me asking me what was wrong. There was *nothing whatever the matter* with me, I said. Isn't that what Dr. Holmes said to Septimus. Nothing a little fresh air and some distractions wouldn't cure. *Nothing whatever the matter with me. I'll be getting up in a moment,* I said rolling on to my side. What was I doing lying in bed?

I couldn't imagine Mrs. Dalloway lying in bed. She'd have no patience for me at all. When I sat up and read my book I was disoriented by the prose, the way it slithered through my mind with all these voices on its back. I couldn't stop the Rezias and Drs. Holmes and Bradshaw from entering my mind. Couldn't stop lines like, *It could be possible that the world itself is without meaning* from sticking in my head. So I put it down.

In mid-July we left Portugal for Berlin. Since the Wall had come down there was much to see, a real cultural revolution going on, and we wanted to witness it. By this time I had started seeing rings around the sun and occasionally people's heads even when I wasn't drinking absinthe. I felt as though the air around me was elastic as a balloon, a membrane I could put my hand through. Occasionally I felt as though I was watching my life unfurl on film, the edge of my vision scratched up and bubbling like the tape had melted on to the bulb. The dark and jagged outline of a pine tree against the bright blue sky seemed violent. I would go into a sort of state, a daze, sometimes for many minutes on end, as though the needle of my consciousness had gotten stuck in a groove. I couldn't speak though I could hear others around me speaking. I was unable to break out of this space of suspended animation, and after a while I didn't even try. I sank down into the nothing, telling myself that eventually, I would come back out.

Then one day I didn't.

When we arrived in Berlin it was gray and misty, and in my mind it never changed, although I know this isn't true for I have seen the pictures. The picture taken outside the ruined church the day our friend appeared from Portugal. For a time we lived in a school dormitory that rented rooms, then when the money ran out squatted in an old building whose courtyard boasted an accordion-crushed Wartburg sedan, and bullet holes deep enough to swallow your index finger. We salvaged furniture out of the dumpsters and slept on old blankets that

had been put out for the trash, we shared a filthy toilet with pale belea-
guered-looking heroin addicts who you usually only heard skittering
like starved mice in the hall. Because there was no hot water, we ran
the cold we got at the gas station through an old coffee maker we'd
found on the street, and bathed by standing up in a bowl, and soaping
our body in full view of the open window so as to catch whatever
warming sunlight there might be.

We had no money, I lost weight. I missed home. One night drunk
and exhausted I snapped. I threatened to throw myself out the window. I wanted to jump. I wanted to just drop out of sight. I wanted to
hit the ground and have my bones break. I wanted it to kill me. I
wanted out. Septimus wasn't so crazy, he was just tired and scared.

I remember little from that time. The wail of a cricket echoing in
the marble stairwell of the hotel we moved into until we could fly
home, lying on the roof feeling pinned down by the sun which spun
above my head like a fiery rope, the ice cream bar served to me at
breakfast time on the plane. My husband whispering in my ear, holding my hand telling me he was going to get me back; my father having
trouble unlocking the car door in the airport parking lot; my mother
crying in the doctor's office when I told him I had wanted to kill myself, and still did.

Seeing my husband's face when I came out of a seizure, or my parents' faces peeping through the crack of the door when they thought
I was sleeping, I would sometimes think in the voice of Dr. Holmes,
*Didn't I have a duty to my husband? How unfair it was that I was scaring
everybody like this.*

I remember my father cutting flowers for the house, for my room,
irises, and magnolias, dahlias and foxgloves. When I remember my
father then, he is always coming in with flowers. Flowers, there were
always flowers. How could I have laughed at Mrs. Dalloway selecting
the flowers for her party? How delicate a task this was. How very, very
important.

After leaving Portugal my husband and I moved back to New York
City, and later to Brooklyn. Here behind my Victorian-era brown-
stone I have my own garden. It is a very English garden in some re-
gards, the high fences are overgrown with ivy; pink and white
climbing roses scale the back deck, fragrant honeysuckle and clematis
vines lattice the trellis, and here and there appear patches of violets,
snapdragons, bleeding hearts, and lavender. Every springtime now for
fifteen years my husband and I throw a spring feast to celebrate the
season, it has, as I have gone into my thirties, become a bit less pagan,

and more gustatory. I take joy in shopping for the supplies. I buy champagne and morels, fiddlehead ferns and salad greens that get tossed with pansies and nasturtiums, I choose handmade cheeses and fresh breads, select sausages and shellfish for paella. Like Mrs. Dalloway I would trust no one to pick the flowers but myself. There is pleasure in sorting through the buckets of cabbage roses and irises, the daisies and hydrangeas. Carrying home my bouquets of butcher-wrapped flowers, parrot tulips and peonies, lilacs and lilies, I see people stare and smile.

Standing at a traffic light a man inquires, *Are you having a party?*

I am, I say, feeling slightly embarrassed. Here I am off spending a week's salary on flowers and wine when children are starving in my city. Here I am, my head filled with recipes for cheese puffs and escargot, while our government is taken over by a dictator.

Later, however I am in the moment. As I watch my friends take the stairs to my door, entering my home shucking off coats and wraps, I savor the bittersweet collision of past and present. My daughter, in conversation with her godfather smiles at me across the room, while her little brother, at my hip, steals slices of orange dipped in chocolate. A woman I have recently become close with laughs. A man I love browns butter on the stove beside me, and I realize staring into the face of a beautiful friend, that she is prettier for the lines around her eyes, and that I too am aging. As my husband goes out to call in the children's cat, I am filled with thankfulness. I would not have these children with another man. That other man I sometimes think about. I would not know what it was to be loved and necessary if it were not for these people in this room. Isn't that what Clarissa wanted? And so for a night, this is the most important thing to me, this party. It defines me, and gives me shape, a past and a present, and perhaps a path to my future. For an evening the perfect party, the perfect dress, the perfect flowers, really do matter.

I know what it's like to be that sort of woman.

JULIE SCHUMACHER

Resurrection Hockey

Though I'd been told there is no stepping into the same river twice, I waded deep into familiar water when I opened the flyer inviting me to join the Mt. Carla Women's Field Hockey Resurrection Team, Vera LaVelle, coordinator, weekly practices to begin on the twelfth of June.

My old pal Agnes read the flyer over my shoulder, and neither of us could believe what we were reading: pale and unexercised as eggs, we hadn't played hockey since the infamous afternoon, almost twenty-four years earlier, when—held back from victory by a questionable last-minute foul shot followed by some public misbehavior on the part of Coach LaVelle—we had lost the chance to be high school champions in the Diamond (Small Wonder!) State of Delaware. Going into the tournament we'd been the favorite, the Tri-State area's glorious unstoppable Mt. Carla, a team whose fans shouted our moniker at halftimes like a sexual recommendation, *Mt. Carla!*, even exhibiting a dog in heat (her name was Carla) at crucial games. Miss LaVelle resigned in protest after the tournament. Some said she had been forced out: there were rumors that in addition to being overly aggressive she was a proselytizing lesbian (a gym teacher, unmarried, what kind of role model was that for Mt. Carla's girls?).

Agnes, my oldest and dearest friend on the planet, turned the flyer over to double-check that it was addressed to me, Miss Jorie (Marjorie) Hand. "We're sunk," Agnes said. There could be no other Mt. Carla field hockey team. "We're dead," Agnes said. There could be no other Vera LaVelle.

It's hard to get away from the past in some sections of the country. The suburbs of northern Delaware, for example, encourage stay-at-home behavior. Most people linger around the neighborhoods that spawned them until they inherit their parents' houses or, in the case of parents too stubborn to expire or move to Florida, until they can buy the house next door. As a group, the people I knew in high school were in general still locally accounted for, like birds that had failed to migrate. We often pretended we didn't see or still know each other, but inevitably we found each other everywhere—at the Safeway, at the bank, the bars, the track. Of course I was still very much accounted for myself, more severely so than others: I taught history in the same senior high school building that I had graduated from. Though Mt. Carla had been redistricted and renamed, it was still the same school: gunmetal gray floors and orange lockers and a smell of institutional disinfectant. Agnes offered me condolences when I landed the position. But I don't plan to be a history teacher forever; I like to tell myself that the future is ever fungible, unknown.

Agnes insisted that we talk strategy that night at her house over Chinese food and ice cream. By the time I walked into her kitchen the greasy cardboard cartons were open, and half-empty, in the sink. "You couldn't have waited?" I asked. "It's only five-fifteen."

Agnes waved a second flyer in front of my face. "I got one, too," she said. "What does she mean by *Resurrection?*"

I explained that I'd heard that Miss LaVelle had found religion.

Agnes barked. "I can't believe she acknowledges any other god but herself. Almighty LaVelle. Remember when she used to make us pass to each other with our eyes closed? I was a walking bruise for four years. My shin bones were pulp. And remember about five years after the fiasco we saw her in that home decoration store, wearing a *dress?*"

"That was her brother's store," I said. "He took pity on her and gave her a job after she quit."

"Like Argentina took pity on the Nazis." Agnes handed me an unbreakable dinner plate with yellow daisies around the rim. She had acquired her parents' old dishes along with their house; though she had fixed up most of the rambler, the kitchen still looked just like it had when we were fifteen. Sometimes I expected her mother, now living in a trailer in Sarasota, to shuffle in in her snap-front dress and remind us that we were old enough to clean up after ourselves.

"You know you loved playing hockey," I said. I opened a beer. "The harder it was the better you liked it."

Agnes smiled. She had a sly smile, as if she were hiding a piece of lemon in her cheek. "I knew it," she said. "You want to go to the first practice."

"I didn't say I wanted to go."

"You didn't have to say it. You want to go. It probably has something to do with history. One of your theories. You want to be condemned to repeat the past to prove you forgot it."

"You're the one who wants to go," I said. "Otherwise you wouldn't have brought it up." Agnes shrugged and taped the flyer to her refrigerator door. Outside, in her quiet neighborhood, the streetlights were ticking on one by one; she started walking through the house turning the indoor lights on to match. Agnes and her former husband Brian had a son who died at the age of seven, and in the weeks before he died he lost his sight and wanted all the lights burning because he was terrified of the darkness coming to get him. At the very end Agnes would sometimes shine a flashlight into his eyes while she sang him a song. After his funeral she began to keep the lights burning all night, either in sympathetic fear or as a monument to her son's final wishes. She and Brian divorced within a year after Peter died.

"I wonder if LaVelle looks the same," Agnes said, coming back into the kitchen where I sat at the enamel table. "She's probably even meaner and uglier. More sadistic. She probably dreams about chewing my ass off for no reason."

"Oh, come on," I said, "she didn't dislike you. In particular."

"She detested me," Agnes said. "Everyone else back then detested me, too, unless the ball was headed to right fullback. Then I was popular. Then I got my fifteen seconds of fame."

I stirred a forkful of egg fried rice. Agnes was never easy to get along with. Even before Peter's death she was moody and judgmental, prone to depression. Periodically, she disappeared into silent chasms of sadness as suddenly as if she were dropping off to sleep. I used to picture her moodiness as a giant slab of Swiss cheese—she had to walk across it with her eyes closed, her feet sensing where the awful vacancies lay.

"It's possible that all of us are meaner and uglier," I said. "Maybe we were all at our prime back then. Maybe our best days are behind us."

Agnes stared.

"Sorry," I said. Sometimes I opened my mouth and heard the most extraordinary statements, things that had very little to do with who I was, or what I believed. There was another version of Jorie Hand that lived inside me. "We could stop by tomorrow," I said. "Just to humor ourselves. Just for kicks. Pure pleasure."

"Don't joke around," Agnes said. "You don't believe in pure pleasure." She opened another beer. "The truth is that we were all misfits, Jorie, that's what it comes down to. That's what kept us all together."

"We weren't misfits."

Agnes held up her fingers as if to tick off a number of items. "A degenerate from a broken home—that's me; a pathologically shy person terrified of her own potential—that's you; a stuck-up perfectionist who couldn't make friends—that's Alice; a set of psychological Siamese Twins—the Rinaldis; a dwarf—"

"Beth wasn't a dwarf."

"Then how'd you know I was talking about Beth? And what about Virgin?" Virgin was short for Virginia, the nickname used ironically. "We were girl jocks at a time when it wasn't fashionable to be a girl jock," Agnes said. "We were too short, or too homely, or too tall or loud or aggressive. We were together because the boys didn't want us. Or in Virgin's case, because they wanted her too much."

I pushed my plate toward Agnes, who had been filching the largest mushrooms with a pair of chopsticks. It's true there was some kind of sublimation involved in our practices and play. Hockey came before everything. And Miss LaVelle did encourage us to be aggressive. As a team we hit too hard and fouled too often; we chewed through our mouth guards and wore out the towel grips on our sticks. We even borrowed—this was partly P.R.—the football players' blocking sleds, foam-and-metal dummies we crashed into while shouting something primal about the other team. We played fervently, desperately, to win.

"We were a great team," I said, tipsy with justice and nostalgia. "We deserved to win the tournament. We should have won it." Secretly, in a kitchen drawer, I kept a photo of our last and best varsity, the Mt. Carla Comets, where I could study it in moments of self-doubt.

"That's the problem," Agnes said. "We shouldn't have *cared* so much about winning it. We were *girls*. We should have gone home and set our hair and painted our nails and gossiped and had sex with some awful loser and gotten over it."

"You did all those things," I pointed out.

"That's true, I did. But I never got over it." Agnes tapped my wrist with an oily chopstick. "Neither did you."

We decided to drive by, not even to enter the parking lot. We were wearing shorts and T-shirts and golf shoes, not cleats, and I tried not to notice our four white thighs spreading out like pancake batter on the gray upholstery. I'd brought some books and my big keyring as if I could be planning to do some copying in the school office. But I made Agnes put our hockey sticks in back.

The first time we cruised past the school we saw only two cars in the lot. The second time around there were three, and beyond them we saw a figure chalking lines on the bumpy field. Over Agnes's protests I pulled into my usual spot under a pair of maple trees in the shade of the gym. We hunkered low in the bucket seats, laughing and pinching each other, rocking back and forth with senseless mirth, braying like donkeys. Then Agnes froze. A car pulled up beside us and in the driver's seat was a woman with a nearly recognizable face, hard to decipher with twenty years and probably fifty additional pounds on it, but certainly someone we once knew, someone we'd spent years with and had intimate conversations with and sworn always to be loyal to and remember. "I'm Beth," the face said, evoking the idea of a pie speaking, and before Agnes and I could react, before we could see the previous version of the face swimming up through the decades and the added flesh, there was a knocking at the opposite window. "You're late," a voice said. It was Miss LaVelle.

I don't believe in reincarnation or even life after death except in the metaphorical sense, which made it difficult to confront the second, earthly version of Vera LaVelle. In her previous existence, she had looked and dressed like an aging girl: a kilt and a T-shirt and ankle socks, and two black pigtails that made her reddish middle-aged face look steamed and bewildered, as if she'd just removed it from boiling water. Now she wore neat blue sweatpants and orthopedic-looking shoes and she was thin, just shy of frail. The dark braids were gone, replaced by blunt, shoulder-length white hair that looked as if it had been trimmed at home with a kitchen shears. Her ears parted the hair on both sides of her head, like rocks protruding from running water.

"Hey there," I said, stupidly. Miss LaVelle nodded and walked toward the field.

"Warm welcome." Agnes got our sticks from the back seat, re-expressing her theory that my interest in history and war and weaponry had its source in too many afternoons spent with Coach LaVelle.

"Look at her," I marveled. "She has to be sixty at least. She looks pretty good. She was probably forty back then. Do you think she's more than sixty-five?"

"Sixty-eight," Beth said. "I asked her. She has a cataract in one eye. And she had a mastectomy."

"Did you interview her dentist, too?" Agnes asked.

Beth didn't hear her. She was foraging in her trunk for the goalie pads.

"Let's get this painful episode over with," Agnes said. She goosed me with her stick and we walked to the field.

Miraculously, eight players showed up that afternoon: Miss LaVelle; Agnes; me; Beth; the Rinaldis, Renee and Roberta, ten months apart and still indistinguishable; and two other women I gradually recognized as Alice Canfield—an elegant perfectionist nicknamed "Polo" because of the extent of her family's money—and Heather Kline, otherwise "Pluto" because of the distance at which she kept her mind from the game.

I hadn't held a stick in almost a quarter of a century, and I had every reason to feel disgusted by the human condition and my own status within it as a specimen of physical disgrace. But it was a warm afternoon, the grass was long and uncut, sensual and verdant—that was the word that came to mind. There was something ideal about the ordinary scenery: the trees at the edge of the field were round and green and full like the artificial trees in an architect's model; even the sun, butter yellow, looked more like an artist's rendering than the real thing. The air was warm and fragrant with pollen, and soon I felt a hole in the day open, a void in time that allowed me to step into the past as if walking through a door. The eight of us didn't talk much to each other but entered our own thoughts in a way that only physical exertion allows you to do. I could ignore my extra fifteen pounds, the knot in my back from hunching over student papers, and the rest of my banal and pointless history, the mediocre events that appeared to have made me who I currently am: college; a Master's degree; marriage to a fellow student followed by the period in which Agnes told me I'd behaved with all the fortitude of a sacrificial lamb; divorce; and finally a truncated doctorate ending in a job for which I was hired by the very teachers I had admired, the ones who had inspired and mentored and encouraged me, and who quickly revealed themselves to be a group of stilted and humorless old men.

With a stick and a ball in front of me I could dwell exclusively in the moment. I could concentrate on the physical motion of the hard white ball parting the grass, the wooden stick curved like the J in my name, the sun on my arms. This was what I had loved best. This simple action, this small and single-minded pursuit, defined who I was, told me what my function in the greater scheme was supposed to be.

The best class I ever taught, the most stimulating class, the most intellectually fulfilling, was an honors section on European wars. We started with the Crusades and Pope Urban II at the Council of Clermont, and worked our way toward World War II, time predictably stretching and thinning and moving faster as we approached the present day. Because of the subject matter, almost all of my students were black-T-shirted boys, the kind that played war games on the computer in badly lit basement rooms, shy unsocialized seventeen-year-olds who would have been better off taking dance lessons or paying for dermatology. But during our daily sessions we lit up the classroom with a shared passion, discussing methods and strategies of warfare, the development of armaments, the pathologies of violent behavior. I showed my slide collection from the Tower of London and lectured in the dark about the cruel efficacy of torture. The class provided us with a bird's-eye view of human history and endeavor from the vantage point of a booth shielded in unbreakable safety glass—we could look, we could observe, but we wouldn't get hurt.

Agnes found my specialization very humorous. "Jorie, the pacifist war scholar," she said. "You can't tell me you aren't feeding their bloodlust. One of those kids is probably getting ready to kill his parents with an arquebus."

"They're good kids, Agnes," I told her. "They're learning something. Most boys go through this phase and move on. That's what kids do." I realized too late that I'd been tactless: Agnes's son Peter didn't have a chance to go through such phases. For almost two months after he died Agnes refused to leave the house, even to step onto the sidewalk to get the paper. She told me his death was like a curtain with the rest of her own life waiting behind it, and she had no interest in parting or walking through the curtain to find out what was there.

"I don't know what that statement says about you," Agnes said. "Aren't you planning to pass through this militia-girl phase yourself, eventually?"

"For me it's different," I said. "I get paid to be stuck in time. If I grow out of it I'll be fired." I'd be lost, too, I thought. I study history because I believe in the passing of time, in its ability to make chaotic, disparate events seem almost orderly, coherent, the cliché being that time heals all wounds.

"Getting fired would be an act of mercy, in your case," Agnes said. "Wasn't there a song about living in the past? I never listen to music anymore. I forget to turn it on."

"There are a million songs like that," I said. "But I never listen to them, either."

During our second and third practices, we scrimmaged for over an hour. We practiced our hallmark moves and several extras: the weave, the dodge, the back-pass, the feint. There were ten of us now, one person short of a team. Sue, our old high scorer, had come, wearing a beeper because she was on call as a pediatrician. And Mary Ellen, our long-legged center halfback, had shown up with four-month-old twins, identical pale boys she parked at the edge of the field in a wicker basket. The babies twitched their small, soft limbs in the shade of the bleachers, out of the sun, wailing and waiting for Mary Ellen to drop her stick, lift up her shirt to reveal sweat-glistening breasts, and lean over the two open mouths that had learned to suckle simultaneously. Agnes referred to this interlude as our half-time show.

At the end of our third practice, while we sat in the shade, gulping water, Miss LaVelle handed out copies of a schedule.

"What's this?" Beth asked.

Miss LaVelle continued handing out the slips of paper, licking her finger with a whitish tongue before separating each page from the top of the pile. Her voice was raspy and high-pitched, nearly falsetto. "Our first game is on the second Saturday in August. We'll play at the Tatnall Fields in Greenville."

"What do you mean, our first game?" Agnes asked.

Miss LaVelle looked fixedly at her clipboard as if hoping that it would offer insight into Agnes's behavior. This was classic LaVelle; it seemed stunning that I'd forgotten such a hallmark gesture when right now it was so familiar. It made me believe I was capable of forgetting my own face, my address, anything.

"There's no way we're playing against other teams," Agnes said. "Who would want to play us? What would be the point?"

Miss LaVelle continued gazing at her clipboard. She seldom looked anyone in the eye; the lore when we were in high school was that if she looked at you directly, you'd be turned to stone. Slowly, deliberately, she explained that we were registered as a club team in the summer league. That meant we would be playing against other club teams during what was called hockey weekend. Some of the teams were from the high schools and some were made up of anyone who wanted to play. She needed ten dollars from each of us for registration, plus another fifteen dollars for T-shirts and a medical kit. Hockey weekend was four weeks away.

Agnes hooted. Polo looked thoughtful. Sue said she was on call on occasional Saturdays but that she'd be happy to provide the medical kit.

"You can't be serious," Agnes said. "We used to *be* a club team during the summers. We were good. We were sixteen, seventeen. There's no way we're going to play in that league now."

"Anyone can register, I remember that," I said, thinking aloud and trying not to sense Agnes's rank astonishment beside me. She knew what I was thinking: this was the moment. This was the moment in the village when the ordinary citizens made up their minds whether to stay indoors with their eyes shut, commending their souls to god, or to throw the doors open and take up the pitchfork and the axe.

"I could rearrange my schedule." Sue looked at her watch. "If I had some notice."

"I could play," Polo said.

"I don't believe this," Agnes said. "This is way beyond nostalgia."

Miss LaVelle shifted her gaze to Agnes's shoes. "If you don't want to play," she said, "then why are you here with us, wasting our time?"

I tried to hold onto Agnes's ankle when she stood up but she kicked me in the chest and headed across the parking lot to her car.

Miss LaVelle went on to explain that practice would now occur twice a week, Wednesdays and Saturdays. We should each be running two miles on nonpractice days. We needed good, new cleats as soon as we could get them. I almost expected a lecture on proper support and hygiene for the older girls.

"We'll need more people," Sue pointed out.

"More are coming," Miss LaVelle said. It was hard to tell if she spoke from clairvoyance or senility. She leaned over stiffly, gracefully, for her stick and her whistle. "Next session," she said. "Bring twenty-five dollars if you want to play."

Who could have guessed, at the start of the Delaware Diamond state girls' field hockey tournament, what the future would contain, what it would ask of us? Who could have seen that it would offer Agnes a dead child, that it would include both of our marriages and divorces, my failed doctoral thesis, and a hundred other joys and humiliations? That single bright generic morning seemed to hold within it only the possibility of itself, nothing beyond a supreme present in which no other time existed. How could we lose? There was a late, angrily debated foul, a tenuous judgment by the referee, the usual trivia and scandal. Miss LaVelle swore at the opposing coach, then at Mr. Till, the referee—eventually she was accused of physically attacking him, though Polo swore he had shoved her clipboard into her chest—and was ejected from the field. When the game was over we were too stunned even to assemble a list of excuses: if only Beth hadn't let in the first early shot, if only so-and-so hadn't fouled, if only Pluto hadn't tripped over the bench at halftime and ended up with seven stitches in her arm. That's what history is: hindsight and intelligence and information mixed with regret, a pursuit of truth and knowledge after the facts, at a time when truth and knowledge are no longer as useful. Fort Ticonderoga, the Archduke Francis Ferdinand, Mr. Till in his black shorts and stripes, the fall of Madrid. How did it happen? That's the question we ask ourselves over and over, tossing in threadbare sheets at night. How did we allow this future to happen? How did it come?

By the fifth week of practice there were thirteen of us—a full team of eleven with two substitutes. Virgin had shown up, on the cusp of her third divorce, swearing that she would substitute hockey for men. And with difficulty I'd convinced Agnes to come back, arguing that her Saturdays were vacant and that on the field we could recapture a sense of ourselves before jobs and marriages took hold; we could rediscover who we *purely* were. Agnes was sullen and tentative: I accused her of considering herself undeserving of fun.

We scrimmaged six against six, not counting the goalie, LaVelle making everyone except for Beth, mired in her pads ("cageface," Agnes called her), play both offense and defense, switching positions every half hour. After we ran our two miles, LaVelle brought out a miniature chalkboard, resting it on top of her Velcro shoes. "This is how we used to set up," she said. "Five forwards, three halfbacks, two fullbacks, and a goalie."

```
    X     X     X     X     X
       X     X     X
          X     X
             X
```

She erased the board. "This is how everyone has been setting up in the years since we haven't played: four forwards, two links, three halfbacks, a sweeper and a goalie."

```
    X     X     X     X
       X     X
    X     X     X
          X
          X
```

She erased it again. "This is how we're going to set up."

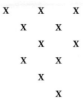

We stared at the chalkboard. The little x's weren't in any particular places. They were haphazard, misaligned.

"There's no clear offense or defense. I can't tell who's who," Pluto said.

"Neither can the other team." Miss LaVelle quickly wiped off the board, as if spies were lurking at the fringes of the field. She reached into a grocery bag behind her and brought out a stack of folded T-shirts, gold with white lettering on the front and back. Agnes was the first to notice that we had all been assigned the numbers we'd sported twenty-four years earlier. Miss LaVelle had a stellar memory. ("Creepy," Virgin said. "She probably has our heights and weights charted on her living room wall.")

"There's no team name here," Polo said, taking one of the shirts. "I guess we can't be Mt. Carla anymore. Do we need another name?"

"How about the biddies?" Mary Ellen said.

"Hens," someone added.

"Divorcées."

"Carlas unmounted."

"I should have asked." Miss LaVelle's voice cut through conversation. "I just assumed." No one said anything. I was beginning to develop a degree of sympathy for Miss LaVelle. I had a theory that she suffered from low self-esteem, and that her inability to look directly at us stemmed from a time when someone had told her she was unattractive. ("Probably her parents," Agnes said. "Probably the midwife who delivered her.")

"You picked a name?" Sue asked.

"I just assumed," Miss LaVelle repeated.

Our official team name: *Resurrection.*

The first team we drew on hockey weekend were the Milford Stars. "Any of them menstruating yet?" Virgin asked when we saw them practice in their size two kilts. They were perky and cute and wore

ribboned ponytails, and gave each other secret good-luck handshakes
before the game.

I noticed that Agnes wasn't wearing her cleats. I'd had trouble getting her out of the house that morning; she was sluggish and argumen-
tative, and forced me into offering ludicrous peptalks in the car,
shooting them down before I could finish them.

We drew into a huddle around Miss LaVelle. "Their only skillful
player," she said, her voice a high growl, "is the center. Sue will take
her and everyone else will take turns double-teaming. Don't leave her
open. Their halfbacks are nonexistent. Remember: we have experience
on our side. Any questions?"

Furtive, we looked the girls over. They were too young for makeup,
too young for beer and cigarettes and even coffee.

"How old are they?" Virgin asked. She had cut the sleeves and the
neck off of her T-shirt, and she was wearing a red bandanna in her
hair—strictly prohibited in the old days; bandannas were sloppy. Virgin always looked good in her uniform.

Miss LaVelle didn't answer. I waved at the Rinaldis' mother, sitting
in the bleachers in a black dress next to an enormous hamper of
snacks. She had never come to a game when her silent and identically
talented daughters were in high school; her home had been a Mt. Ev-
erest of soiled diapers and cooking pots. Now that her husband was
dead and her innumerable children were grown, Mrs. Rinaldi was
cheerful and boisterous.

"I really want to know," Virgin insisted. "How old is that team?"

"Middle school," Miss LaVelle mumbled. "Maybe twelve."

Sue noticed a newspaper reporter and a photographer on the side-
lines, the photographer snapping pictures of Mary Ellen's twins.
"We're a news item," she said. "Aging women, former athletes, return
to hockey." I looked at Sue, who was fit and smooth-faced and professional and successful and lovely, her blond hair in a perfect little ponytail.

Miss LaVelle blew her whistle. "Resurrection!" We took the field.

During the first game, we were aggressive, we were high strung, we
were needlessly ferocious. This was a match between past and present:
we were playing against girls young enough to be our daughters,
against the generation behind us, against people who, when we were
in our prime, inhabited a future that didn't exist. Title IX, for the Milford Stars, was the name of a brand of sportswear. They had no idea
of the context and sweep into which they fit. Besides, the Stars didn't

seem to care if they won; they let by a goal in the first three minutes that left us hacking and wheezing with unfettered joy. At one point Miss LaVelle and Mary Ellen switched positions, Miss LaVelle executing a dodge so quick and graceful that I was caught flat-footed, admiring its skill, its rare, deft beauty. I watched her jog back into position, tongue dampening a corner of her mouth, head tipped to the side (the cataract), wrists flexing, powerful tan legs and agile stick work daring the oncoming offense to approach her segment of the field. "Move it, Jorie!" Polo said. We won five to two, and when they shook our hands after the game the Stars smiled at us with demure uncomplicated happiness, then trotted off, Agnes surmised, to make paper dolls.

Sue handed out a round of ibuprofen.

"Already took some," I said, proud of myself for thinking prophylactically.

Sue took in my glazed expression and reddened skin and continued to hold the pills toward me. She was a certified physician. I swallowed them.

"You played well," Sue told Agnes. "You had a couple of great stops in the second half."

"Thank you very much," Agnes said. "I'll try to keep up the good work. I know everyone's counting on me at this crucial time." When Sue walked away Agnes said, "If it rains, don't think I'm going to keep playing. I'm not going to be a martyr to this game."

"It's barely cloudy, Agnes," I said. "And you'll want to stick around to see how it all pans out."

"You'll fill me in on it," she said. We had thirty minutes of rest before our second game.

Mainly because of Polo and Sue and Miss LaVelle, and because Beth let very little past her into the cage, moving her feet much faster than a person her size could reasonably be expected to do, we won our second game almost as easily as the first. The other team was faster, they were younger, they were stronger, they were in shape. We were experienced. We had the stickwork. We passed backwards, faked, and dodged. We remembered and reenacted our best moves from two decades before. We set up differently each time, shuffling defense and offense, moving inners to link positions, fullbacks to halfbacks, center to wing. We never let them guard the same person, but shifted positions midplay. Flexibility and surprise were our major assets.

What I'd forgotten about hockey weekend—or what I had never noticed in my prime—was that it involved playing one game after another until a single, exhausted team was left. Our third game was scheduled for just over an hour later. "Ridiculous," Agnes said. There were thirty-two teams enrolled at the outset; now there were eight. Amazingly, we had made it to the quarterfinal.

Sue had to leave: a fifteen-year-old patient with hepatitis. I took off my shoes and discovered a blister on my heel the size of a quarter. Renee was wearing a knee brace; Beth had welts on her thighs from the goalie pads. We were all sunburned, depleted.

Meanwhile, Agnes had slipped past my mood-monitoring radar. She was beyond sarcasm and well on her way to anger and despair.

We sucked on ice cubes in the shade, in the lee of the gym. Some of us dozed and some of us waited.

"Is everyone else going to be here for the third game?" Polo asked. "Miss LaVelle needs to know if anyone's leaving."

Agnes was digging a hole in the ground with the toe of her sneaker. "No one's leaving," I said.

One of Mary Ellen's twins began to cry.

As soon as we lined up for the third game I had a bad feeling. In the first five minutes Pluto missed an easy pass across the open goal, Virgin was called for obstruction, and Roberta Rinaldi was warned against raising her stick, golf-style, above the waist. I tried to take a Zen-like approach, to enter the game as a whole and picture what we must have looked like from above—our front line an invading army, our two sturdy links faithful support, our fullbacks a final defense against the godless hordes. We were an army dedicated solely to good; we were virtue and grace and aggression rolled into one.

Agnes was looking morbidly at the clouds, which did seem thicker and darker than before.

Polo drove upfield with an offensive play she'd perfected in practice but they cut her off easily, intercepting. They seemed to see everything we did before it happened, the future illumined before them like a simple map. They turned our skill into clumsiness, our finesse into ragged failure. I turned around to check on Agnes. She seemed to have aged several years in a single morning, and was barely paying attention. The clouds came to a boil over our heads; Mary Ellen's husband lugged the twins into the van and drove away.

When Peter first got sick, I tried to hide my dread by chirping at him, bringing him presents, inventing senseless games. Then one afternoon he told me, "you don't have to look at me anymore, Aunt

Jorie, you can just sit here and be quiet." I was always amazed at Agnes's calm strength during the long awful months at the end of his life. Then I realized it was a *show* of strength, a display, and that internally she suffered a helplessness that bred unending rage.

The sky was as dark as evening. I could feel Agnes's sorrow and depression welling up behind me, and I turned around to try to offer her some kind of comfort. "Agnes!" I yelled. The ball was headed in our direction. She looked up and I knew she was angry, furious with *me:* what was she doing here on a darkening field at the age of thirty-nine, overweight and empty-handed, and without her son? For a moment I imagined that she blamed me for Peter's death.

In the awful light of the coming storm the field, the trees, the players, everything took on a strange patina, as if we had all been out in the humid air too long.

"Agnes!" I yelled again. I wanted to tell her that I could see the future. Though the sky was dark, and though we were caught beneath it in this one small place, I could feel the weeks and the years rolling away under our feet toward a time when I would be able to remind her what it was like to live suspended in a single moment, your very existence a series of small but crucial gestures on a brilliant field.

Without turning around again I knew that Agnes had walked off the playing field behind me. Pluto missed a tackle and let a darkhaired opposing forward into my territory, my region, and as I got ready to meet her I could hear myself describing it all for Agnes: the feeling of being a healthy functioning body in a larger body, marvelous cog in a marvelous wheel. So temporary, I'd tell her, and yet this is what we live for. You were behind me, you felt it, too—the green field a horizon, disaster near but not yet upon us, the day lit with potential like an unencumbered future, the wide open world an unopened book.

DAVID SCOTT

Delaware

Lord De La Warr never saw this flat land.
Had he not been too wearied

from years of civilizing Virginia
with salt spoons and tea cozies

he might have toured Delaware, before retreating
to his feudal estate and taken his name back,

dreaming of something larger, unnamed.
Ohio, Nebraska, North Dakota, Oregon.

But here she lies, Delaware, his name-seed
spread into the future of chicken coops

and combines scraping crop fields clean.
Once, I thought I was De La Warr, war-made.

An old thief coughing into my soup,
but if you stay and stay, there is even

beauty in Kirkwood highway's strip malls
and the litter of so many golden arches

and beyond it all, I'm discovering
my own new country of Iron Hills,

rusted soil, and waving sedge.
I've become more native, more Lenni Lenape

than De La Warr. I gather with the original people
by the beaches welcoming boat-loads

of clothed, unbeaded, unwashed, blank-skins.
I've got my basket of sweet mussels and clams

I've rooted and raked from the muck. I see mostly sky
as the warships' masks rise constantly out of the sea.

W. D. SNODGRASS

Cherry Saplings

—for Russ

You turn your back on them no more
    Than for ten seconds—somebody's got to them.
Weed trees crop up, shadowing them under,
    Tent worms or aphids waste the leaves,
Rot leeches down from a torn branch,
    Woodrats gnaw them, girdle them around.
Take the whole Fall setting them in
    Sunlight, shaping, firming in their soil,
Come Springtime, find some Skidoo
    Snapped them clean off, back to the root.

When white men came to the continent
    First, they grew four feet through the trunk.
Try buying some new cherry, say,
    Six inches wide. Oh, you can find
The old boards still—whole table tops—
    The way you'll still see chestnut cupboards
Or find cross-grained elm chairs for some
    Years yet. We're good and done, though, with
Those broadest old trees, with the tallest.
    Cherries; these are merely the loveliest.

You'd think it was hard for them to take.
    They used it up in horse stalls, barn planks;
That curving tough grain went to roof in
    Dry lives, got buried in the walls
That fixed their hungers, their old wounds, their pride.
    That long-hardened heartwood with its clear

Rays quartering, spreading from the core,
    The ways they stained it—dried milk, dried blood,
Tobacco juice—until it gave way
    To the numbed image ruling their desires.

You'd think they thought it had grown too fine.
    They *never* thought of it. They had their dream.
The saplings stay, though, small stands of them,
    Or alone, there, under other trees,
The satiny red bark, the blown white flowers,
    Their thin trunks leaning outward, outward,
Feeling toward some memory of sun. It is
    Too late to cable them back upright,
Too late to cut down anything around.
    We have no right but to our own grounds.
What will we leave here still worth our hate?

W. D. SNODGRASS

The Marsh

Swampstrife and spatterdock
    lull in the heavy waters;
some thirty little frogs
    spring with each step you walk;
a fish's belly glitters
    tangled near rotting logs.

Over by the gray rocks
    muskrats dip and circle.
Out of his rim of ooze
    a silt-black pond snail walks
inverted on the surface
    toward what food he may choose.

You look up; while you walk
    the sun bobs and is snarled
in the enclosing weir
    of trees, in their dead stalks.
Stick in the mud, old heart,
    what are you doing here?

CRUCE STARK

Getting Out More

"So what you gonna do," Walter said. "You gonna just sit there the whole rest of your life?"

"I'm not sitting, Walter," I said. "I'm standing. In the kitchen. You're lucky I even answered. This time of day, you had to be selling something."

"I am, Sammy, I am. You gotta get back on your feet. You gotta get back into circulation."

Walter didn't say anything else for a moment and I could hear my own breathing through the telephone.

Walter's a good friend. A pain in the ass most of the time, but he's a good friend.

"She's just a woman, Sammy," Walter finally said. "You can't let it get you down."

"She isn't just a woman, Walter. She was my wife. Betty was my wife."

"So she was your wife. But not *now*, Sammy. You got to get on with it. You got to get on with the rest your *life*. "

"I was, Walter," I said. "I was getting ready to have supper. Until I had to answer the telephone."

"You're young, Sammy, you're a good-looking guy."

"I'm forty years old, Walter. She left me for a younger man."

"You're still a good-looking guy, Sammy. You gotta get out of the house. Tell you what. Sheila's gone visiting her mother. She's gonna be there all weekend."

"That's different, Walter. She's going to come back. Monday, she'll be back."

I could hear Walter sighing, all the way down the telephone lines. I wish I had my marriage back. But I wouldn't want Walter's.

"So what I thought," Walter said, "there's this restaurant, up in Pennsylvania. By the river."

"What river, Walter. There's lots of rivers in Pennsylvania."

"The Susquehanna," Walter said, "on a hillside, right on the river. I read about it in a magazine. They said the food was real good. We could start in the afternoon. Have a few drinks. Enjoy the fall. Maybe see the leaves turn."

"It's too early for that, Walter. It's only October. The leaves are still going to be just the way they already are."

"So you want to do it?"

"Do what, Walter?"

"You want me to make the reservations? So we can go?"

"I don't know, Walter. I'm not sure I'm in the mood."

"Saturday," Walter said. "How's that? I'll come by about three, that'll give us plenty of time. We won't need to be in a hurry."

"I don't want you driving," I said. "A couple of drinks, you're not too good at it."

"That's what Sheila says, too."

"She's right, Walter," I said. "You need to listen to your wife."

So I picked him up Saturday in the '92 Corolla. Betty took the Subaru. Only about 60,000 miles. But she said she needs a station wagon. So what was I going to do, she needs a station wagon. Not for her stuff. She hired some college boys in a U-Haul to do that. Or Roger did. He probably wouldn't want to show up himself. So he probably hired the college boys.

Walter lives outside of Wilmington, on the Newark side. It's a nice house, better than when he and Sheila lived right next to us. But he got promoted, Sheila got some money when her daddy died, they moved on.

"So you okay?" he asked after he got into the Corolla. "You look good," he said, but he was really making sure I was dressed right for a nice restaurant.

"I know how to eat at a nice restaurant, Walter," I said. "I don't need to ask Betty about that."

Walter laughed. He was glad to be out, to be going someplace without Sheila.

"Put your seat belt on, Walter," I said. "I don't want you messing up my windshield."

Walter laughed again and buckled on his seat belt. "You sure you didn't call up Betty to make sure you got the right tie?"

"That's not funny, Walter," I said. "I'm not ready to joke about that yet."

"You're right," he said. "It's still too soon for joking around. From now on, I'll be more careful."

We wanted to go the back way, out of Delaware and then up through the Amish country. I wasn't sure at first. That's where Betty and I used to go driving. Back when we did things on Sundays. We'd drive up the country roads, past barns with hex signs. Laughing together when we got stuck behind the buggies, not minding that it took forever. What were we in a hurry for? We were together, we weren't going anywhere, anyway. We were just out for a ride.

It wouldn't be the same with Walter, of course. But I had to stop thinking like that. It'd be different. But that didn't mean it couldn't be fun. So I got off the turnpike at the 896 exit. I'd already checked and the University of Delaware Blue Hens were playing out of town this weekend, so there wasn't any traffic going past the stadium. I didn't want to get stuck in that. And since it was Saturday, there weren't many students around when we drove by the campus. Maybe they were in the library or somewhere studying. Or maybe they were like me when I was a student. They had jobs so they could pay their tuition. Like the boys who took away Betty's things. But I didn't hold that against them. They were probably just trying to stay in school.

"Not a lot of kids out today," I said to Walter.

"It's Saturday, Sammy," he answered, as though what I'd said was obvious. "They're probably getting over their hangovers."

We drove on into the countryside, then past a tiny corner of Maryland into Pennsylvania. The road was only two lanes, but we weren't in a hurry. There wasn't any problem about driving.

Walter didn't seem to be in much of a mood for talking, but I didn't mind. I liked looking at the fields on both sides. Nothing much was growing in them, but it was nice to be away from all the strip malls and traffic lights. It somehow made it easier to breathe. I know that was just in my head, but it didn't matter. I liked feeling that way, whatever the reason.

After we'd been driving awhile, Walter seemed to start getting restless. He was paying more attention to the roadside, as though he was looking for something. We were coming toward a small community, it wasn't even a town, just a group of buildings.

"You about ready for a drink?" he said.

"It's only four o'clock, Walter."

"It's Saturday, Sammy. It's boys' day out. You got to loosen up. There's nobody gonna be waiting up when we get home, Sammy. It's not gonna matter if we can't walk a straight line."

"I know that, Walter," I said. "There hasn't been anybody waiting in my house for awhile now."

"I did it again, didn't I, Sammy? I got to be more careful. And I will, Sammy. I'll be more careful. Over there," Walter said, and pointed to a tavern that was a little ways back from the road. "That looks like a nice place."

I pulled into the parking lot. The bar didn't look very different from any of the others we'd already passed along the roadside, just places where people could go and have a drink. It was made mainly of concrete block, but that didn't matter. Whoever had built it hadn't planned for people to stand around and look at it.

Inside it was dark and smelled of cigarette smoke and beer, which was about the way it should have.

"You want to sit at the bar?" Walter asked.

I shrugged and Walter picked out a stool and I sat down beside him. There were other patrons at the tables near the door, but we were the only ones sitting at the bar.

"My friend and I need a couple for the road," Walter said jovially to the bartender, a short man with a long nose and a narrow face. The middle of his head was completely bald, but the hair on each side was black and thick, although it looked like it needed combing.

He didn't respond at all to Walter's friendliness, just kept washing glasses in a sink, like he was waiting for Walter to finish.

"Make mine a bourbon and branch," Walter said.

The man looked up at me and kept waiting.

"I'll have a beer," I said. Since I'd been living alone, I was being careful. I didn't want to be one of those people who try to drown their loneliness in alcohol.

The man was still waiting, so I told him, "It doesn't matter. Anything you have on draft."

I could tell that Walter was looking at the bartender carefully as he measured out the bourbon into a shot glass, probably making sure it was enough but also hoping the man would be generous and give him a little more. That was one of the problems between Walter and Sheila. She kept saying that she didn't mind Walter having a drink every now and then, but he was beginning to abuse the privilege.

"So how is Dorothy?" I said after we got and paid for our drinks. I knew Sheila's mother from when she'd visit while we were still neighbors. I liked her, although she wasn't the type to put up with much nonsense. "There's nothing wrong, is there? She's not sick or anything?" She wasn't getting any younger and she was living by herself since her husband had died a few years ago.

Walter sighed. He'd already finished half of his drink. "Nah," he said, not seeming as jovial, as if there was some sadness he was trying to get through, "she's fine. Sheila just thought she ought to go see her, get out of the house for a couple of days. You know how they are. Some free time from the job, got to go see their mothers."

"I guess," I said, but I didn't. Betty and her mother never got along. About half the time it was me that had to call her up on her birthdays and the like. Betty wasn't as bad with her daddy. Although it was kind of funny. When they'd come visit us, all Calvin, her daddy, would do was sit and read the newspaper or watch television, and Betty and her mother would spend all their time in the kitchen or going through clothes as though they were best friends. But once they left, it went back to the way it was before. We almost never went to visit them. Betty said it had taken her long enough to get away. She wasn't in any hurry to go back.

Walter was looking around the room now, curious about who else was there. There wasn't a whole lot to see, just four or five men sitting together at a back table. They looked like farmers, but I know you can't tell a whole lot by the way people dress. So I turned back around toward the bar and took another drink.

Of course, maybe it'd have been different if we'd had kids. That probably would have made Betty and her mother closer. It certainly wasn't our fault. We gave ourselves enough chances. Those first years after we got married, we loved being in bed together. There wasn't any place either one of us would've rather been. We did things, different positions, things neither one of us had ever even thought about until after we got married. That was probably the best time of our marriage, of our lives, or at least of mine. I can't say about Betty's. I thought I could, but now I can't be sure.

Back then, when we were spending so much time in bed, it seemed that everything was possible. I didn't care about my job or that Betty had to work longer at the hospital. She's a nurse and she's good at it, although now they don't get to do as much of what they like to do, really taking care of people, the reason they got into the job in the first place. Now there's too much busy work going on. But back then, life seemed so *open*.

And maybe it still would have been if we'd been able to have kids. That's probably why Betty wanted to spend all that time in bed, that's what I think now. But it didn't happen. Nobody knows why. We both got checked. Betty knew the right doctor because of her work at the hospital. Nothing seemed to be wrong with either one of us and Betty didn't want to adopt. She said it somehow wouldn't feel natural, and I guess it's a good thing we didn't. It'd make things a lot more confusing now, having a kid who couldn't understand any of it, why grownups do these sorts of things.

Walter finished off his bourbon in a big swallow and put his glass down on the bar with a flourish. "Well," he said, "we got that taken care of. You about done?"

"Just about," I said and drank the rest of my beer. I put fifty cents on the bar as a tip and wanted the bartender to notice that I was the one who'd done it, but he didn't look up from washing the glasses.

Once we were in the car, Walter got quiet again. It's just his way sometimes, after he's had a drink. That's probably what was happening now. He just didn't want to talk. I hoped it wasn't because he wasn't enjoying the trip. I didn't want him to be disappointed, because he'd been right. I'd stayed inside the house way too long, and it was nice out in the country. The sun was coming down kind of in a slant, not really bright, you could tell it was October, but it made everything along the roadside seem to shine. The leaves on the trees were still green, I'd been right about that, but they wouldn't be that way long and that could have made things sad, things changing, everything getting ready to die in the winter. But for some reason I didn't feel that way. Maybe it was the beer, but I didn't think so. I think it was being out of the house, going somewhere with Walter.

We had to take even smaller roads to get over to the river, which was fun. It made me feel like we were doing something off the beaten track, and I guess we actually were. Pretty soon we were behind a buggy and the road was so curvy there wasn't any way to pass, but I didn't really care. We weren't in any hurry. Walter was leaning back, I couldn't tell if he was napping, but there wasn't anybody behind us trying to hurry us along, so I was happy to just keep following. I even lowered my window so I could hear the sound of the horse's hooves on the pavement.

They had their bad weather cover around the buggy, everybody closed in so the wind couldn't get to them, but I could still see through the clear plastic or whatever it was, probably not isinglass curtains like in the song. But whatever it was, I could see the family inside, all dressed in their black, the father with his hat and long beard, the wife with a cloth over her head and in between them a little boy, maybe nine or ten years old, all of them squeezed together on the seat looking like a family is supposed to look.

"Hey, Walter," I said.

Walter kind of grunted.

"That's nice, isn't it?"

"What's nice, Sammy? I was taking a nap."

"Up ahead. In the buggy."

"You mean the horse?" Walter said. "Yeah. It's a nice-looking horse."

"No, I mean the family. Out for a ride like this."

"This is Amish country, Sammy. This is what we're supposed to see. That's why we left so early."

"I know. But I think it's nice. A family. Out for a ride like that."

"They got nothing else to do," Walter said. He still was unhappy about my waking him up. "They don't have televisions. They got to find other stuff to do."

Seeing the buggy put Walter in a bad mood, so I didn't try to keep talking. And he probably wouldn't have agreed, anyway. Walter Junior was away at school. He hadn't wanted to go to the university. It was too close to home, he said. And he and his Daddy hadn't been getting along the last couple of years anyway, so Walter probably wasn't in the mood to see a family out enjoying a buggy ride together.

So I told Walter to go back to sleep. I wasn't in any hurry. Even where there was room to pass, I decided not to. Walter was right. This was the reason we'd left early, to enjoy the countryside. And I liked to imagine what it was like, not having television or electricity or worrying too much about getting on in the world. Where when you got married, you already knew what the future was going to be like. All you had to worry about was to make sure things stayed the way they were when you started.

That's what I'd tried to tell Betty. She kept saying, how can you be satisfied with your life, sitting behind the same desk, answering phones all your life? And I tried to tell her, but I never could find the right words.

It's something I'm good at, I said. We can't all get up every morning and go to the hospital knowing we're going to save somebody's life. I'd like doing that. It'd make me feel a lot better than answering phones at the credit union. But that's not something I can do. You're luckier than me. But I do make people feel better sometimes. Other people could be more unfriendly than me, so sometimes I make a difference even if the people I'm talking to don't know it. They don't know there are other people who aren't as friendly, because all they know is they got me.

But Betty would just say I don't understand how you can keep doing it. And what I wanted to tell her and I tried—but I'm a lot better at talking over the phone sometimes than I am talking to Betty—is that if my job was the only thing I had, it *wouldn't* be enough. But the job was just the in-between time, so I could come home and we could be together. So we could make supper and go for drives and since we have electricity, watch TV and then go to bed together. That's what I think about when I'm at work, when other people might be getting bored, I just remind myself that I'm killing time before I can go home where my life really is.

But Betty had a hard time understanding that. She'd say, it doesn't make any sense, Sammy, just working at the same job until you retire. You've got to reach out. You got to do something with your life *now*. You keep waiting, it'll be gone.

And I wanted to explain to her that I didn't need to do anything with my life. I already had more than I'd ever expected. But when I tried to tell her she just shook her head and smiled and said I needed to learn how to want more. So I guess I probably should have been Amish. I think it'd be great on a Saturday, to eat lunch around a table in a toasty kitchen, right next to a wood stove, and then go hitch up the horse and then you and the kid and the wife scrunched up against each other, with the kid in the middle, and maybe you'd let him take the reins, and he'd be excited but probably wouldn't want to show it. He'd try to look serious and businesslike, but you and your wife would look at each other over his little shoulders and smile at each other, because you'd know that this was what is most important about life. And there'd be a car slowing down behind you, because the man in the car liked watching and that made you even happier, because everybody could see that you were a part of a family that had found what it was looking for.

"Hey, Sammy," Walter said, "sooner or later we're going to have to get around that buggy. We got plenty of time to get there, but not if we don't go a little faster."

"You're right, Walter. I was just enjoying being behind the buggy. But I guess we can go ahead and pass them now."

I waved when I did, but the man seemed to be concentrating on his driving, and because of the bad-weather enclosure. I couldn't really tell much about the wife and the son. Still, I was glad I waved. I wanted them to know I hadn't been bothered by their being so slow.

After we'd been driving awhile longer, I looked over at Walter. "You better sit up," I said. "I'm not sure where I'm supposed to be going."

Walter checked some notes he pulled out of his sports jacket's inside pocket.

"We turn right, just up ahead," he said. "We're almost there."

I'll have to say this for Walter. Wherever he'd read about the restaurant, he'd made a nice choice. It was up a long driveway, hidden back in the trees on the side of a hill. There was lots of room in the parking area. It was still early, even though the sky was overcast and the days were getting shorter, so it was already almost dark.

We got out of the car and Walter seemed happy. He walked over beside me and hit me jokingly on the arm. "Looks good, huh, Sammy?" he said.

"It sure does, Walter, " I answered. "It looks like the right kind of place."

Inside it was all wood everywhere and dark. The maître d' found Walter's name on the list and smiled just the right amount. Friendly, but dignified, letting us know that we might be the ones being waited on, but that not just anybody could be a waiter, much less a maître d' in a place like this. He was about our age and wore a dark suit, not a tuxedo like in a lot of places. He got our menus and motioned for us to follow him and Walter went first.

The maître d' stopped by a small table nestled up against a working fireplace. Even the fire was just right, enough to look nice but not enough to make it too warm. When we got there, the maître d' hesitated and glanced at Walter, not like he wasn't sure what to do but like there was a choice and he needed us to make it about where we wanted to sit, whether we wanted to sit side by side or across the table from each other.

It took Walter a moment to realize that's what the maître d' wanted to know, then he started to grin, but then stopped and indicated to the maître d' that he could put the menus on each side of the table, so he did and we sat down.

After the maître d' left, Walter said, "Did you see that, Sammy? He thought we were a *couple*, like we were here on a date."

"He sure did," I said.

I looked around the room. It had several different levels and a lot of plants in pots on the floor, but I could see where a few of the other diners were sitting, and most of them were couples, but we were the only table with just two men, at least that I could see. "I thought you handled it just right," I said.

"That's funny, though, isn't it. Like we were out on a date."

That's one of the things that irritated Shirley. For some reason, the last year or so, Walter had started saying things about being attracted to men, mainly I think to upset Shirley. It was a game he was playing. If anybody had ever taken him up on it, he'd probably run as fast as he could back to Shirley.

He was probably just wanting something different. But only inside his head. He probably knew that he wouldn't happy if he really did something like that. It probably just makes him forget about whatever's making him unhappy with what he's already got. But I may be reading too much into it, because I never felt that way about Betty. I knew what we had, or at least what I had. I just didn't know how to keep it.

Almost immediately our waiter was at the table, filling our water glasses and telling us his name was Eric and asking about drinks. I said water would be fine, but Walter shook his head and told Eric he knew what I needed and ordered each of us a bourbon and soda. Then Walter leaned back and sighed. "Look out the window, Sammy. You can't see that back in Wilmington."

I looked and Walter, of course, was right. Even though it was just about dark, you could look through the big picture windows that covered all one wall and see out on the Susquehanna, way down below. You could see the water shining even though the banks were almost black, and you could see some kind of water birds flying low, probably ready for their dinners, too.

Walter was right. I was glad I was here.

I had duck with orange sauce. Walter had a steak. He ordered the wine, and I enjoyed it. We talked about things that didn't seem to matter, but they really did, because I knew Walter was trying to make me feel better.

Eric the waiter stayed close by. It was still too early for most people to eat dinner, although more were coming in. Walter was probably drinking a little too much. The food hadn't had time yet to absorb all the alcohol, and he'd insisted on ordering another bottle of wine. But we were taking our time. Nobody was rushing us. It was that kind of place. And, to be honest, after awhile, the wine was tasting good. I wasn't worried too much about driving back. Maybe I should have been. I wasn't too familiar with this part of Pennsylvania. But once you start drinking, I guess your judgment's the first thing to go.

That's probably why Walter started his game-playing with Eric, becoming more friendly than the occasion called for, trying to make jokes and smiling a lot. And Eric *was* a good-looking young man and he kept being attentive and nice, but I felt sorry for him. He was just doing his job. He didn't need to have to put up with Walter. But there were more people eating, now. So Eric could excuse himself and take care of them.

So Walter and I kept talking, about the Eagles, about the Phillies next summer, things we could have opinions about without having to worry about disagreeing. But while we were talking, Walter kept looking around for Eric. I didn't really mind as long as he wasn't actually bothering Eric, and I was used to this in Walter, and I certainly didn't care about what other people did in their bedrooms, although I knew Walter was still just playing a game.

I wonder if Eric could tell that, or if he thought maybe Walter was just trying to make me jealous. I thought about Walter and me as a couple, but I couldn't, not in any real couple sense.

Then I tried to think of Walter, not like we were a couple, but as a special kind of friend, someone you could feel close to about really personal things, things you wouldn't tell anybody else. Betty had friends like that, women she could talk to in ways she couldn't talk to me. At first I got jealous. Which is kind of funny, being jealous of her women friends. But I was—almost as much as I'm jealous of Roger now. Because they got to see a side of Betty she wouldn't show me. Maybe that's because she was talking to them about us, about how she'd stopped being happy about our marriage. But she told me it was just something they did together. They talked to each other in ways men couldn't understand. And I said I'd try. But she just smiled and then talked about something else.

I looked over at Walter again and wondered if I could do that with him, if I could tell him things I couldn't tell anybody else. After all, he's probably my best friend. Nobody else called me up and worried that I wasn't getting out of the house.

So I kept looking at Walter for a moment, but it wouldn't work. There's no way I could tell Walter what I was feeling. And it wasn't just that. It wasn't just that I couldn't. I didn't really want to. It didn't make sense, but the only person I wanted to talk to about the way I felt was Betty. And she was the one that was making me feel this way in the first place. And if I could talk to her, I wouldn't even try to change her mind. I'd like to do that, but that's not going to happen, not now, but she's still the only one I want to tell about it.

But I probably wouldn't be able to find the right words, even if I had the chance. And maybe Betty would understand that, too. Because there've been times before when I needed to tell her things and I couldn't and it didn't matter, because we were both feeling the same thing. Like when we were trying to have a kid and we couldn't. I understood the way she felt because I felt it too. We had to try to get it into words, but we both understood that we couldn't. I don't think I'd ever feel that way with Walter.

"Why're you smiling, Sammy?"

I told Walter it was nothing. But that wasn't true. Thinking about how Betty and I had shared the bad times had started me remembering the good ones, too, back when we'd been happy in bed together, and how close you feel to each other, not just when you're making love, but after it's over, when you're lying in bed naked. There's nothing between you and the other person, not even the sheets. You're just there with each other, and you're talking but you don't really need any words. What you're saying is just a way of making being together last longer. And it felt natural, the way things are supposed to feel. I think you've got to feel that if you're going to try to talk about some things.

I looked at Walter, cutting into his steak, and I did feel fond of him, I had to admit that. It was good to have a friend, even though it was Walter, I thought, and smiled.

By the time we got through eating and paid the bill and got back into the Corolla, it wasn't only dark, it was raining. I was glad I was driving. I'd had more than I usually drank, but even so, I'd rather be driving on the country roads instead of Walter.

"These roads, you've got be careful," Walter said. "They might start to get icy."

At first I wanted to tell Walter he'd had too much to drink and to just be quiet and take a nap. But then I remembered what I'd been thinking back in the restaurant, about how Walter was the only person who'd called me up, so I said, "It's not cold enough for ice, Walter, it's only October."

"You'd better turn right at the driveway, Sammy. Stay off the back roads. We can get back by going through Lancaster."

"That's going the wrong direction, Walter."

"I know, Sammy," Walter said, "but we can hit Route 30, then go back down through West Chester. Those are bigger roads. We won't have to worry about buggies."

I started to say there probably wouldn't be any buggies, this time of night and in the rain, but I remembered again and so I didn't. I simply turned right instead of left and started driving toward Lancaster.

I have to admit I was feeling kind of light-headed. But it wasn't bad. It was raining, of course, and maybe it was getting colder, only not anything like Walter was talking about. Still, it was getting late and I wasn't real familiar with the roads, not out here in the country, and Walter wasn't a whole lot of help. I don't think he went to sleep, but he might as well have, for all the help he was giving me.

So I got a little lost, but not bad. And besides, we weren't in any hurry and I had plenty of gas. Like Walter had said, it wasn't like there was anybody back home, keeping the home fires burning.

So I wasn't surprised when I wound up in Lancaster from a direction I hadn't been expecting. I knew if I kept driving around enough, I'd see a sign for Route 30. Lancaster isn't all that big a city. So I wasn't worried. It was probably the street lights that got Walter's attention, because that's when he sat up straight and said, "Tell you what, Sammy, what we could use about right now is a nightcap."

"We've already had enough, Walter. We probably ought to get home."

"It's early," Walter said. The clock on the dashboard said 11:15. "It's our night out on the town. And here we are, we're in town. We got to take advantage of what we're being offered, Sammy."

I didn't say anything. I was still hoping he'd go back to sleep or maybe change his mind.

"Over there, Sammy," he said. "That looks like a nice bar."

It looked like a bar, that was true enough. It was in the middle of the block with the usual neon beer signs in the windows high up on the outside brick wall.

"You sure about this, Walter?" I said, but I'd made the mistake of already slowing down to look where he'd been pointing.

"Sure I'm sure," Walter said. "We got a long drive, Sammy. You need to take a break. And besides, there's entertainment." He pointed to a sign in a window lower down, on the other side of the bar's front door. "It says country and western music. You like to listen to that. Pull up in front there and let's go in."

Walter was right. He and Sheila used to make fun of Betty and me because we liked to go out and dance to country music. I wasn't much good on the dance floor with any kind of music. But with country music it didn't seem to make much difference. So I parked right in front of the bar's door and we got out.

"I don't think that sign goes with this bar, Walter," I said. "It looks like it belongs to the building next door."

"Sure it does," Walter said and headed for the entrance. As soon as we got inside we were hit by the smell of beer and cigarette smoke. And it was really dark. I guess most bars are dark, or at least the ones I'm used to, but this one was probably darker than it needed to be.

The front door let you in about halfway down the length of the room, and at first all I could see was a stage built into the wall off to our left, about four or five feet off the floor. That's where most of the light was coming from, even though there wasn't anybody on it. The bar itself made a sort of semicircle in front of the stage, like it was a moat protecting whatever went on behind it, the country band or singer, whatever the sign outside was advertising. By the time I'd taken all this in, Walter was already heading for one of the stools, so I followed him, and we got our choice since there wasn't anybody else sitting there.

Between the bar and the stage there was a space where the bartender fixed drinks and served the customers, except at first I couldn't see anybody back there. But once my eyes got adjusted, I could see the bartender down at the far end, leaning against the edge of the stage where it made kind of a ledge. She had one arm resting on the stage and was smoking a cigarette, waiting I guess to make sure we were going to stay.

She was staring at us like she'd be happy if we'd change our mind and go back out the front door. You couldn't blame her. You couldn't tell who might wander off the street into a bar this time of night. But she finally gave up and decided we weren't going to leave. She wasn't that old, maybe forty or so, but she moved toward us like she was tired, the flesh on her cheeks sagging down like they'd already given up the struggle. She didn't say anything, just stood there holding a dish towel in one hand and a burning cigarette in the other one.

Walter ordered a double bourbon and I said I'd just have a beer. I was going to tell her what kind, but she didn't wait for that. She turned and walked down the bar to where there was a sink and some glasses and got a bottle of beer from a refrigerator under the counter. She didn't bother looking at what brand, but I didn't care either. Then she poured Walter his bourbon and handed me the beer. She waited again, so we paid her, then she moved a few feet down the bar and leaned back against the edge of the stage.

I stared at the empty stage like I was waiting for somebody to come out on it, though I really wasn't. I was just waiting for Walter to have his drink so we could go home. I'd enjoyed our day. It'd been good to get out. But now I was ready to go home.

Walter was looking around back of us, trying to tell what else was happening. I did, too, and it took a moment or two for my eyes to adjust to the darkness in the rest of the room, but even when they did, there wasn't much to see. Just a few men sitting at tables. Everybody seemed to be with someone else, except for one man sitting in a corner, staring at a glass half filled with something. In the darkness I couldn't tell what. Walter nudged me.

"I think I'm gonna go talk to that fellow over there," he said.

"What for, Walter?" I said. "Let's just have our drink and go home. We've had a good time. But it's getting late. You're just going to get things confused."

Walter grinned kind of goofily. He'd had more than I'd had to drink. "Who knows, Sammy?" he said. "Maybe I'll make a new friend."

"The guy's probably drunk, Walter. You don't need to do this."

"Besides," Walter said, "there's going to be a band. We don't want to miss that."

I sighed and turned back around. I might as well let Walter play his little game. Nothing would come of it. That was part of the point. But he could feel he was being adventurous, doing something he knew Shirley wouldn't approve of. He'd probably tell her about it later.

So Walter got up and headed toward the other side of the room and I turned back to my beer and started staring again at the stage. My eye caught a sign for the first time, tacked just underneath the ledge, that said, "Customers are not allowed to talk to the performers." That confused me. Maybe it was because I'd been drinking, but even if I'd been sober I don't think I'd have understood why you couldn't talk to a country and western band. The performances I'd been to before, the musicians hadn't been very articulate, but they'd made an effort to be friendly.

When the bartender came over to see if I wanted another beer, I asked her. She was actually a lot friendlier than the way she'd been acting had led me to believe. It was probably because you can't be sure who's going to be walking into a bar in the middle of the night. You have to be careful.

She wiped the bar a bit with her rag and smoked her cigarette a minute and then said in a surprisingly clear and pleasant voice, "Oh, sometimes the wives hear about it and get mad, and that's bad for business. It's better to have the rule. You ready for another beer?"

That confused me, too. Not about the beer. I said yes to that, not because I really wanted one, but I looked back into the room and could see that Walter was doing his best to get into a conversation with the man, who was still just more or less staring at his glass, but Walter had a serious and committed look on his face, so I assumed he was going to be at it for awhile longer. That meant I had to drink something if I was going to stay sitting at the bar, so I said yes.

But I still didn't understand about the wives getting mad, or for that matter, what wives she was talking about, the wives of the band members or the customers or what? I knew I'd been drinking so I didn't want to get into any long conversation, but when she brought me my beer, I asked her if the wives ever came themselves to hear the band play.

She looked at me strangely. She wiped a spot on the bar, which didn't need it. "What band you talking about?" she said.

"The country and western band, the one on the sign outside the door."

She thought about that for a moment then said, "That place's been closed for more than a year. Couldn't get any business. Nobody wants to hear that kind of music." She took another swipe with her cloth. "Can't figure out why. Sounds better than the stuff we got in here." Then she went back to her place at the back of the bar and concentrated on her cigarette.

I didn't know what kind of music she was talking about. Whatever music they played here must have already been over. But that meant I wasn't going to hear a country and western band, and that was okay. The bar was warm and I wasn't worried about driving home. I'd had enough to drink so that I felt a little woozy, but it was a good sort of feeling. The weather was bad, but pretty soon we'd find Route 30. As a matter of fact, I was kind of looking forward to the drive home, just Walter and me, and he'd be a little drunk, but that'd be okay. He'd tell me about his encounter with the man at the back, and most of it would be made up, but that was okay, too. It was better than spending the evening back home in an empty house. So I took a swallow of my new beer and sat there and waited for Walter to finally give up and decide to go home.

I was drinking my beer and then for some reason, I don't know why, I was looking toward where there was a jukebox, off to the side where all the tables were almost lost in the darkness, and I hadn't noticed it before, maybe because nobody'd been playing it. Then everything was like in a dream. For a moment, I thought it had to be.

There was a halo of light surrounding the jukebox, coming from inside it and making everything close seem to glow. And in front of it, there was a beautiful naked woman.

I knew I was imagining it, but that didn't matter. It didn't matter at all, because she was so beautiful. She was facing the jukebox, looking down like she was selecting music and all I could see at first was her shape, just a silhouette surrounded by light. But then I got over my surprise, and I could see things more clearly, the softness of her skin, the way the light from the jukebox made shadows across her back, her behind, the slender curves that made me think she was probably young.

And she was standing there like some angel that had lost its way, in her halo of light as though all she had to find for salvation was the right song. Her head was bent over the jukebox's buttons, and I could see now that her hair was light and cut short, her neck really slight, and she looked terribly vulnerable, standing naked and all by herself in front of the jukebox, nobody but me even seeming to notice she was there.

It was like time completely stopped. And I hoped it wouldn't ever start again. I wanted to sit where I was, on my stool, and watch her standing there forever, just the way she was, surrounded by the light and the quietness. Because if she moved, or if I did, or if anything changed at all, I knew she'd have to disappear.

Then all of a sudden the world changed. There was a throbbing all around, some rock song, lyrics I can't, I don't even want to remember. All I remember is that she stood there a little longer and then she started to turn around and in that moment, in her starting to turn, my heart almost stopped. She was so beautiful the way I'd been seeing her, to see her any other way was almost more than I could imagine. But I didn't need to worry about being disappointed. Everything about her was already too magical, none of it could be real. But when she did turn, when I saw her face, the front of her body, it took my breath away, and I felt like I was drowning.

She wasn't totally naked. She was wearing some kind of thong that covered her in front, but the back strap was so slender it got lost between her cheeks. And once she turned, the light caught her breasts, small, young and seeming to reach out, welcoming the world, even welcoming my eyes on them, and she started toward the stage into the brighter light, and I could see her face better now, and it was what I'd hoped it would be, almost round but not quite, and innocent looking. She wasn't really young. She was a grown woman, but not old, not by any consideration, maybe in her late twenties. She walked up onto the stage and stood there listening to the music, as though she was waiting to hear something that she knew she'd be the only one able to hear, all the while looking out into the darkness, and then she looked down at me and she smiled. Then she started to dance.

I'd never been in a bar where girls danced. I'd never really wanted to be. And I knew without thinking that I'd been right. Because this one was different. This wasn't just someone dancing to entertain dirty old men. She was dancing because of the joy of it.

I stared at her almost without breathing. The music seemed to fade into the background. The sounds of the drums and the electric guitars, that was still there, but all of it became softer and seemed to surround her body, to be controlled only by her movements. If I tried to describe what they were, it'd probably sound like what you're already imagining. Only it wasn't like that. There wasn't anything vulgar about them at all. But if I tried to go into detail, you'd probably think so. There were the jerks and the bumps, all the motions you probably associate with this sort of thing. But it was different in ways I can't possibly find the words for. There was an innocence about the way she did them, as though her movements weren't for anybody else, just for herself. And what she was feeling was the joy of having a way to let things that were inside her come out.

She looked out over my head into the darkness, and there was a slight smile on her face and I looked at that for as long as I could, because there seemed to be something indecent about looking at her body, at the way it moved, at the way the light glistened off her skin. Because it wouldn't be fair looking at her that way. It would cheapen what she was doing, the way she was changing the whole barroom from a place all darkness into something bathed in light.

There wasn't even any bar smell now. The odors of beer and cigarettes were suddenly gone, and all that was left was just the empty light and the shape of her body moving through it, twisting, bending, and every now and then she'd glance down at me and she must have seen how I was feeling, because she'd smile, then she'd look up again and out into the darkness, and then she'd seem to go back into a world all inside herself. And I knew now why the sign was there, telling people not to talk to her, not because there'd be anything actually happening between the customers and her. She was way beyond that, and besides, there was the castle wall, the moat in between her and the rest of the world. But that wouldn't be enough. There needed to be the silence, with only the music, so she could stay inside her world.

And so I tried to keep paying attention just to the dance, to keep my mind on the way her body moved through the light, through the tiny space of the stage, I tried hard. But I couldn't help thinking about her, about her life, about why she had to come here, to do this, to reveal these things about herself. And I wondered, maybe she went to college in the daytime, maybe one of the community colleges around here. Her face was intelligent, the kind that went along with reading books, with thinking about things. You could tell that, just by looking. So maybe she had to work here at night so she could do those other sorts of things during the day. I knew about having to work like that. But it was different for her. She'd found a way to express things, to put her feelings into something you could see, that everybody, just looking, could understand. Most people aren't lucky enough to find that.

But then I wondered what it was like most of the time, when somebody like me wasn't there. When there wasn't anybody to watch and understand and then applaud, and I could see her in my mind, dancing her heart out in all the emptiness, with only the bartender leaning against the bar, still smoking a cigarette, and the men back in the darkness, but nobody with her here in the light, caring about what she was doing, what she was saying in the only way she knew how. So it didn't matter that after every song I was the only one applauding. At least somebody knew. Somebody was there trying to understand. Now she didn't glance down as much. She knew I was paying attention, even if nobody else was. She'd gaze out over my head, her eyes about half-closed, a little smile on her face. And she danced.

And then the music started getting louder, and she was moving faster, her little breasts trembling, her hair shaking back and forth and the sweat on her body seeming to glisten. And that's when I started clapping.

Even before it was over, before the music had really stopped.

And when it did, when she was standing there on the stage and not moving, looking lost in the light and all the emptiness, I still couldn't stop. I was making the only sounds in the room now, and she was looking down at me strangely, and I looked over toward Walter, but he was looking back at me smiling, as though he liked seeing me happy. And I knew I should stop, I should let her get on with her dancing or whatever she planned to do next. But I couldn't. Even if I tried, I knew I couldn't help myself. So I did the only thing I knew how to do, I kept right on clapping.

BILLIE TRAVALINI

To My Quaker Grandmother

All I ever wanted was to be like you,
To have a strong back and a strong mind,
And do that magic thing you always did
Whenever you looked someone straight
In the eye and knew when *not* to talk.

At thirteen I was eager to please,
Eager to see March's final snowfall gone
And cherry blossoms show up along
The Brandywine the same way they
Showed up every April, sweet-smelling
Petals blowing this way and that, reminding
Me of the sweet-smelling confetti my sister
Once made out of pink construction paper
She soaked in Evening in Paris perfume.

I didn't need Paris back then.
You told me that the Brandywine
Was the most beautiful place
In the whole wide world
And I believed you.

You also told me that silence
Can be more powerful than words,
And I believed that, too. I could see
The power of silence, not in the river,
But in the faces of the giant rocks
That held the river up and the ground down
Without asking for a thing.

"They sure are beautiful," you said.
I remember how I wanted to say something

Important, maybe something about
How George Washington might have
Seen those same rocks on his way
To the Battle of the Brandywine.
I almost said it, too, but just then
I saw a school of sunfish swim between
The rocks, and, like pure magic,
I swallowed my words just in the nick of time.

BILLIE TRAVALINI

At ten, Betsy's life was going fine until the day a Family Court judge ordered her to leave Mama Cope, her foster mother—the only parent she had known—and live with strangers: her biological parents. Before she was able to understand what it all meant she had gone from feeling safe and loved to unsafe and unloved and from middle-class Catholic to lower-class Protestant. But the heart of the memoir, *Bloodsisters*, is not the abuse she endured as the result of one bad decision made by one rushed judge. It is the power of sisterhood. It is the story of how Bootsie, a tomboy and their father's favorite, willingly gave up her favored place in the family to protect Betsy—the sister she never knew she had—from their father's demons. And, how, together, they learned to never give up hope, no matter what. This is how it begins.

Bloodsisters

Wilmington, 1960

The driver's name was Woody Hicks. He lived next door to my real mother and my real father. The garbage truck we were riding in was his. And I was going home. None of which pleased me.

"The missus sure seems nice," the driver said, trying to make small talk. I wasn't interested. He didn't know Mama Cope and I resented his sliding in some comment like he did. I pushed myself closer to the door and stroked Sissy Jupe's big, orange head. "My pretty kitty," I said, cutting him off. Sissy was sleeping in the folds of my pinafore, hiding the pink tulips that Mama Cope had embroidered into the shape of a heart. Mama Cope was my foster mother. When she put my suitcase on the seat next to the driver, she straightened my ponytail with her long, soft fingers. Then she told me to be good and promise I wouldn't be so stubborn. I did, but she knew I was hopeless so she just gathered me up in her arms and laughed.

"Just don't go gettin' yourself in any trouble," she said, pulling a hankie out of her pocket and dusting the tops of my new pink leather shoes. "I'll try to visit you real soon." Then she let go and I could see her eyes filling up with tears.

That was two years and thirty-six days ago. I was ten. And before my real parents came into the picture, I was happy. Mama Cope had raised me from the time I was two months old and we had gotten used to each other. Her husband, James, died when I was three. I don't really remember him, except that he was a quiet man and smoked fat, smelly cigars from a can.

After he died, Mama Cope did her best to bring me up right. She taught me how to garden and talk to Jesus and make cutout snowflakes from tissue paper.

Suddenly I was supposed to forget all that. Give it all up as if it were nothing more than a big balloon with the air sucked out. Gone. And all I could see I had for it was a ride in a smelly garbage truck and Mama Cope's sweet face looking after me as we pulled away. When we were almost out of sight, I saw her pick a marigold from her garden and wave it back and forth above her head. I didn't wave back. I wanted to, but I didn't. Waving was too much like saying good-bye for good. So I leaned my face to the window and watched Mama Cope fade from view like a passing road sign. Then . . . everything was gone. Mama Cope . . . the red maple tree she and I grew from a seedling . . . the metal rooster standing on the roof pecking at the wind . . . even the pale chalk lines of my last hopscotch game. I remembered how Rita Rosini and I had stood in the street, drawing. The sun beating down on our bare shoulders. As usual, I won. Rita had as much coordination as a cow. And that's the truth. But we both collected baseball cards and liked Shirley Temple movies and Nancy Drew mysteries. I would've liked her even more if she wasn't such a big bragger. I never had much use for braggers, but I sort of made an exception in Rita's case. Part of the reason was she loved baseball almost as much as I did. Before moving to Delaware she lived in the Bronx, one block from Yankee Stadium. There, she said, statuettes of ballplayers like Babe Ruth and Lou Gehrig stood at every intersection and if she opened her bedroom window she could hear the announcer's voice almost as clearly as if she were sitting behind home plate. The Yankees was my team—reliable, handsome—and I didn't even mind when Rita got some of the details mixed up and moved the stadium to Brooklyn and Lou Gerhig's statuette over to where Babe Ruth's used to be. Rita was different than most braggers. She had a soft heart. When she learned I was moving she gave me every one of her baseball cards for keeps. Even her Mickey Mantle and Roger Maris cards.

Anyway, I was thinking about all this, when what happens but I catch a glimpse of Rita in her mother's station wagon. I ducked real fast because the last thing in the world I wanted was for them to see me riding in a garbage truck. Even so, I had to fight the urge to take one more look around. I don't know why, but I had this terrible fear that I had to hold on to every last detail or one day I might start to forget who I am. And I had vowed that I would never let that happen, no matter what.

"Couldn't help noticin' your cat's blind," the driver said. He was puffing on a Lucky Strike, which hung from his lip, cowboy style. He steered with both hands, letting the ash fall onto his lap, then brushing it off every so often without taking his eyes off of the road. "Got a glass eye myself."

I didn't answer, but he was saying all the right stuff. I couldn't help being interested. I twisted sideways and rested my feet on the metal hump in the floor over the engine. Then I locked my vision on his eye. It looked real enough, though it didn't move at all. Just sat there. Like a pale blue star with its light almost gone. I kept hoping it wouldn't fall out.

"Mighty healthy-lookin' cat," he said, between puffs. I noticed that his voice was softer than his face, which was the color and texture of worn leather. But it was a nice face, and his glass eye, as smooth as a robin's egg, gave it character. Every now and then I would check his eye to make sure it was where it was supposed to be.

Sometimes, when I was checking, I almost said something. Once I was about to call him Woody, but I caught myself just in the nick of time. I didn't want to rush things. After all, I reasoned, if I let my guard down, my memory might start to go soft and I might change into somebody I didn't even know. I saw it happen on *Wagon Train* once. An Indian boy went to live with white folks and, in no time flat, he forgot all about being Indian.

Anyway, I lifted Sissy's head and smiled into his glowing gold green eyes. "Good boy," I whispered. Sissy's eyes didn't have pupils; light bounced off of them like two colored mirrors. I put Sissy's face to the window so he could see what was going on. Of course he couldn't see, but I liked pointing things out to him anyway.

"Guess you thought you had yourself a girl cat when you named him," the driver laughed.

I wasn't about to let myself get trapped into a long conversation, so I directed my words at the half-closed window: "You don't know anything," I mouthed.

We drove onto a two-lane highway. I was getting sort of bored so I unzipped the front pocket on my suitcase and slid my hand in. The pocket was deep and I had to push aside a pile of baseball cards to find what I was looking for. "There you are," I whispered, opening a small book to page two twenty-three. There, as smooth and pretty as a store-bought hankie, was the last tissue snowflake that Mama Cope made me. It was pink and had a house in the center and lots of flowers around the edges. I was about to read, but I decided against it. Instead, I put my book back and zipped the pocket closed.

The driver threw me a glance.

"What's your book called?" he asked.

"*Hard Times*," I mumbled. I could've said how the man that wrote Scrooge wrote it and how Mama Cope read it to me and how it's a hard book to read, but I didn't. I could've also said how Sissy Jupe, a smart circus girl, is in the book, and that would've cleared up his question about my cat's name. But I didn't mention that either. Instead, I slid closer to the door without saying another word.

It stayed quiet for a long while. Then the driver pulled his cigarette from his lip and his voice came back.

"Feel free to roll your window down more," he said, throwing his cigarette out. "Gets pretty hot in here."

He didn't mention the smell, so I pretended not to notice. I thought about how when somebody farts, they look around hoping they're the only one on earth who can smell it. Of course, they aren't. Even so, Mama Cope said it's good to let them think so. I reasoned the same kind of thinking applied to this situation. So I lowered my window and stretched my arm across the empty space.

"That's better, huh?" I said, and with my free hand I rested Sissy Jupe's chin on my arm.

The sun was strong and a gentle breeze lifted my newly trimmed bangs. We were in the center of a big town and it sort of looked familiar and it sort of didn't. The town had a Warner movie theater and a Woolworth's and an old train station with fancy brickwork and high windows. When we passed something interesting, I pointed Sissy's head in the right direction and explained what we were looking at.

The driver signaled to the left and we turned onto a one-way street. Along the curb, farmers, with straw hats pulled down over their eyes, sat in the back of pickup trucks, shouting: "Chickens. Come get ya fresh chickens." Up the block were the corn farmers and they were shouting, too, and so was the egg man, and the string bean man and the string bean man's wife. She was real fat and was holding up fistfuls of beans, smiling.

"Ever been to Wilmington before?" The driver's voice was a lot stronger with the cigarette gone.

I wasn't sure, but I shook my head, no, just the same.

"Well, on Friday and Saturday farmers drive up from Kent and Sussex counties," he said, "and sell just about anythin'. I don't see him today, but one fella carves fruit outta wood. People buy 'em too. Mrs. Hicks bought a few an' Boy-Boy, that's my son, lost a tooth on an apple one night."

It seemed to me that only idiots and blind people would buy fruit you can't eat. Even so, I appreciated the information, so I nodded my thanks. Then I spoke my mind: "Dumb," I said.

"Can't deny that," he laughed.

As we moved up the street a ways, the farmers were replaced by men selling ice cream from metal boxes strapped to their chests. I saw a clown, too. He had orange hair and baggy pants and giant balloons tied around one hand. I stuck my head out the window to get a better look. Suddenly I smelled something good.

"Mmmmm," the driver said. "Fresh-roasted peanuts."

As I pulled in the aroma, I studied passersby determined to find the source. "Over there on the corner," the driver said, excitedly.

My eyes nearly fell out of my head.

"Holy cow, Sissy, a real peanut man." I was staring at a six-foot burlap peanut, shouting, "Peanuts. Get ya fresh roasted peanuts."

"Must get pretty hot in that costume," the driver said, slowing down. "Think we oughta buy some and help the fellow out?"

"No thank you," I said.

The driver called the peanut man over and bought a bag, just the same. Then he cracked a few and threw the shells out the window.

"Sure you don't want any?" He waited for my reply, and then popped the peanuts in his mouth.

Slowly, the truck started moving again, then stopped unexpectedly.

"Damn women," I heard the driver say. "Can't park a car to save their lives."

I looked through the front windshield just in time to see a green Chevy jump the curb and hit a parking meter. The driver looked a lot like Sister Catherine, my third grade teacher, only she wasn't wearing nun clothes and had a frown on her face.

"She had enough space for ten cars," the driver said, moving down the street.

"Look Sissy," I said, changing the subject, "a poster. That's the circus Mama Cope was talking about."

"An awful lot of folks are goin'," the driver said. Suddenly, it occurred to me that the driver's voice sounded genuine. I was glad because people with phony-sounding voices always get on my nerves. The social worker who told me I had to live with my real mother and father and how it was all for the best had a voice like that. Her name was Miss Reinheart, or something like that, and she had the phoniest voice in the whole world. I hated it.

I turned so Sissy Jupe was facing the driver, then I said: "We love the circus, don't we Sissy?"

After a long pause, as if he was sorting out something important in his head, the driver said: "You and Mister Jupe are quite a pair, aren't ya?"

"Sissy Jupe," I corrected.

"I'm not sure Sissy Jupe'll be allowed to go to the circus, but I overheard Bill and Virginia talkin' about going. Don't quote me on that, though."

Bill and Virginia were my parents, but it sounded funny hearing them referred to by their first names. Mama Cope had always called them "your real mother and father" and Miss Reinheart would say "Mr. and Mrs. Toppin." I figured it was her way of reminding me that I had their last name and that was supposed to mean something. Of course, it didn't.

When the light changed, the driver pulled over to the curb and got out. I watched him walk over to the poster and catch his thumbnail under the staples and pop them out one by one. Then he tucked the poster under his arm and got back in his truck.

"Thought you might like to have this," he said.

"Thank you." I might have said more but I was too shocked and impressed to keep a record of it. I never saw anyone take something in plain sight like that, snatch it as casually as if he were picking an apple off his own tree, as if he had every right in the world to it. It raised my opinion of him, considerably.

When he handed me the poster I did another quick check of his eye, without him spotting me. I felt a little guilty, knowing how hard he was trying to be nice and all. Besides Mama Cope said people with glass eyes and missing legs don't like you staring at them. And I knew she was right, it's mean to stare. So I gave him a little smile and lowered my head.

Anyway, that's when I noticed, for the first time, the leather belt he

had wrapped around his waist. The belt was as thin as a lasso and spun
through his belt loops two or three times, until only a foot or so was
tied off in front like a double-laced boot. All of a sudden it occurred
to me that the driver was a poor person. Since he lived next door to
my parents, I wondered if they were poor too, and, if they were, did
they wrap their belts and a drive smelly garbage truck.

"Do Bill and Virginia have a car?" I blurted out. Mama Cope had a
thing against children calling elders by their first name, but I had a
feeling the driver was different. He hesitated a moment, then said: "A
Ford wagon. It broke down or they would've come an' got you themselves."

"I wish they'd disappear," I thought, standing the poster on one leg.
"King the Lion, Brooks International Circus, Thursday through Saturday Only," I read out loud.

"Might be nice to show Carole and Bootsie," the driver said.
"Maybe you can all go."

I kept my eyes on the poster. The truth is I couldn't have moved if
I had wanted to. My insides froze up. I had forgotten all about having
sisters. Mama Cope had told me about them, but I didn't know them
any better than I knew my real parents. Which is saying I didn't know
them. I only met all four of them once. Miss Reinheart made the ar-
rangements shortly after Mama Cope petitioned the court to adopt
me. Mama Cope said being I was ten, it was time we made things legal
between us. The words hit my ear sweetly, like the words of a sweet
song. B-E-T-S-Y C-O-P-E, I said, trying out my new name. I reasoned that if I had Mama Cope's last name, I would be her daughter
for keeps. Then my real mother and father couldn't show up and ruin
things.

It was a sound plan but it backfired like an old shotgun with a bad
load. Just when I was accepting my new sense of permanence, I
learned that being adopted was hard work. Mama Cope explained how
we had to go to family court in person so a judge could decide if she
could keep me. I told her straight out that I had a bad feeling about
the whole thing. It seemed to me that talking to a judge would only
complicate things. After all, I reasoned, he didn't know a single thing
about us that he hadn't heard secondhand. Mama Cope said my faith
was sagging and things would work out. I decided to take her word for
it because I wanted to believe she was right. Besides, I knew I wouldn't
have a moment's peace if I believed otherwise.

Anyway, that May a judge finally found the time to see us. We all
met in a big courtroom. The room had a high ceiling and a marble

floor the color of cooked shrimp. The judge's bench was the same color only it had a lot of dark veins in it like the tops of old people's hands. The judge was fat-faced and had Miss Reinheart's eyes. He sat behind all that marble like an old king on a throne. I grabbed a piece of Mama Cope's dress and didn't let go. Every so often she would give my arm a little pat to calm my jitters. It worked, too. Once the judge starting talking, things proceeded pretty quickly. I tried real hard to keep on track. And I did right up until Miss Reinheart and the judge starting throwing around a lot of big, legal-sounding words I didn't understand.

I used those occasions to look over my real mother and father. It felt strange, like staring at strangers at the supermarket and thinking you might know them and you might not. My father had an old face and wide shoulders and, except for a tattoo of a rose just above his right elbow, he was plain looking. What was left of his hair was brown. He didn't have my nose, my chin, my lips, nothing. Anyway, he noticed my gaze and returned it with a dime-store smile. The smile was stiff and looked forced and made his cheeks and lips lift up unnaturally. His eyes were as black as crow's eyes and stuck in my mind. I looked up at Mama Cope but she was busy trying to figure out what Miss Reinheart and the judge were getting at. I felt Mama Cope's dress balled up in my hand and my fingers squeeze into a fist. I was reminding myself to hold onto my faith, like Mama Cope told me to, when I heard Miss Reinheart say: "Your Honor, Mr. Toppin is now gainfully employed and I have a doctor's report confirming Mrs. Toppin has regained her health; therefore, it is the position of Children's Services that the natural parents be given full permanent custody of their daughter."

Slowly I turned and looked at my mother. She was a short, slim woman and wore a white dress with tiny red roses on it. Her hair was a pretty auburn color and shiny. I studied her for quite awhile before she returned the attention. When she did, she looked at me with pale eyes that were soft and sad looking. Then she glanced over her shoulder at Carole and Bootsie and slowly turned her eyes back on me before pointing them at the judge. Carole and Bootsie were skinny and had my father's plain looks. I could tell by their bored expressions that they didn't want to be there any more than I did.

When the judge and Miss Reinheart were done, my father spoke. Seems he was willing to give me up, but my mother said: "Blood is blood. Can't change that by turning our daughter over to some stranger to be raised."

I heard my mother tell the old, fat-faced judge those exact words. Then I saw the judge nod his head as if what she was saying made perfectly good sense. "In the best interest of the child," the judge concluded, "effective today, June 1, 1960, I am granting the natural parents, William Henry and Virginia Toppin, permanent custody of Billie Elizabeth Toppin, also known as Betsy Toppin. I further order that all contact with the foster mother, Rebecca Cope, immediately terminated." When he was done, I saw Miss Reinheart's skinny lips part in a smile and Mama Cope crying. My father was smiling, too, a real big smile that came out through his eyes.

Slowly the scene faded and, in the back of my head, Mama Cope was standing by her flower garden, waving.

My eyes started watering. The driver was looking straight ahead, but I knew he was watching me with his good eye. The way he kept cocking his head to the side gave him away. But he had sense enough to keep quiet and I was grateful for that. I stoked Sissy Jupe a few times to settle myself. I wasn't much for crying. Mama Cope said it had to do with me being stubborn. I saw Mama Cope cry twice: when the fat-faced judge gave his ruling and when Woody Hicks showed up in his garbage truck. They were the two worst days of my life.

"Almost there," the driver said.

We were on a four-lane highway. There was a Goodyear Tire store and a Texaco gas station on one side and a Gulf station and some houses with tall hedges on the other. When the houses ended, there was a big empty field and, in the distance, on the top of a high hill, I could see a large brick building.

"Veterans Hospital," the driver offered. "When it snows, the kids go sledding there."

It was a good hill for sledding, all right. But, I didn't plan to stick around long enough to see snow. We drove a little ways more, and then turned off the highway onto a side street. The street was marked by a steel pole with a rusted street sign at the top that read, "Brighten Avenue." An old house with a bakery sign on the lawn sat behind the pole. The bakery didn't have a big window for displaying creampuffs and cakes and lemon meringue pies like "Nappi's." Nappi's was my favorite bakery and when I was good Mama Cope took me there and let me pick out anything I wanted. I always picked a creampuff.

Brighten Avenue was long and skinny and had a drainage ditch dug down one side of it. The driver was riding the brake, as if he was expecting some sort of danger ahead. I eyed the street closely. It was full of potholes and, in between the potholes, there were lots of little stones with pieces of glass and dirt mixed in.

"You ever need anythin', anythin' at all, you come an' see me," I heard the driver say.

On both sides of the street narrow houses were bunched together in rows like seats in a movie theater. The houses all looked the same, white with high front steps and porches. On the porches, sitting in wooden rockers, or leaning on stair railings, I saw plain-looking women talking to tired-looking men. Children, wearing T-shirts and no shoes were jumping rope, laughing. Suddenly I realized this was what Mama Cope was talking about when she said: "Everybody doesn't live the way we do, people have their own way of doing things."

Anyway the more I saw, the more nervous I got. Then from out of nowhere a big, white house came into view. The house was made of stucco and had a large yard and a horseshoe-shaped driveway edged with all sorts of colorful flowers.

"Look snapdragons," I said, pointing Sissy's face at the window.

"That's the Benson's house," the driver said. "Got two girls. Sarah and Jean Ann. Their daddy works for the State; he does all right for himself."

I thought about quizzing him about Sarah and Jean Ann's ages, but I decided against it. Instead, I mumbled something dumb, and followed it up by asking if we were still in Delaware.

"Didn't even leave New Castle County," the driver replied. "Just looks different 'cause you're used to livin' in the country. This *was* country but the city keeps creepin' up on us."

His words made me think about Mama Cope's house. First, I saw the whole thing. The lace curtains. The rooster sitting on the roof pecking at the wind. The brass doorknocker shaped like a pineapple. The garden. Then I saw Mama Cope waving that picked marigold. It seems I couldn't get that picture out of my head no matter what.

"Not me," I said, firmly, "I can leave anytime I want." It was a lie, but I knew that Mama Cope wanted me back. It was just that the truth didn't make much sense any more, so I had to tell myself a few lies to straighten out everything in my head.

"Well, Betsy," the driver said, calling me by my name. "I hope you won't leave before you give everybody a chance to get to know you."

I lowered my eyes, without answering. "My pretty kitty," I said, stroking Sissy Jupe's head.

Suddenly I felt the truck jerk forward and come to a full stop. I

looked up. On the driver's side of the street was a big empty lot with
some junk cars on one side of it.

"We're here," the driver said, pointing at the end house. It was the
ugliest house on the whole street. The paint was peeling and giant,
ugly weeds had taken over the front yard. Sitting alongside the curb
was an old red Ford with one wheel missing and white letters on the
side that read, "William H. Toppin Home Improvement Co. Inc."

"Looky there," the driver said, turning sideways to see out my window. "Everyone's on the porch waitin' for ya. The tall one's my missus
and that's my son, Boy-Boy next to her." He took a long look, and
then added, "Welcome Home."

I told him I already had a home.

The driver opened his mouth to speak but no words came out. I
followed his eyes out the window and found myself staring point-
blank at my father. He was standing on the porch and his crowlike
eyes were locked on mine. I swallowed hard and studied the rest of his
face. He was still wearing a dimestore smile and I tried to work up a
smile of my own but I couldn't. Every time I went to part my lips, they
stuck to my teeth and my eyes dropped in a squint. I wanted Mama
Cope. I wanted her to tell me that everything was going to be fine,
although I knew by the look on my father's face, it wasn't. Even so, I
longed to hear the sound of her voice. I would've given away every
one of my baseball cards if I could've heard Mama Cope speak right
then. But the only voice I heard was the driver's.

"Remember, you ever need anythin'; you come see me," he said,
pleasantly. I knew he was trying to cheer me up but it didn't work.
Seeing my father again took the wind right out of me.

Standing behind my father was Mrs. Hicks. She was as big as a man
and wore her hair in a tiny bun at the nape of her neck and gold, wire-
rimmed glasses. She reminded me of the Amish women in Dover, who
sell homemade jelly and pies at the Farmers Market, only she didn't
wear a white doily on her head.

When I was done with her I swept my eyes over the whole bunch
of them. I noticed that they were dressed poor and stood with their
heads lowered a bit like once a year churchgoers. The sight of them
made my stomach drop. Mama Cope said it's no sin being poor but I
wondered how I was supposed to act now that I was one of them, being
I lacked experience in such matters. From the looks on their faces, I
assumed being poor was awful and made people frown. Their frowns
were nervous, the kind people wear to the dentist. After a moment,

cautious smiles came onto their faces and got mixed in with their frowns. My mother waved at me and the rest of them did the same.

"Time to get out," the driver said, gently.

"Nooooo," I replied, dragging the word out. I was looking at my father. His smile was bigger than any of the others. Even so, I had a strong feeling that he didn't like me. I don't know why, but I did.

"Hold onto Mister Jupe," the driver said in the same gentle voice. "It's a big step down."

"His name's Sissy," I said, pressing Sissy Jupe against my chest. Then I pushed open the heavy truck door and half-slid and half-stepped down to the street.

"I want to go home," I said over and over in my head. I said it until by brain got tired and I saw my mother walking toward me with a sad, childlike smile on her face. She was wearing the white dress with the roses on it and high-heeled shoes. When she was just a foot or two away, her eyes dropped and she paused a moment, the way Mama Cope did when she put my suitcase on the seat next to the driver. Suddenly a sense of panic came over me. I felt tears, hot, heavy ones, trying hard to get out, but I didn't let them. I wrapped my arms around Sissy Jupe and followed my mother to the porch and slowly went inside.

ANTHONY VARALLO

In The Age of Automobiles

Cody was surprised to see Mr. Turner getting into a Toyota Tercel. He would have imagined Mr. Turner driving something more like his mother's car, a Pontiac Bonneville, or maybe even a Town Car. But of course Mr. Turner couldn't afford a Town Car on a teacher's salary. Mr. Turner wore polyester blend dress shirts, and had a habit of taking large swallows of coffee from a Colonial Williamsburg coffee mug, a souvenir from last year's disastrous field trip. That was the day Cody had been sent home for fighting, but hadn't even thrown a punch. He'd cried in front of the entire seventh grade, a humiliation he couldn't afford to think about if he wanted to get home before his mother's shift at the supermarket ended at four-thirty.

Mr. Turner had already started the engine when Cody put his hand to the passenger window and knocked. A loose beard of snow fell from the window. "Mr. Turner?"

Mr. Turner rolled the window down. "Well, hello Cody," he said. He was wearing the fake fur that students called the Beaver Cap behind his back. "Didn't see you there for a second, then voila, there you were."

"Sorry," Cody said.

"Everything okay?"

"Uh-huh."

"Did you miss your bus?"

Cody hadn't missed his bus. He'd stayed late for band practice, then got off the activities bus when Jason Kiefer and Mike Mott threw his snow boots out the window. "Yeah," Cody said. "I guess maybe I need a ride. I'm real sorry about asking. I really am."

"Don't be," Mr. Turner said. "Hop on in."

"I'm really sorry," Cody said. Again. When would he stop saying sorry so much?

"It'll warm up in here in a minute," Mr. Turner said. Inside, the car smelled faintly fusty, like a library book. A tape deck was plugged into the cigarette lighter. The defroster made widening, half-moons of clear glass across the front windshield. "You can put that in the back seat if you want," Mr. Turner said, pointing to Cody's clarinet case.

"That's okay," Cody said. "I can just keep it at my feet."

"Is that an oboe?"

"Clarinet."

"Ah," Mr. Turner said. He was wearing his new oversized glasses, the ones that had accidentally removed all skill in caricaturing him. " 'The clarinet, the clarinet, goes doodle-doodle-doodle-det!' "

"Yeah," Cody said.

"Don't ask me how I remember that," Mr. Turner said.

They pulled out of the parking lot, where Cody could see the snow beginning to adhere to the highway. The sight of snow always pleased him, since he felt in some way responsible for it, although he knew he really wasn't. It was amazing, all the dumb things he thought he might be responsible for.

"Everyone keeps telling me I'll get used to this cold weather eventually," Mr. Turner said, "but—" he reached across the wheel to pull the turn signal. A car even smaller than Mr. Turner's turned past them, an enormous Christmas tree stuffed into its hatchback. A yellow tag hung from the tree's sappy stump. Although Christmas was less than a week away, Cody's mother still hadn't gotten a tree. He would have to remind her of that.

"Who's driving who, right?" Mr. Turner said.

"Yeah." Cody tried to laugh, but nothing came out. The defroster had worked its way to the top of the window. The noise of it offered comfort, the way his vaporizer did. That was a secret Cody was glad no one knew: he still slept with a vaporizer.

"I don't miss the lightning, though," Mr. Turner said. "That's one thing I can say about this weather: at least there's no lightning." Mr. Turner was from Florida. "No hurricanes either." It was embarrassing the way Mr. Turner wore leather sandals in the springtime, the way he cheered for incorrect sports teams like the Miami Dolphins, the way he pronounced lawyer as "law-yer" instead of "loi-yer," the way everyone else did. A part of any respectable Mr. Turner impression included grabbing your crotch, saying, "Who would *layk* a Floorida *oor*ange?!"

"—but this is as far north as I could ever live. I've got a brother back in Tampa, says he could never imagine living north of the Carolinas, but I always say to him, you know, they get snow there too. Some-times. Not all the time, but sometimes."

Cody nodded. He tried to think of something to say about Florida, but the truth was he'd only been there once, when he was five. His memory was of a crowded beach where his bucket was dragged to sea, a strange solitary cactus that grew in his grandparents' stony lawn, and an alligator farm where his grandfather had encouraged him to throw a fistful of feed from a fenced-in footbridge. The feed had dispersed in the air, like chimney ashes, and landed on an alligator's back, who neglected to lick it away. This depressed Cody.

"—but I've got a good little car." Mr. Turner was telling Cody about driving the car from Florida to Delaware, all in one shot. Twenty-one hours.

"Wow," Cody said.

"I tell you, by the end I was seeing phantom deer, if you know what I mean." Cody didn't know. "I know what you mean," he said.

They took a right onto Naaman's Road. The snow had picked up and Mr. Turner had to use his wipers. The movement of the wipers helped to cover the silence that had sprung up between them. Again. It was horrible, trying to think of things to say. Cody wondered how adults always managed to think of things to say. Whenever his father took him to the movies, he'd tell the ticket girl, "We'll make do with two for what's new."

"I'm glad, actually, that we ran into each other today," Mr. Turner said. "I've been meaning to get back to you about your research paper."

Cody felt his face grow warm. "Sorry," he said. "I'm real sorry about that."

"No need," Mr. Turner said, then sneezed. Cody wasn't sure whether to say bless you or not. "Have you given any thought to our agreement?"

Cody nodded. "I'm real sorry about that," he said. "I'll get it to you after the break." The paper had been about the moon, a topic of Cody's own choosing, but he'd forgotten about it until the night be-fore it was due. The only reference books he could come up with were the paperback dictionary his mother kept in her sewing table, and his father's old 1961 encyclopedia set, still smelling like aftershave, with its short, but rapturous entry about the possibility of a manned moon landing. Cody had lifted most of his paper from the text—it was fun, figuring out how to reword things—using the dictionary for long, un-necessary definitions of words like *crater*, *atmosphere*, *gravity*, and *gal-*

axy. His mother typed the paper up on her old Royal typewriter while the two of them watched *Dallas*.

"That would be terrific," Mr. Turner said. Outside, cars were slowing to a stop. Cody watched a white station wagon pull up alongside them. "I'd be glad to read your revision." A woman sat behind the wheel. Cody stared, but the woman didn't notice him. "I'd be glad to read anything you might like to write," Mr. Turner was saying. "You've got quite a flair for words."

"Thanks," Cody said. The woman reminded him of something he hadn't thought about until now: the year before, Mr. Turner had been engaged, but his fiancée had broken it off. It wasn't even a secret, really, except that Mr. Turner never said anything about it. Cody remembered the one time the fiancée had come to school, sitting at the back of the classroom reading a magazine while Mr. Turner lectured about the Marshall Plan. The fiancée was pretty, clearly ten years younger than Mr. Turner, with a habit of tapping her pen across the edge of the page, then laughing when she read something amusing. "Does anyone have any questions?" Mr. Turner had asked, and the fiancée had raised her hand. "Does everyone know that Lawrence and I are engaged?" she said. Cody had joined the others in a low, sustained oooooh until Mr. Turner said, "Gentlemen, *please*, let's give it a rest." But it was too much to think about. Lawrence!

"Plus a vivid imagination," Mr. Turner said.

Cody nodded. Students made jokes about Mr. Turner, lousy puns about being turned down, turned away. Nothing too mean by school standards. Pretty mild stuff. That was the thing, Cody thought, you couldn't really like Mr. Turner, but you couldn't really hate him either. He was the kind of teacher your parents forgot to mention after parent-teacher night. He didn't have Mr. Olsen's good looks or Ms. Trent's affability and sly English accent. Students saw his picture in the yearbook and didn't even think of cutting it out and gluing it to a bobblehead doll, a ritual reserved for Mr. Thomlinson and Principal Wallace. No one thought anything of Mr. Turner, really, not even the time last spring when he paused in the middle of his lecture and said, "Don't you think I know that everyone in this classroom is smarter than me?" His voice had sounded on the edge of tears. A U of sweat showed through his shirt. "Don't you think I know that?" Looking back, Cody realized, that must have been around the time his engagement had ended. Students did impressions anyway. "Don't you think I'm aware of that?" someone would say, then everyone else would break out laughing.

The traffic began to move again. Across the windshield, snow landed and was wiped away over and over again. Cody watched, wondering if his mother would leave work early because of the weather. Sometimes her boss, Mr. Jackson, let her out early when the roads got slick. She'd show up at three-thirty with bags of day-old bread and overripe fruit, right in the middle of Cody's after-school snack, cinnamon toast with double butter. Cody thought it was awful when she came in, spilling bruised plums onto the kitchen linoleum and telling him to wake her for dinner; she was going to take a nap. He was embarrassed to see her winter coat, twenty years out of style, with its fake fur hood and humiliating trim, still torn from the time she'd caught it in the car door. It would be a disaster if she was home by the time Mr. Turner dropped him off. What if she was on the front porch, where she sometimes let the newspapers collect for days? What if she greeted Mr. Turner in her Phillies sweatpants?

"Is that your bus?" Mr. Turner said. Cody could see the bus ahead of them, stopped at a traffic light. He felt as if someone had casually handed him a two-ton refrigerator.

"I dunno," he said.

"I think that's the activities bus," Mr. Turner said. "But I can't read the insignia."

Cody could see the bus driver, Captain Leroy, shouting through a rolled-up *Sports Illustrated*. *You're toast, Hitchens!* he'd say when Cody lingered at the door's edge. *Toast!*

"Too short," Cody said.

Mr. Turner pulled closer. "Bluebird," he said. "I think ours are Bluebirds, aren't they?"

Cody saw the back of Mike Mott's head, the cowlick no one had ever thought to mock, not once, not ever. Mott's teeth wore the most awful chain of braces Cody had ever seen; these, too, were granted acceptance, as was Mott's sometime stutter, and habit of saying "templature" for "temperature."

"I dunno," Cody said.

"I'm pretty sure," Mr. Turner said. By now Mr. Turner had pulled so close that Cody could see Jason Kiefer propped against his Eagles coat, its green and white logo pressed against the window. Jason had thrown the coat over Cody's head while Mott unlaced his snow boots. Its lining smelled like old butter.

"Wouldn't mind having that kind of traction," Mr. Turner said. "Those tires." Cody reached for his clarinet case. If he had to, he could run. Sure, it would be awkward, explaining it later to Mr.

Turner—there was no getting around that—but at least he would have the Christmas holiday to divide him from his actions. He'd play his new video games, watch football, slice the gift fruitcakes and smother them with grape jelly.

"But I could live without the manual steering."

But what about the few days left before the holiday? Those would be excruciating, Mr. Turner greeting him in homeroom with a phony smile, not wanting to make him feel embarrassed. Perhaps pretending like nothing at all had happened, the worst. Perhaps asking, after everyone else had left for recess, how things are at home.

"And the noise," Mr. Turner laughed. "Right?"

They had pulled so close it seemed to Cody they were under the bus. The bus's bumper wore a ledge of dirty snow. "Right," Cody said. The bus pulled forward, then stopped with a rocking motion. Cody felt the Tercel lurch forward. "What's the prob, buddy?" Mr. Turner said, but the problem was clear: they were now inches from the bus's rear, where Jason Kiefer and Mike Mott's faces could now be seen, laughing. Soon their faces were haloed by other faces and fingers were pointing at Cody and Mr. Turner and Mr. Turner's sad brown car.

"It *is* one of ours," Mr. Turner said.

Cody had looked away the moment Jason's eyes met his, but now he chanced another glance, and saw Mott licking the window.

"Oh, boys," Mr. Turner sighed.

Jason's face, which always looked as if had just registered horrible news, contorted itself into a pained kiss—an idea the other boys quickly cribbed, puckering their lips and hugging themselves like zealous lovers.

"Comedians," Mr. Turner said.

Mott pressed his hands and face to the glass, puffing his cheeks. This distorted his usual towheaded expression, but Cody felt he could still read its single, urgent question: should I imitate fellatio or not? Mott's imitation was pretty good, what with the way he closed his eyes and made mmm-mmm sounds the way everyone knew adults did, but part of its power was its infrequent use, judiciously saved for ripe moments like the time Cody accidentally wore his mother's tennis socks, and the time a bus of cheerleaders waved hello.

"Real jokesters," Mr. Turner said, but Cody detected a whiff of unease. The semester before, someone had nailed Mr. Turner's roll book to a drafting table.

"Yeah," Cody said. He wished he could laugh whenever and throw back his head after hearing a dirty joke, saying, Good one. But he couldn't. He was the other kind of person. He felt himself beginning to cry.

"I'll tell you something," Mr. Turner said. "Sometimes I think about all the things you kids are going through, the teasing and peer pressure, and I want to stop classes for a week and talk. Put it in the open, you know?" Mr. Turner looked over at him. "What would you think about that?"

Cody nodded, but he was already practicing his anticrying exercise, envisioning a series of double-hung numbers collapsing into themselves, one through ten, like the ones his clock radio wore. He had failed to summon them the day at Colonial Williamsburg.

"It's something," Mr. Turner said, "I've given a lot of thought to." As the bus was pulling away, his eyes met Mott's; Mott's eyes conveyed his satisfaction in these unprecedented events, shaping them into legend. He would, his smile informed him, never let Cody forget. To give the legend its necessary conclusion, Mott raised both middle fingers and pretend-humped the emergency exit door.

"—thought about it so often my friends say they're sick of hearing about it," Mr. Turner was saying. "'Just do it,' they say. It'll be tough, but the most important things always are. The things most worth doing—"

The problem was getting from 10 back to 1. If Cody imagined the 0 falling away, this left the 1 on the wrong side of things, requiring the 0 to acrobatically jump the 1 so that the numbers might ascend from 01 on.

"—the next light, or should I cut through this shopping center? Cody? You okay?"

Cody gripped the clarinet case to his chest. "Sorry," he said, but the sound of his own voice only made things worse. He began to cry. He couldn't stop. When Mr. Turner pulled into the shopping center, he took a deep breath and dried his eyes with his palms.

"I was fat," Mr. Turner was saying. "Did you know *I* was a fat kid?"

Cody, twirling a French fry in ketchup, said no, he didn't know that.

"Honestly—do you want me to tell you something honestly?—I was a fat teenager *and* a fat twentysomething, too." Mr. Turner made his eyes wide.

They'd stopped at Howard Johnson's the moment Cody told Mr.

Turner he could walk home from the shopping center. It wasn't far; he'd walked it a hundred times. But not in this weather, Mr. Turner had said. He wouldn't think of it. After a snack, Mr. Turner would drop Cody off at the front door. He'd even go inside, explain things to Cody's mother, if that was what Cody wanted. If not, fine, he would just drop Cody off in the driveway. He wanted Cody to know that whatever he chose would be fine with him. That was an important thing to know, he said.

"Do you know what it's like being the only fat kid in a family of four boys? *Four.*" Mr. Turner held up four fingers. "One All-State track three years in a row, one the local high dive record holder, one model good-looking with a voice like Neil Diamond, and one, well," Mr. Turner raised his hands in an Oh, well gesture, "one kid so flabby and pale and lonely he fell asleep on the beach one day and woke up in the hospital. The *hospital.*" Mr. Turner waited until Cody had registered the necessary look of surprise. "Nearly died," Mr. Turner whispered.

"Wow," Cody said.

"Exactly."

A plate of salad greens sat between them, untouched. A fly toured a lone yellow raisin.

"You see? That's what I remember about growing up. Feeling humiliated. Feeling alone. Feeling like I was somehow not allowed into everyone else's happiness. That's a state crime, by the way, in Florida. Not feeling tan and happy." His look informed Cody that this was a kind of joke.

Cody attempted a laugh. "Not feeling tan," he said.

"In grade school they called me Lardwrence. 'Lardwrence, how did you get to be so fat?' or 'Hey, Lardwrence, what's shakin—besides you?' Go ahead, laugh. Some of it seems funny, doesn't it?"

Cody shook his head.

"Well, you better believe I laughed it off. What else could I do?" Mr. Turner forked a lettuce leaf without bringing it to his lips. "I imagine you know that."

Cody tugged at his coat sleeve. "I dunno." Suddenly, he felt stupid; stupid to let the incident get to him; stupid to ask Mr. Turner for a ride in the first place; stupid to cry in front of his teacher; stupid to accept Mr. Turner's offer of a quick meal.

"That's something we have in common, isn't it?"

Cody nodded, a gesture he felt was required of him.

"I've seen the way they tease you." Mr. Turner took a bite of lettuce. "I've seen it for a long time now."

Cody shrugged. "It's not so bad."

"No, Cody." Mr. Turner shook his head. "Do you know what you
just had?"

Before Cody could answer, Mr. Turner said, " A Junk Thought. Do
you know what a Junk Thought is? It's all those thoughts in your head
that keep telling you things are okay when things are definitely not
okay. Accepting things the way they are is hard. Really hard. But
worth it, Cody, so, so *worth it*." He gave Cody a look above the rims
of his glasses. "Trust me. It took me a long, long time to figure this
out. My life was a series of Junk Thoughts. It was like I woke up in the
morning feeling lousy about myself, spent most of the day feeling
worse, went to bed feeling even worse than when I started. Just like
they say; it's a cycle. Right? It's like—" Mr. Turner described a circle
in the air. "You know? Like, 'Help! I'm trapped! Who can help me?
I'm all alone!'"

"Right."

"Well, you're *not* all alone," Mr. Turner said, as if Cody had been
arguing this. "No one is. That's something Justine helped me to see.
Justine helped me to come to terms with my Junk Thoughts." Mr.
Turner nodded. "That's something I'll always owe her."

"That was nice," Cody said.

Mr. Turner went on as if he hadn't heard. "Do you know that Justine was the first woman I was ever seriously involved with? I mean
seriously. I never even went to my senior prom. I never really even
went on a date until my senior year of college. That's the truth. Do
you know how old I was the first time I even kissed a girl?"

"Well—"

"Twenty-*two!*" Mr. Turner said. "Twenty-two years old and kissing
a girl for the first time." Mr. Turner clicked his tongue. "Tough to
think about."

The waitress brought the bill, which Mr. Turner tucked beneath his
placemat. "In college I was always hitting the library when most guys
were in fraternities, partying it up, having a social life I could only
dream about as I sat in the reading room and wished I was anywhere
else." He shook his head, ruefully. "Justine couldn't believe it. She was
the complete opposite, of course. Studious, but fun."

Cody understood that it was his job to nod.

"Oh, she knew how to have fun."

Outside, the snow had stopped, but it looked deeper than Cody had expected. If it snowed tonight, maybe he wouldn't have school tomorrow. A blizzard and he might not have to return until after the holiday.

"People say, 'Sorry to hear about you and Justine,' or 'Sorry to hear things didn't work out,' and I always say 'Why? There's nothing sorry about it.' Am I sorry we're not together? Well, yes, I admit that. I'd be lying if I said otherwise. But the fact is, Justine was the greatest thing that ever happened to me. Ever. And there's no way I can look back at that kind of experience as—" he held his hands apart, "as, as anything to be sorry for." When Cody chanced a look, he saw that Mr. Turner had his eyes closed.

"Do you know why I'll get over Justine?" he heard Mr. Turner whisper.

Cody didn't say anything.

"Because I've got *self-respect.*" Mr. Turner brought his hands to his face and made tiny whimpering noises. "That's what I've got."

Cody imagined Mr. Turner telling his mother about missing the bus, and the taunting, and Justine. He imagined him saying he loved her. It was the idea of Mr. Turner sitting at their kitchen table, whose fourth leg sometimes fell off for no reason whatsoever, that made Cody realize he had to do something. He had to make a choice. But it wasn't until Mr. Turner announced he'd left his wallet in the Tercel that a decision revealed something of itself to Cody. Mr. Turner said, "I'll be back in a second," and stood up. "You hold the fort, okay?" Mr. Turner donned his furry hat and pushed through the heavy glass doors to the parking lot.

A burst of cold air came in. Cody waited a moment, then walked toward the side door to the hotel parking lot. It was the lot he cut across coming home from Happy Harry's, his pockets stuffed with trading cards. Once outside, his eyes focused on a stand of pine trees, whose snowy boughs hid the entrance to a dirt path that led to his neighborhood. The sight of virgin snow pleased Cody, as did the view the path afforded him: the front lot, Mr. Turner riffling through the Tercel, searching for his wallet. For a moment Cody wondered if he should call out. Should he? Should he let Mr. Turner know he was heading home? Should he say thanks for the ride? Didn't he owe that to Mr. Turner? He couldn't decide. And that was the thing: even as Cody entered his neighborhood, even as he shook snow from the heels of his boots, even as he opened his front door, he felt like he was still deciding.

JEANNE MURRAY WALKER

Betting in Bright Sunlight at Delaware Park

—for Rick Smyth

He leans against the fence where he can see
long shots parade before him to the track:
Calamity, Jay's Boy, Timbuktu.
Grabbing a pen, he figures on his pass.
Numbers spin like women in his head
and while he handicaps, the crowd grows still.

The sun flips like a coin up in the still
white sky while he adjusts his eyes to see
what he'll recoup this race. Glare splits his head.
She left like moonlight gone. He can't keep track
of why or what it means. He lets that pass.
At least he doesn't have to bet for two.

Until the fanfare shakes out flags at two
he figures: Even odds that she will still
come back. Satisfied to wait and see,
he ambles off to watch the new field pass.
One moons at him like a young cousin, head
as dark as rumor in the paddock. The track

is fast. Her name is Come Back. He keeps track
of her sweet swerve with one good eye and runs to
lay his paycheck on her gorgeous head.
Lord, he needs something finally to stand still.
He'd like to close the track tonight, to pass
home to a wife as true as Middle C.

We bet the way we have to bet, The sea
of nags rolls off and he begins to track
her on the flat, the curves, He sees her pass
the roan, the chestnut mare, until she's off to
Jesus, kneecaps flying to heaven, still
true, still on track. The jock gives her her head.

Rags shaken in the wind, her mane. Her head
eats light, drinks furlongs. He can't even see
the blur until the photo. There she's still.
And first. And his. He rises beyond the track,
beyond his hands, his rings, his blue tattoo,
his shoes. The crowd divides to let him pass.

He floats above us like wash still blown ahead
of its own sleeves. We see him pace the track
to her bare arms, bare hands, sweet back.

JEANNE MURRAY WALKER

Driving North to the Headwater

All day, the radio blares news
of twelve people who lost their lives on a showboat
overturned by a tornado in Ames, Iowa
while I start north to find you, my dark
headwater, my father. After twenty dry years
would you ask how it was? Would you be waiting
at the end as you must have waited
at the beginning? I will tell you.
Not to remember why I started
was the most blank forgetting of all.
While the white lane markers
sutured Delaware to New Jersey, New Jersey
to New York. I watched for signs
and grew thirsty. The highway played its hand
of green aces from Philadelphia
one after another, to Saratoga Springs.
Coming into Schenectady, I drove
through a wide band of country music
which somewhere further north began to fade,
the voices growing invisible as ghosts.
Rusty harvesters stood beside barns
which collapsed into waiting fields.
How was it? I will tell you.
I traveled all day without stopping,
without food, without water
for fear the car would not start again.
I kept my distance from the Kozy Kamper
full of children I could see
for a hundred miles in the rear view mirror,
its tire promptly buttoned onto its bumper.

Beside me trucks snarled up the mountains
corseted with rock, while I looked for you.
The roads grew narrower
until I turned down a lane beside an old lake
with reeds whiskering the shore,
trees up to their knuckles in sweet water.
When the needle on the gas gauge
registered EMPTY I thought:
Now come. Or don't come.
I am driving down the final lane and
daylight is shutting down. The only sign
reads NIGHTCRAWLERS FOR SALE. Finally I can see
nothing but the muscles of my arms, stiff
on the steering wheel, curving like yours
used to curve. Ahead I can feel
the bridge falling
asleep over the river, the fields
pulling up their covers to the road.
I can hear the lock lock lock
of the wipers which my hand has turned on,
the clouds finally having begun to give rain.

LARA M. ZEISES

Me and the Bean

We ran into the Stringbean at Denny's, of all places. The one next to the roller rink on Route 273. It had been two, three years since I'd seen him last, though I'd hear stories about him from time to time. Chelsea Donovan told me he'd had a threesome with Kelly Simons and Stacy Hartnett at a pool party Stacy hosted the summer after his graduation. About nine months after that, Eddie Royer called to tell me the Stringbean had been arrested pushing pot to twelve-year-olds behind the playground at George Reed. The last I'd heard he was scrubbing dishes at an old folks' home, preparing for a surgery that would remove a weak lung damaged by too much dope.

Me and the Stringbean dated once, a high school fling thing birthed out of a mutual loneliness we tried to kill with pilfered booze and raw, backseat sex. He had a real name, of course, but I always thought of him as the Stringbean on account of his pale body, stretched long and thin. Despite this—despite the toothpick arms and bony legs and sharp ribs that bruised my middle with every thrust—I loved the guy. Loved the way the ends of his white-blond hair always stuck up from his scalp at odd angles, and how his enormous star sapphire eyes—the only spots of color that appeared on his whole self—how those eyes ate my face every time he looked at me. In those eyes I could almost pretend I was a pretty girl.

So. Denny's. It was going on two a.m., and me and Sam and Jessie had just wrapped up Girls' Night at the Bowlerama. I needed caffeine, Sam needed to pee, and Jessie needed a Moons Over My Hammy. Sam saw him first. She let out a low, "Oh god," grabbed my shirtsleeve and said, "Let's go somewhere else." I was all ready to be annoyed with her but then I saw him. My Stringbean. Sitting around one of those small round tables with that evil munchkin Justin Benson and their dealer, Chris Hicks. My mind kept spinning the *ohmigods*. Jessie said, "No. No no *no*. Not *again*." She turned as if to leave, but I had the car keys and therefore the luxury of pretending not to hear her.

"Hey, you," I said, swooping in for a quick kiss to the Stringbean's cheek. Out of the corner of my eye I saw Justin Benson make a face. What a retard. The Stringbean swiveled in his seat, slowly. He looked terrible. He was skinnier than ever, if that was possible, and he had an oozy sore on the corner of his mouth. Plus his skin had taken on the nasty gray hue of someone who's used too long. I thought, *My sweet boy, what have you done to yourself?*

Some more facts: The Stringbean forgot to tell me he loved me until after I broke up with him, and even then, I wasn't sure he was being so sincere. I think that's what did us in. It was never really the drugs. I didn't touch them, but I didn't mind them so much. What I minded was the emptiness that crawled into the Stringbean's eyes. How they stopped being hungry for me, even when we were doing it. He used to keep them open, especially when we were kissing. But at the end, they were always shut tight, like he was battling a demon in the darkness behind his lids. I guess I started wondering if that demon was me. He tried to tell me different, but those were just words.

The Stringbean rose, threw his lanky arms around my back. He smelled like stale smoke, but at least it was the tobacco kind. How could he smoke with only one lung? He squealed, "Yo, Jules—what up, girlie?" but before I could tell him my "what up" he was kissing me, tongue and all, right in the middle of the Denny's. I could hear Sam and Jessie groaning in the background. I could hear Justin Benson snickering and Chris Hicks blowing dirty-boy whistles through his coffee-stained teeth, too, but I didn't care. I didn't even mind the oozy lip sore, that's how dumb the Stringbean made me.

There was this one time, when I was a sophomore and the String-bean a senior, he convinced me to skip out on my geometry mid-term—skipping out on a midterm! Me!—and we hopped into his mom's Subaru station wagon (circa 1984, with genuine wood paneling and everything) and drove to the beach. He'd said he needed to go—not just wanted, but *needed*—and my stomach got all tingly, because who knew he could be such a romantic?

Two hours later, when we hit the outskirts of Rehoboth and my midterm had already ended, I realized why he "needed" to go. He pulled into a trailer park, stopped outside a double-wide, lemon yellow model that actually had a screen porch, and told me to stay put, that he'd be back in a few. I couldn't believe it. He was gone maybe fifteen, twenty minutes, and in that stretch my anger grew from a baby seed-ling into a prize-winning pumpkin. By the time he finally emerged, I was *this close* to taking the car and leaving him behind.

"Hey, beautiful," he said, after slipping behind the wheel and stashing a suspiciously shaped brown paper bag in the glove compartment. "Where do you want to go now?"

"Home," I said through gritted teeth.

"Home? But we just got here."

"Home," I repeated, waiting for a fight—waiting for him to ask me why I was so angry, or at least explain why he thought a drug run was a good enough excuse to make me flunk a test worth 25 percent of my final grade. Instead, he simply shrugged and did as requested. We made it back before dinner.

The Denny's was pretty full, but there was a handful of empty chairs at the table next to the Stringbean's. After our lengthy embrace he motioned to them and said we should pull up some seats. But Sam had already disappeared to the bathroom, and Jessie just stood there, hip jutted out, arms folded crossed across her chest, glaring at me.

"C'mon," I said. "Let's sit down, we'll a grab a bite, no biggie."

"I need to talk to you," she said. "Now."

Chris Hicks made an *ooh* sound and said, "Some*one*'s in trouble!" My face flushed hot but I knew if I didn't go talk to her we'd have an even bigger scene right at the table. So I let Jessie pull me into the ladies' room, where Sam was washing her hands all OCD like Lady Macbeth.

"What are you doing?" Jessie hissed.

"Yeah," Sam chimed in. She turned off the faucet and said, "We should just go."

I said, "But I don't want to go."

"Of course not," Jessie said. "Which is exactly why you *should.*"

"Oh my Christ," I said, rolling my eyes. "How old are we again?"

Jessie stamped her foot like a little girl. "This is ridiculous! I'm not going through this again. We'll stay, but I don't want to hear that lowlife's name ever again, you got me? This is your choice and it is your problem. Period." With that, she punched the door open and stormed back into the restaurant. Sam just shrugged and followed her back out, leaving me standing there alone.

And even though I knew Jessie was playing the drama queen, and Sam her supporting flunky, I couldn't blame them. Once I'd decided to end it with the Stringbean it took me almost a year to emotionally detox fully, and even then I'd still have fantasies about running into him somewhere and us starting up again. Kind of like this, actually, only before.

I looked in the streaked mirror that hung crookedly over a yellow-stained sink. Earlier that evening I'd thrown my long brown hair into a low ponytail, but the broken bits around my face had escaped and frizzed into a fuzzy frame. I had two fresh zit scars on my chin, and a recent sinus infection left the bridge of my nose swollen and two bluish banana-shaped bruises underneath my eyes. Even worse, there was a small chili stain on my T-shirt, near the right boob, from our dinner earlier at the Dog House. Beautiful, my ass. I looked like a junkie coming off a six-day binge. Then again, maybe he found that sort of thing appealing.

I splashed a little water across my forehead and blotted with a paper towel, trying to get rid of the oily sheen my skin accumulated over the course of the day. Then I pinched my cheeks, hard, to give them color, and shaking slightly I headed back out.

Immediately I saw that Sam and Jessie had rebuffed the Stringbean's invitation and were sitting at the adjacent table instead. Jess had pulled out an empty chair next to her and when she saw me, she patted it cattily. I shook my head and made a beeline for the Bean.

"Here," he said. "You can sit on my lap." Before I could protest he'd reached an arm out and snaked me to him. I couldn't help but giggle, and I tried to block out the sound of Jessie's disapproving snorts. Justin Benson hailed the waitress—for my benefit, I thought— but it turned out he only wanted the check. I managed to ask for a cup of coffee before she ran off again, and felt much relief when Chris Hicks pushed his chair away and said that he and Justin were "outtie."

"You coming with?" he asked the Stringbean, who shook his head no. "Didn't think so."

"You can give me a ride later, can't you Jules?"

"Sure," I said. I'd counted on it.

Then it was sort of stupid, Sam and Jessie sitting at a separate table, but I knew if I'd asked them to move that Jessie would've started in on me again. So I let them stay there and whisper terrible things about me while I turned into my fifteen-year-old self again, high on the wild buzz of making time with a past love. I ordered a Grand Slam and the Stringbean asked for the same, even though he'd already had one before I'd arrived. When the food came we ate quickly, me still in his lap, the Stringbean nuzzling my neck between bites, and I guess there was talking too but I don't remember much of what was said.

Pretty soon Jessie was all, "Can we go now? Some of us have actual jobs and need to work tomorrow." She slapped a twenty on their table and stormed outside, not even bothering to get change, and Sam tailed her. The Stringbean pulled out a twenty of his own and said it was his treat, and I nodded even though I didn't know where that money came from, whether it was plate-washing money or profit from his lucrative junior high drug ring. Then we all piled into my car, Sam and Jessie in the back, the Stringbean on shotgun, his fragile spidery hand groping for my knee whenever I wasn't shifting gears.

Sam opted to get out at Jessie's place—I'm sure, in part, so they could spend more time talking about what a loser I was and how they'd failed in their efforts to reform me. Then Jess tapped on my window; I rolled it down and she said, "For god's sake, promise me you won't go to France," which was our high school euphemism for sex, obscure enough that anyone who wasn't me, Sam, or Jessie wouldn't have a clue as to what we were talking about. I told her it had been a long time since I'd traveled and I couldn't promise her anything, but that I'd be sure to fly safely and would call her in the morning. Disgusted, she turned on her heel and walked away without even saying goodbye.

"What was that all about?" the Stringbean asked.

"Nothing. So where to?"

He grinned. "Wherever you want to take me, beautiful."

"Stop that," I said, turning away from him. "I look like hell and you know it."

The Stringbean sighed. "I would've thought you'd learn how to take a compliment by now."

I turned back to face him and said, "I can too take a compliment—when it's warranted, that is."

He shook his head. "Whatever."

It irritated me, his tone, but I wasn't sure why I had to make such a big deal out of some harmless sweet talk. It's not like everything had to mean something.

"So are we going somewhere or what?" Could I be any bitchier?

He shrugged. "It's kind of late—maybe I should just head home."

"Oh."

So then it was just me and him, parked outside of his parents' white clapboard house on Tiverton, where he still lived, if you can believe it. He took a deep breath and said, "God, Jules, you even smell the same." I wanted to ask him what exactly I smelled like, but I thought it might piss him off again, so I didn't.

We talked in nostalgic terms of Top 40 songs and themed "socials" held in our high school's cafeteria. He reminded me of the first time we slow danced, how I tried to match his height by climbing onto a plastic chair. And how he swooped me up off that chair into his skeletal arms, swirling me around until I was dizzy enough to puke.

I wondered if were going to do it, or at least make out some more, but the Stringbean had stopped trying to fondle me even before we got to his house. There was a light on over the driveway and in its dim glow I searched his eyes, tried to see if some of the old hunger was there, but it was either too dark to see, or I was too afraid to look hard enough.

He coughed then, a deep, wet cough that made me want to gag. It was an old-people cough, and afterward the Stringbean wiped a string of phlegm from his mouth and onto his jeans. Then, as if nothing had even happened, he pulled a pack of cigarettes from his shirt pocket, tapped them on his leg, and took one out.

"You're not going to smoke that?" I asked, suddenly alarmed.

"I was going to," he said. "Why? Is this a nonsmoking car?"

"Yeah," I said, because I didn't have the balls to say what I really wanted to, and I didn't have the stomach to watch him kill himself anymore.

"What if I roll down the window?"

"Please—no."

He sighed. "Okay. So Jules—what are you up to these days? You haven't said."

"Oh, you know—school, work, the usual."

"Didn't you graduate yet?"

"Uh, yeah," I said. "But I'm in college now."

"Right, right," he said. "College."

"What about you?" I asked, already knowing the answer.

"The same," he said. "The usual."

A heavy silence filled the car, making me feel claustrophobic. This wasn't what I had imagined. I'd pictured him stroking my hair, telling me I was every bit as beautiful as he remembered. I pictured him cupping my face in his hands, kissing me, soft at first but then maybe harder, pulling me to him like he would die if I didn't make love to him right that second. I pictured me gently pushing him away, saying no, we can't, it wouldn't be right, and him telling me that it would always be right between us, that after all this time he had never loved anyone as much as he'd loved me.

Instead, he was slumped down in the seat and closed his eyes, like he was too tired to even look at me. Tentatively, I reached a hand up and smoothed some hair by his ear, and he smiled like a puppy being petted but that was about it. I turned on the radio and pressed #6 on the pre-set, knowing that the Saturday-night love songs would be

playing and hoping they'd inspire the Stringbean to want to take a trip
to France with me after all.

Then this great Marvin Gaye song came on and I contemplated the
merits of trying to use it as some cheesy pick-up line, like, "You know,
I'm in need of a little sexual healing myself." But it seemed too overt,
too *desperate*. So I kept my mouth shut until the Stringbean opened his
to speak:

"Hey, Jules—why'd we break up again?"

The words startled me. "You know," I said. He had to know—I'd
given him a big speech about it at the time, all about how it felt like
we were going through the motions, that I didn't feel like he really
wanted to be with me anymore, that I was tired of faking it and maybe
we should quit while we were ahead. I was half-bluffing; I'd expected
him to argue with me, tell me I was wrong and show me how much he
really did want to be exactly where he was. Instead, he nodded like he
understood and said, "Whatever." Two weeks later was when he told
me he loved me, but we'd been at a party and I figured it was just
horniness. It wasn't until that summer, when the scab had already
healed and I was in an antiboy phase, that he sent me a two-page letter
telling me how sorry he was that he always acted like I didn't mean
anything. "You meant everything," he wrote, "but I understand why
you never want to see me again. I wouldn't want to see me either."

It was the kind of letter that, had I received it even two months
prior, would've sent me straight back into his arms. But the timing was
wrong; I stuffed the letter in a box and forgot about it for awhile, and
by the time I remembered we'd already drifted too far apart.

"I forget," he said. "Was it because I hooked up with that redhead
at your birthday party?"

"What? No. What redhead?"

"You know, that girl you used to hang out with all the time. What
was her name? Spe . . . Seagull?"

"Speigel," I said. "Jessica Speigel."

"Right," he said. "Spiegel."

"Are you kidding me? She was just *here*. In the car."

"What? Oh, shit. Yeah. Yeah, I guess she was. How about that?"

How about that.

"God, we were so drunk that night. She gave me a hummer in the
downstairs bathroom and then barfed, right on my johnson and everything. She never told you?"

"No," I said. "I never knew."

"Oh. Man, I'm sorry."

"It's okay. Ancient history, right?"

So many things were beginning to make sense. Jessie's hatred, for one. The Stringbean's deadness, for another. And me—what to make of me? I wished I hadn't seen him tonight. Some things were better left in the past.

He asked, "So if that wasn't it, then what happened?"

"Nothing happened," I snapped. "It's what *stopped* happening."

"I don't get it."

"You never did."

"Huh?" the Stringbean said, clearly confused. "What are you trying to say?"

"Nothing. Never mind. Look, I should get going. It's late and I—"

"—need to get going," he finished for me. "Sure. I get it. Just— before you go? Tell me: what's the one thing you remember most about me?"

My head was cloudy; it was like my memories had been poured into a blender with a cup of fantasy and a strong dose of reality, mixed until I no longer knew what was true and what I'd made up on my own.

"C'mon," he said. "You must remember something."

I could've lied—could've been mean and said something about how he was always getting high, how I knew he'd never go anywhere in life, how even back then I knew there'd be better men who'd break my heart. But I couldn't do it. So I said, "You were the first boy to tell me I was beautiful." He grinned when I said this, and I hated the grin almost as much as I'd craved it. Before I could stop myself I added, "You were probably lying, but still." And then his grin faded and I wish I hadn't said that second part. What's the use in hurting someone who's already broken?

So then I asked him, "What about you? What's the one thing you remember most about me?" His fingers reached out again for the hair grazing my right shoulder, and he rubbed a few strands between his thumb and his pointer finger. "Well?" I pressed. "You made me do it. So what's the thing?"

He raised his head so that his big sad eyeballs bore holes into my own, and he unlatched the door, swinging it wide with a rusty creak. Finally he said, "You always looked at me like I was a liar." It was the second-to-last thing I ever heard him say, the thing that haunts me even more than his gray skin and dilated pupils.

"Like a liar," he said again. "That, and the fact that you were damned beautiful."

Contributors

JULIANNA BAGGOTT grew up in Newark, Delaware, where she lived until recently. She is the author of four novels for adults, including *Which Brings Me to You* (2007) coauthored with Steve Almond, as well as three books of poems, including *Lizzie Borden in Love* (2006). She also writes novels for younger readers under the pen name N. E. Bode—namely, *The Anybodies Trilogy* (HarperTrophy, 2004–2006). Her work has appeared in the *Best American Poetry* series, *TriQuarterly*, and *Ms Magazine*, and has been read on National Public Radio's Talk of the Nation. N. E. Bode is a recurring essayist on XM Radio. Baggott teaches in Florida State University's creative writing program and lives in Tallahassee with her husband and four children.

JOANN BALINGIT grew up in Lakeland, Florida. She has lived in Morocco, Portugal, and western Kentucky. Her poems have appeared in *Salt Hill*, *Smartish Pace*, the anthology *DIAGRAM.2* (Washington, DC: 2006), and elsewhere. Her awards include an Individual Artist Fellowship from the Delaware Division of the Arts. She teaches poetry at The Wellness Community in Wilmington, Delaware, and lives with her family in Newark.

LINDA BLASKEY's work has appeared in *Literary Mama, Terrains, Milford Chronicle, Beltway Poetry Quarterly, The Broadkill Review*, in the Biggs Museum's anthology *Art and Poetry*, and in a privately printed chapbook, *The Poet Laureate Presents: Eight Delaware Poets*. She has work forthcoming in *The Farmer's Daughter* and *A Cadence of Hooves*. A short story was recently presented at the Adrienne Theater in Philadelphia by InterAct Theatre's Writing Aloud program. She was a recipient of an Individual Artist Fellowship from the Delaware Division of the Arts. Her manuscript, "Leaving Arkansas," was a finalist in the 2006 Dogfish Head Poetry Prize competition. She lives in Lincoln, Delaware.

FLEDA BROWN was poet laureate of Delaware from 2001–7. Her sixth collection of poetry, *Reunion*, won the Felix Pollak Prize and was published in 2007. She is the author of five previous collections: *The Women Who Loved Elvis All Their Lives* (2004), *Breathing In, Breathing Out*, winner of the Philip Levine Prize (2002); *The Devil's Child* (1999); *Do Not Peel the Birches* (1993); and *Fishing With Blood*, (1988), winner of the Great Lakes Colleges New Writer's Award. Her poems have appeared in *Poetry, Kenyon Review, Southern Poetry Review, American Poetry Review, The Georgia Review*, and many other journals and anthologies. She has published a number of essays in journals such as *Image, Prairie Schooner, Shenandoah*, and *The Journal*. She has written on teaching poetry and on the craft of writing, and she is coeditor with Dennis Jackson of *Critical Essays on D. H. Lawrence* (1988). She taught at the University of Delaware for twenty-seven years, where she directed the Poets in the Schools program. She is now on the faculty of the Rainier Writing Workshop, a low-residency MFA program at Pacific Lutheran University in Tacoma, Washington. She lives in Traverse City, Michigan, with her husband, Jerry Beasley.

WILLIAM CLAIRE was founding editor and publisher of *Voyages*, a national literary magazine, which won five national awards for excellence. He has edited three books: *Alan Swallow: Publishing In the West* (1974), *Selected Essays of Mark Van Doren, 1924–1972* (1980), and *The Physician as Writer* (1984). He has also won National Endowment for the Arts awards, a Yaddo Fellowship, and a Rockefeller Foundation Fellowship for Residency in Bellagio, Italy. He has published poems and essays in more than fifty national publications, including *The Antioch Review* and the *American Scholar*.

ANNE AGNES COLWELL, a poet and fiction writer, is associate professor of English at the University of Delaware. Her work has appeared in numerous journals, including *California Quarterly, Mudlark, Evansville Review, Phoebe, Eclectic Literary Forum, Southern Poetry Review, Stickman Review, Poetry Bay*, and *Octavo*. An online chapbook of her poems appears in *The Alsop Review*. Her first book of poems, *Believing Their Shadows*, has been a finalist for the University of Wisconsin's Brittingham Prize, the Anhinga Prize, New Issues Poetry Prize, and the *Quarterly Review of Literature*. Her critical book, *Inscrutable Houses: Metaphors of the Body in the Poems of Elizabeth Bishop*, was published in 1997. She lives in Milton, Delaware, with her husband, James Keegan, and son, Thomas.

TOM COYNE is the author of *A Gentleman's Game* (2002), named one of the best twenty-five sports books of all time by *The Philadelphia*

Daily News. He cowrote the screen adaptation and worked as a copro-
ducer on the firm version starring Gary Sinise. The movie was nominated for an ESPY award as best sports movie in 2002. His second
book, *Paper Tiger: An Obsessed Golfer's Quest to Play with the Pros* (2002),
was an editor's pick in *Esquire Magazine* and *USA Today.* He is a con-
tributor to *Golf Magazine.* A 1993 graduate of Archmere Academy, he
earned his MFA in 1999, and won the William Mitchell Award for
"Distinguished achievement in the Notre Dame Graduate Creative
Writing Program." He currently lives in Philadelphia where he
teaches creative writing at St. Joseph's University.

DEBORAH CREASY was recently awarded a Mid-Atlantic Arts Foundation Creative Fellowship to the Virginia Center for the Creative Arts.
Her poems have appeared in *Tar River Poetry, The Broadkill Review,
raccoon,* and *Delaware Beach Life,* and are forthcoming in an anthology,
Six Delaware Poets (2007). Her poems were included in the "Poetry in
Public Places" traveling exhibit in Sussex County in 2004. She has
been a bookseller and event coordinator in independent bookstores
for more than ten years. She lives in Ocean View, Delaware.

ROBERT HAMBLING DAVIS's fiction has appeared in *Antietam Review,
The Sun, The University of Alabama Review, Phoenix, Homestead Review,*
and elsewhere. He has won two Individual Artist fellowships from the
Delaware Division of the Arts, most recently for an excerpt from his
novel-in-progress, *High Invisibility,* which was a semifinalist in the
William Faulkner Creative Writing Contest. His short story, "Death
of a Deer," originally published in *American Writing,* was nominated
for a 1999 Pushcart Prize and featured in the debut issue of americans-
tories.org. A Delaware native, he lives on his family's farm in Newark,
Delaware, and teaches yoga at Hockessin Athletic Club.

ED DEE, after twenty years with the New York Police Department,
earned an MFA in Creative Writing from Arizona State University.
His first novel, *14 Peck Slip* (1994), was a *New York Times* Notable
Book of the Year. *Bronx Angel* (1995); *Little Boy Blue* (1997); *Nightbird*
(1999); and *The Con Man's Daughter* (2003) followed. He lives in
Lewes, Delaware, with his wife, Nancy, a native of Rehoboth Beach.

MARISA DE LOS SANTOS holds a PhD in Literature in Creative Writing
from the University of Houston. She has published poems in many
literary magazines, and her poetry collection *From the Bones Out* was

published in 2000. Her first novel, *Love Walked In,* was published in January 2006. Foreign rights have sold in fourteen countries, and the novel was optioned by Paramount, with Michael London attached to produce and Sarah Jessica Parker attached to coproduce and star. Marisa lives with her husband and two children in Wilmington, Delaware, where she is working on her second novel.

LIZ DOLAN's poems, memoir, and short stories have appeared in *Delaware Beach Life, Delmarva Quarterly, New Delta Review, Prism International Quarterly, The Cortland Review, Rattle, Mudlark,* and *National Bridge,* among others. She has won a fellowship and grants from the Delaware Division of the Arts, and received a Pushcart Prize nomination in fiction in 2005. Her work in *Mudlark* was chosen for The Best of the Web by Web Del Sol. Recently, she was accepted as an associate artist in residence with Sharon Olds at the Atlantic Center of the Arts and was appointed a poetry board member for *Philadelphia Stories.* She lives in Rehoboth Beach, Delaware.

MARIBETH FISCHER is the author of *The Language of Good-Bye* (2001), which won the 2002 Virginia Commonwealth University Award for Best First Novel, and *The Life You Longed For* (2007). Her essays have appeared in *The Yale Review, The Iowa Review, The Pushcart Anthology XXI,* and *Best American Essays 1995.* Her essay, "Stillborn," won a Pushcart Prize. Her essay, "Lottery," won the Smart Family Award for Best Essay, and was named a Notable Essay in *Best American Essays 1997.* As lecturer and as founder of the Rehoboth Beach Writers' Guild, in 2004 she organized "Writers At The Beach: Pure Sea Glass," an annual conference dedicated to raising money for charity. She lives in Rehoboth Beach, Delaware.

ALLISON FUNK grew up in Wilmington, Delaware. She has published three books of poems: *The Knot Garden* (2002); *Living at the Epicenter* (1995); and *Forms of Conversion* (1986). She has received a fellowship from the National Endowment for the Arts and prizes from *Poetry* and the Poetry Society of America. Her work has been included in *The Best American Poetry, The Paris Review, Poetry, Shenandoah, Image,* and other journals and anthologies. She is now Professor of English at Southern Illinois University Edwardsville, where she is also an editor of *Sou'wester Magazine.*

DANA GARRETT's poems have appeared in numerous magazines, journals, and anthologies, most recently in *The Homestead Review, North-*

east Corridor, American Writing, ACM, and *Grrr: An Anthology of Poems about Bears.* He has won Individual Artist fellowships from the Delaware Division of the Arts and has graduate degrees in English and philosophy. He lives in Stanton, Delaware.

VANESSA HALEY has received grants from the Virginia Commission of the Arts, the Delaware Arts Council, and the Astraca Foundation. She was a resident at the Virginia Center for the Creative Arts and the first recipient of the John Haines Award for Poetry in 2001 from *Ice-Floe: International Poetry of the Far North.* Her poems have appeared in numerous journals and anthologies, including *Poetry, The Gettysburg Review, Karamu, The Alaska Quarterly Review, The Hampden-Sydney Poetry Review, Reading Poems: An Anthology of Poetry,* and *Poetry from Sojourner: A Feminist Anthology.* Her collection of poems, *The Logic of Wings,* a finalist for the Lyre Prize, was published in 2004. After a fifteen-year academic career, she returned to Wilmington, Delaware, to practice psychotherapy.

GARY HANNA received the Emerging Artist Fellowship from the Delaware Division of the Arts in 2003. He won the Brodie Herndom Memorial Prize from the Poetry Society of Virginia in 2002 and the Walter W. Winchell Poetry Contest sponsored by the *Connecticut River Review* in 2005. His poems have appeared *in Inkwell, The Common Ground Review, Hawaii Pacific Review, Mid-America Poetry Review, California Quarterly, South Dakota Review,* and many other journals. He is the director of the Poetry at the Beach reading series in southern Delaware.

WENDY INGERSOLL is a piano teacher, a devoted grandmother of four, a member of the Westminster Presbyterian Church's Reverberations Handbell Choir, and a skier, hiker, and traveler. She grew up in Hockessin, Delaware, and now lives outside Newark. Her chapbook, *River, Farm,* about Maryland's Eastern Shore, was published in 2005. Her poems have appeared in *Worcester Review, The Lyric, ByLine, Potpourri, Delmarva Quarterly,* and *Diner,* among other journals, as well as in *PoetsCanvas.org* and *Passagers* online. Her work won first place in the 2007 Rehoboth Beach Writers' Guild Writers at the Beach poetry contest.

McKAY JENKINS is a former staff writer for the *Atlanta Constitution,* and has written for *Outside, Orton,* and other publications. He is the author of four books: *Bloody Falls of the Coppermine: Madness, Murder and the Collision of Cultures in the Artic, 1913* (2005); *The Last Ridge: The Epic Story of the U.S. Army's 10th Mountain Division and the Assault on Hitler's Europe* (2003); *The White Death: Tragedy and Heroism in an Avalanche Zone* (2000); *The South in Black and White: Race, Sex, and Literature in the 1940s* (1999); and is editor of *The Peter Matthiessen Reader* (1999). He is the Cornelius Tilghman Professor of English and a member of the program in journalism at the University of Delaware.

JAMES KEEGAN teaches English at the University of Delaware Academic Center in Georgetown, Delaware. His chapbook of poems, *Of Fathers and Sons* (2003), received the 2003 Dogfish Head Poetry Prize, and his work has appeared in *Southern Poetry Review*, *Poet Lore*, and *Shenandoah*. Keegan is also a professional actor and is currently entering his fifth season as a member of the Resident Troupe at the Blackfriars Playhouse of the American Shakespeare Center in Staunton, Virginia, where he has played many roles, including Iago in *Othello*; Banquo in *Macbeth*; the Ghost, the Player King, and the Gravedigger in *Hamlet*; Dromio of Syracuse in *Comedy of Errors*; and Stephano in *The Tempest*. He lives in Milton, Delaware, with his wife, Anne Colwell, who is also an educator, poet, and novelist, and his son Thomas, who is also an actor and a 2007 graduate of the University of Delaware.

AMANDA KIMBALL has taught poetry at the Ferris School in Wilmington and at Camp Imagine, a division of the Newark Arts Alliance. Her awards include a Merit Scholarship through the *Arts & Letters* journal at Georgia State College and University, and a 2004 Honorable Mention in poetry from the Delaware Division of the Arts. Her poetry has most recently appeared in *The Spoon River Poetry Review* 28: 2 (Summer/Fall 2003): 75.

E. JEAN LANYON was honored in 2001 by the governor and legislature for serving as poet laureate of Delaware from 1979 to 2001. An artist and poet, she has been published in numerous magazines and journals. *The Myrno Bird*, a picture storybook, won the First State Writers' Prize (1970) and was followed by four chapbooks of poetry, including *People Garden* (1976), which was partially funded by a grant from the National Endowment for the Arts, and *The Rose Bush*, a picture storybook (2003). She has won Individual Artist fellowships in painting and poetry from the Delaware Division of the Arts.

EMILY LLOYD is a freelancer by day and a librarian at Delaware Tech's Georgetown campus by night. Her chapbook of poems, *The Most Daring of Transplants* (2004), won the Dogfish Head Poetry Competition. Originally from Washington, D.C., she lives with her partner in Milford, Delaware.

ALEXANDER LONG's first two books of poems are *Vigil* (2006) and *Noise* (2007). With Christopher Buckley, he is coeditor of *A Condition of the Spirit: The Life & Work of Larry Levis* (2004). His work has appeared in, or is forthcoming from, *The Southern Review, Pleiades, Blackbird, Quarterly West, The Prose Poem: An International Journal, Third Coast, 5 A. M., The Cream City Review*, and elsewhere. He holds a PhD in English from the University of Delaware.

BONNIE MACDOUGAL received her undergraduate degree from Bryn Mawr College, magna cum laude with Honors in English literature, and her law degree from the University of Pennsylvania. She is the author of four novels about lawyers and the law: *Breach of Trust* (1996); *Angle of Impact* (1998); *Out Of Order* (1999); and *Common Pleas* (2002). Her novels have been translated into eight foreign languages and are sold around the world. A specialist in complex commercial litigation, she is one of the few lawyers ever to practice with Bill Clinton. She has a long familiarity with the state of Delaware, having spent grueling weeks in Wilmington courtrooms, and glorious weeks in Rehoboth Beach. *Out Of Order* is set in Delaware and reflects extensive research into the legal, political, and social circles of the state. She lives with her husband and daughters in Chester County, Pennsylvania.

H. A. MAXSON is the author of a novel, *The Younger* (1999), and has published four collections of poems: *Turning the Wood* (1976); *Walker in the Storm* (1980); *The Curley Poems* (1994); and *Hook* (2001). He has also published *On the Sonnets of Robert Frost* (1997), and is coauthor, with Claudia Young, of seven works of historical fiction for young readers, including *Zwaanendael: Valley of the Swans* (2000). He holds a PhD in creative writing from the Center for Writers, University of Southern Mississippi. His poems, stories, and articles have appeared widely in magazines and anthologies. He is a founding member of the annual John Milton Memorial Celebration of Poets and Poetry in Milton, Delaware, and of the online magazine *Delaware Poetry Review*.

JANE MCCAFFERTY grew up in Wilmington, Delaware. She is the author of three books of fiction: *Director of the World and Other Stories*

(1992), which won the Drue Heinz Prize from University of Pittsburgh Press; *One Heart*, a novel (2000); and *Thank You For The Music* (2004), a second collection of stories. She has been awarded a Pushcart Prize and a National Endowment for the Arts Fellowship, and her work has been included in *Best American Short Stories* (2004). She credits her professors at the University of Delaware for teaching her most of what she knows about writing. She received an MFA from the University of Pittsburgh in 1989. Currently she is associate professor of English at Carnegie Mellon University.

FRANETTA MCMILLIAN has been active in the Delaware literary community for the past twenty years. She has served on the board of *Dreamstreets*, a literary magazine based in Newark, Delaware. Her zine *Etidorhpa* was featured in the *2001 Zine Yearbook* (2002), and her *Confession of Nathan Cross* (2004) was honored in the 2004 edition of *Best Zine Ever* (2005). Her CD of spoken word and music, *Reveries of the Solitary Walker*, was featured in the August 4, 2005, issue of *The News Journal*, Wilmington, Delaware. Her most recent chapbook is entitled *Down Low* (2006).

DEVON MILLER-DUGGAN holds an MA from the Writing Seminars at The Johns Hopkins University and a PhD in literature from the University of Delaware. She teaches a variety of interdisciplinary courses for the University of Delaware's Honors Program, where she is also the Distinguished Scholars Mentor. She serves as the head of the Flower Guild at St. Thomas's Episcopal Church in Newark, Delaware.

DOUGLAS MOREA was born and raised in New York City, beside the tracks of the No. 7 IRT Flushing Line. Long since a Delaware resident, his poems have appeared in numerous publications, including *The New Yorker* and *Mickle Street Review*.

TRACY STEVEN PEALE, SR., began writing poetry under the tutelage of poet and author Julianna Baggott. His poem "Letter To A Laureate (of the Americas) From One Of The Young Poets" appeared in *New Delta Review* 20:2 (Spring/Summer 2003): 38. He lives in Wilmington, Delaware, with his wife and two children and works as a strength and conditioning coach.

DRURY PIFER, playwright and novelist, founded the Berkeley Stage Company, a theater devoted to new plays and a fresh approach to acting. Over thirty of his plays have been staged in the U.S. and Europe. Two were nominated for the Helen Hayes/Charles MacArthur Award for Outstanding New Play, 1992 and 1993. He has published *Circle of Women* (1970), a novel, and *Innocents in Africa* (1994), a memoir. *Innocents in Africa* was named one of four finalists for the British Writers' Guild Award for Best Non-Fiction Book of 1994. His short fiction has appeared in numerous magazines and journals, including *Harper's* and *Story*. He was the recipient of a National Endowment for the Arts Creative Writer's Fellowship and an Individual Artist Fellowship from the Delaware Division of the Arts. He has taught creative writing at the University of California and the University of Delaware, and has served on the Delaware and Maryland State Art Councils. He lives in Wilmington, Delaware, with his wife, Ellen.

FRANCIS POOLE is editor and publisher of *Blades,* a tiny magazine. He has had poems in *Beloit Poetry Journal, Lost and Found Times, New York Quarterly, Pearl, Rolling Stone, Southern Humanities Review, Shattered Wig,* and *World Letter.* He is the recipient of two Delaware Division of the Arts fellowships in Poetry. He works as a film librarian at the University of Delaware Library.

LYNN PRUETT a graduate of Caesar Rodney High School, grew up in Kent County, Delaware. She has published a novel, *Ruby River* (2002), as well as stories, essays, and poems in numerous magazines, and has received fellowships from Yaddo and the Kentucky Arts Council. She lives in Lexington, Kentucky, and is on the faculty of the low-residency MFA program at Murray State University.

MAGGIE ROWE was awarded a 2004 Fellowship in Poetry by the Delaware Division of the Arts. Her poems have appeared in local and national publications, including *The Sun* and *Oberon* magazines and the *2007 Collection of Art and Poetry,* published by the Biggs Museum, Dover, Delaware. She lives in Newark, Delaware, with her husband and the youngest of her three children.

GIBBONS RUARK's poems have appeared widely for over forty years in many magazines and journals, including *Ploughshares, The New Republic, The New Yorker,* and *Poetry,* and in various anthologies and texts. They have also won frequent awards, including three Poetry Fellowships from the National Endowment for the Arts and a Pushcart Prize. Previously collected in *A Program for Survival* (1971); *Reeds* (1978);

Keeping Company (1983); *Small Rain* (1984); *Forms of Retrieval* (1984); and *Rescue the Perishing* (1991), seventy of his poems appear in *Passing Through Customs: New and Selected Poems* (1999). A member of the University of Delaware faculty for almost forty years, he recently retired and now lives with his wife, Kay, in Raleigh, North Carolina.

ELISSA SCHAPPELL is the author of *Use Me* (2000), which was a finalist for the PEN/Hemingway award and was named a New York Times Notable Book, a Los Angeles Times Best Book of the Year, and a Borders' Discover New Writers selection. She is currently a contributing editor for *Vanity Fair* magazine and is a founding editor and now editor-at-large of *Tin House* magazine. Her work has appeared in, among other places, *The Paris Review, Spin, Spy,* and *Nerve.* She grew up in Hockessin, Delaware, and currently lives in Brooklyn, New York.

JULIE SCHUMACHER grew up in Wilmington, Delaware. She graduated from Oberlin College with a BA in Spanish and from Cornell University with an MFA in fiction. Her first published story, "Reunion," written to fulfill an undergraduate writing assignment ("tell a family tale"), was reprinted in *The Best American Short Stories 1983.* Subsequent stories were published in *The Atlantic, Ms Magazine, Minnesota Monthly,* and *Prize Stories 1990* and *1996: The O. Henry Awards.* Her first novel, *The Body Is Water* (1995), was a finalist for both the PEN/Hemingway Award and the Minnesota Book Award. Her other books include a short story collection, *An Explanation for Chaos* (1997), and three novels for younger readers: *Grass Angel* (2004); *The Chain Letter* (2005); and *The Book of One Hundred Truths* (2006). She is a professor of English and the director of the creative writing program at the University of Minnesota.

DAVID SCOTT is the winner of a PEN Discover Award in fiction and of Individual Artist fellowships in fiction and poetry from the Delaware Division of the Arts. A graduate of the creative writing program at the University of North Carolina, Greensboro, he has published poetry and essays in *New Delta Review, Ecotone, Madison Review,* and *Greensboro Review,* and in the anthologies *About What Was Lost* (2007) and *Red, White and Blue* (2004). His work has been read on the Naturalist's Diary (Sirius Radio). He lives in Tallahassee, Florida, with his wife and three children.

W. D. SNODGRASS's more than twenty books of poetry include *The Fuehrer Bunker: The Complete Cycle* (1995); *Each in His Season* (1993); *Selected Poems, 1957–1987* (1987); *The Führer Bunker: A Cycle of Poems in Progress* (1977), nominated for the National Book Critics' Circle Award for Poetry and produced by Wynn Handman for the American Place Theatre; *After Experience* (1968); and *Heart's Needle* (1959), which won the 1960 Pulitzer Prize for Poetry. He has also published two books of literary criticism, *To Sound Like Yourself: Essays on Poetry* (2003) and *In Radical Pursuit* (1975), and six volumes of translation, including *Selected Translations* (1998), which won the Harold Morton Landon Translation Award. His honors include an Ingram Merrill Foundation award, a special citation from the Poetry Society of America, and fellowships from the Academy of American Poets, the Ford Foundation, the Guggenheim Foundation, the National Institute of Arts and Letters, and the National Endowment for the Arts. He is retired professor of creative writing and contemporary poetry at the University of Delaware, and now lives in upstate New York.

CRUCE STARK is the author of a novel, *Chasing Uncle Charley* (1992). Along with the state's poet laureate, Fleda Brown, he has led the Delaware Writers' Retreat, held regularly in the fall at Rehoboth Beach. In 1996, the readers of *Delaware Today* magazine selected him as Delaware's "Best Writer." A longtime resident of Wilmington, he was for many years a member of the University of Delaware's creative writing faculty. He is now retired.

BILLIE TRAVALINI's memoir, *Bloodsisters* (2005), was a finalist for the Bakeless Publication Prize and the James Jones Prize and won the 2005 Lewis and Clark Discovery Prize and the Delaware Press Association Award for nonfiction. Her essay "Wholeness and the Short Story" was published in 2005 in *Writers on Writing: Short Story Writers and Their Art*. She photographed and wrote *Wilmington Senior Center: Fifty Years of Community* (2006). She has received Individual Artist fellowships and grants in fiction and poetry from the Delaware Division of the Arts. She is a fiction editor of *The Journal of Caribbean Literatures*, director of the Delaware Literary Connection, and founder and organizer of the New Castle Writers' Conference. A Phi Beta Kappa, magna cum laude graduate of the University of Delaware, she earned her MA at Temple University. She teaches at Lincoln University, Wilmington College, and in the Boys and Girls Clubs' Pegusus Art Works Program, and is a teacher-consultant for Delaware's Department of

Children, Youth & Their Families, for whom she edited *Teaching Troubled Youth: A Practical Pedagogical Approach* (2007).

ANTHONY VARALLO grew up in Yorklyn, Delaware. His first collection of short stories, *This Day in History*, won the John Simmons Short Fiction Award (University of Iowa Press) and was a finalist for the Paterson Fiction Prize. A graduate of the Iowa Writers' Workshop, he has published stories in *Epoch, New England Review, Crazyhorse, Story Quarterly, Black Warrior Review*, and elsewhere. He is the recipient of an Associated Writing Programs Intro Journals Award, the *Crazyhorse* Fiction Prize, *The Journal* Short Story Prize, and a National Endowment for the Arts Fellowship in Literature. He is assistant professor of English at the College of Charleston.

JEANNE MURRAY WALKER's latest book of poetry is *A Deed to the Light* (2004). Her poems have appeared in *Poetry, The Georgia Review, Image, American Poetry Review, The Atlantic Monthly*, and many other periodicals. Among her awards are a National Endowment for the Arts Fellowship, a Pew Fellowship in the Arts, and seven Pennsylvania State Council on the Arts awards. She travels widely in the U.S. and abroad to give readings and conduct writing workshops. She is also a playwright whose work has been produced across the United States and in London. Married and the mother of two children, she lives in Philadelphia and is professor of English at the University of Delaware.

LARA M. ZEISES is the author of several novels for young adults. Her first, *Bringing Up the Bones* (2002), was named an honor book for the 2001 Delacorte Press Prize Competition. Her second, *Contents Under Pressure* (2004), began as a thesis project at Emerson College, where in 2001 she earned her MFA in creative writing. The book has been named to the 2006 International Reading Association's Young Adult Choices list and was voted the 2006 Delaware Blue Hen Teen Book Award winner. Her third novel, *Anyone But You* (2005), was a *Teen People* Top 10 Pick. Under the pseudonym Lola Douglas, she has published *True Confessions of a Hollywood Starlet* (2005) and its sequel, *More Confessions of a Hollywood Starlet* (2006). She is a University of Delaware graduate and has taught in the English Department there and at Archmere Academy in Wilmington, Delaware.